Home Schooling:

Political, Historical, and Pedagogical Perspectives

Social and Policy Issues in Education: The University of Cincinnati Series

Kathryn M. Borman, *Series Editor*

Contemporary Issues in U.S. Education, *edited by Kathryn M. Borman, Piyush Swami, and Lonnie D. Wagstaff*

Home Schooling: Political, Historical, and Pedagogical Perspectives, *edited by Jane Van Galen and Mary Anne Pitman*

in preparation

Assessment Testing and Evaluation in Teacher Education, *edited by Suzanne W. Soled*

Children Who Challenge the System, *edited by Anne M. Bauer and Ellen M. Lynch*

Early Childhood Education: Policy Issue for the 1990s, *edited by Dolores Stegelin*

Effective Schooling for Disadvantaged Students: School-based Strategies for Diverse Student Populations, *edited by Howard Johnston and Kathryn M. Borman*

Explaining the School Performance of Minority Students: Anthropological Perspectives, *edited by Evelyn Jacob and Cathie Jordan*

Home Schooling:

Political, Historical, and Pedagogical Perspectives

edited by

Jane Van Galen
Foundations of Education
Youngstown State University

Mary Anne Pitman
Department of Education
University of Cincinnati

ABLEX PUBLISHING CORPORATION
NORWOOD, NEW JERSEY

Library of Congress Cataloging-in-Publication Data

Home schooling : political, historical, and pedagogical perspectives /
  edited by Jane Van Galen, Mary Anne Pitman.
      p.   cm.
  Includes bibliographical references and index.
  ISBN 0-89391-706-0
  1. Home schooling—United States.   2. Home schooling—Law and
legislation—United States.   3. Education—United States—Parent
participation.   I. Van Galen, Jane.   II. Pitman, Mary Anne.
LC40.H66   1991
649'.68—dc20   90-25723
                                                          CIP

Ablex Publishing Corporation
355 Chestnut Street
Norwood, New Jersey 07648

Contents

Introduction
    Jane Van Galen and Mary Anne Pitman   *vii*

PART I: THE PHENOMENA OF HOME SCHOOLING   **7**

1 Home Instruction: The Size and Growth of the
Movement
    Patricia Lines   *9*

2 The Academic Achievement and Affective Development
of Home-schooled Children
    Brian D. Ray and John Wartes   *43*

3 Ideologues and Pedagogues: Parents Who Teach Their
Children at Home
    Jane A. Van Galen   *63*

4 Culture Acquisition in an Intentional American
Community: A Single Case
    Mary Anne Pitman and M. Lynne Smith   *77*

**PART II: THE IMPLICATIONS OF THE HOME
SCHOOLING MOVEMENT**   *99*

5 State Regulation of Home Schooling: A Policy Analysis
    James G. Cibulka   *101*

6 The Best and Wisest Parent: A Critique of John Holt's
Philosophy of Education
    Susan Douglas Franzosa   *121*

v

7   The Shifting Roles of Family and School as Educator:
A Historical Perspective
Joseph Kirschner   **137**

8   Home Schooling Law
Sharon Nalbone Richardson and Perry A. Zirkel   **159**

Appendix: Home Schooling Requirements in the
United States   **202**

Author Index   **211**

Subject Index   **214**

Introduction

Jane Van Galen
Youngstown State University

Mary Anne Pitman
University of Cincinnati

Home education is neither a new nor an unusual phenomenon. What is new in human history is institutionalized, compulsory schooling, and what may be unusual is the inordinate attention and concern being paid to the relatively small number number of families who have chosen to conduct their children's education at home. The growing practice of home education has generated considerable controversy at the state and local levels and has received growing attention in the popular press. Research on home education, however, has been meager, and policy makers have had little substantive information about who is learning at home, why they are doing so, and how well they are doing. This volume represents a significant step toward answering these questions.

While differing in their perspectives, the authors of the following chapters agree that the home-schooling movement offers an intriguing critique of traditional education. While national attention is focused on efforts to improve schools through greater external control in the forms of increased bureaucratization, professionalization, and standardization, a growing number of families are choosing to forego traditional schooling altogether. When these uncredentialed parents assume control over the education of their children, the schools are placed in the position of defending the very structure of schooling. Meanwhile, educators themselves are speculating as to whether that structure itself may be obsolete and inappropriate. When parents withdraw their children from school because of ideological conflicts, educators are called upon to defend a common curriculum and common educational goals in an increasingly pluralistic society. And when parents propose alternative pedagogies, schools are placed in the position of defending traditional pedagogy that is also being widely criticized from other fronts. This volume places the experiences of these families within the broader framework of current debates over pedagogy, the organization and control of schooling, and the feasibility of pluralism in the common school.

What is known about home schools and the people involved in those schools? The chapters in the first section of this book report both qualitative and quantitative studies of the parents and the children who are learning at home. In Chapter One, Lines summarizes what is known about the demographics of the home-schooling movement. Lines argues convincingly that the timeliness of decisions about policy and of data collection for future studies of home education rest in part upon defining the often-elusive population of home educators. Her chapter moves the field several steps closer to an accurate portrayal of the families who are learning at home. She employs innovative data collection strategies to generate her own estimates of the parameters of the home schooling population, and she suggests further strategies that could enable future researchers to further define and describe this population.

Questions of the effects of home education on the academic and social development of the children are addressed by Ray and Wartes in Chapter Two. Basing their conclusions on the growing body of achievement test data from several states and on their own research in the state of Washington, the authors demonstrate that, at least by standard measures, children educated apart from institutional schooling are faring at least as well as traditionally educated children, and in many cases, home-schooled children appear to be outscoring their formally educated peers on standardized achievement tests. The data in this chapter refute the concerns of policy makers and others who envision home-schooled children as isolated and neglected victims. But this report also raises intriguing questions about what may be learned about learning when schooling takes place apart from the constraints of bureaucracy.

The next two chapters present qualitative vignettes of two very different home schooling populations. In Chapter Three, Van Galen analyzes similarities and differences between the ideological orientations of two groups of home schooling parents she studied in one state. The first type of parent—those that Van Galen calls the Ideologues—are home schooling because of strong ideological differences with the content taught in public schools. These parents are primarily fundamentalist Christians, and their disagreements with the schools center around moral and spiritual values and about the authority of parents relative to other actors in their childrens' lives. The second (and smaller) group of parents described by Van Galen are the Pedagogues— those parents who chose to teach their own children because of their preferences for informal learning structured around their childrens' interests and paced to their children's development. For these parents, home education represents an extension of lifestyles that are often characterized by independence, self-sufficiency, and personal efficacy. This chapter raises questions about the adequacy of a "one-best system" of schooling for parents and children whose values and lifestyles are obviously diverse.

Pitman and Smith's research, reported on in Chapter Four, analyzes the day-to-day interactions of children and the adults in home schools. Grounding their research in theories of learning and cultural acquisition, Pitman and Smith offer a rich analysis of children engaged in learning in the home setting. From this chapter, we learn not only about how children learn at home, but more broadly, how children learn. The conclusion these researchers draw from their case study of learning in one household—that "humans are learners and that they cannot be prevented from learning, even in their own homes"—has important implications for education both within and beyond the setting of the home.

Beyond what is known about home schools, questions of the significance of the home schooling movement for education at the end of the 20th century remain. These are the questions addressed by the authors in Part II. In Chapter Five, Cibulka analyzes trends in state regulation of home schooling. He argues that home school policy is best understood within the context of two counterveiling trends in educational policy: the growing state regulation and standardization of education and the growing demand for more family choice in education. Cibulka views the relatively rapid growth of home education and the relative success of home school advocates' lobbying efforts as evidence of growing public concern over public schools and greater public influence over educational policy. Cibulka's analysis enables us to view home education not as an isolated activity of a marginal group of parents, but rather as one of many manifestations of discontent with the current state of public schooling.

In Chapter Six, Fransoza critiques the individualist philosophy underlying home education while agreeing that the growth of the home education movement signals deeper discontent with the goals and practices of public schooling. In her philosophical critique of the writings of John Holt (one of the earliest leaders of the home schooling movement), she notes that the home schooling movement is grounded on the premise that individual autonomy and independence have precedence over social participation and social responsibility. Fransoza decries the loss of a vision of social reform through schooling which she sees underscoring the writings of home-school advocates, and she calls upon those endorsing home education to reconsider society's responsibility for the individual.

It is this loss of faith in the secular mission of public schooling that Kirschner traces in his historical analysis of changing relationships between family, state, and school. Kirschner attributes the loss of faith in the civic mission of schooling in part to the failure (indeed to the impossibility) of schools ever living up to the charges placed upon them by society and in part to the pervasive alienation endemic to an era of rapid modernization. Weaving together these two strands of analysis, Kirschner helps to explain why home schooling has emerged as a major educational issue at the end of the 20th century and why short-sighted regulation of home schools will do little to address either the dilemmas of public schooling or the concerns of parents who choose to teach their children at home.

Specific provisions of the regulation of home education is the subject of the eighth and final chapter in this volume. Zirkel and Richardson offer a comprehensive analysis of home school litigation and of constitutional challenges to state compulsory attendance statutes. Their chapter discusses those cases that have restricted the state's interests in education and those cases in which parents' authority over their children's education have been defined. From their analysis emerge recommendations for policy makers in states in which the regulation of home schooling is still being debated—recommendations that acknowledge both the state's interests in protecting the well-being of the individual and the rights of parents to direct the education of their children.

WHAT HAS NOT YET BEEN ADDRESSED?

While the authors of these chapters have compiled careful and thoughtful analyses of the current home schooling movement, questions remain. As the chapters in Part I illustrate, the analytical lenses of researchers studying home education are most often focused on the families themselves. Yet a common theme implicit in all the chapters is that home schooling is not merely an educational problem, and that the educational solutions usually recommended to manage the home schooling "problem" fail to address not only the broader concerns of home-schooling parents, but also the challenges facing public education that are made explicit by the home-schooling controversy. The studies reported in this volume suggest that the significance of this movement lies in what can be learned about learning, about educational policy, and about the strength and viability of the institution of schooling. Such issues must be taken into consideration in future research on home education.

We hope that this volume answers some of the pressing questions about the home-schooling movement, but we also expect that the collection of studies raises more questions than it answers. Why, for example, has the movement emerged at this point in time? More children than ever before are living in single-parent homes, homes in which both parents are employed, or homes that include adults other than biological parents, yet the home schooling movement appears to be predicated upon a traditional, middle-class, Euro-American family model in which the mother is economically dependent upon the father. Home educators are almost exclusively women, and the significance of this growing number of women who forego their own financial and professional independence in order to teach their own children is an issue that has been largely unaddressed.

Researchers of the movement are just developing a cohesive research agenda, and we anticipate that the work reported here will lead to even more comprehensive analyses of the intersections of family, school, and the state in a postmodern society.

Part I
The Phenomena of Home Schooling

Chapter 1
Home Instruction: The Size and Growth of the Movement

Patricia Lines*
U.S. Department of Education

Home instruction:

___ *was the mainstay of education on the American frontier.*
___ *is a do-it-yourself family enterprise.*
___ *is a flight from modern American schools.*
___ *is a thorn in the side of school professionals.*
___ *became a visible and energetic movement over the past decade.*
___ *All of the above.*

Home schooling, once a necessary mainstay of education on the American frontier, waned in the late 19th and early part of the 20th century, retreating before the drive for compulsory schooling and a public goal of seeing all children graduate from high school. In the past

* Ms. Lines is a senior research associate in the Office of Research, Office of Educational Research and Improvement (OERI), United States Department of Education. She is grateful to OERI for granting her leave, and to Catholic University of America for appointing her to a visiting chair, enabling her to complete this chapter. She also wishes to thank all of the individuals who contributed information permitting construction of the tables; and Thomas D. Snyder, Branch Chief, Compilations & Special Studies, National Center for Education Statistics, and Paul M. Siegel, Chief, Education and Social Stratification Branch, U.S. Census Bureau, for their helpful critiques of an earlier draft of this chapter.

The opinions reflected in this chapter were developed by the author acting in her private capacity. No official support or endorsement by the Department of Education or other governmental agencies is intended or should be inferred.

two decades, the practice has reemerged as a popular option for parents desiring more direct control over their children's education. John Naisbitt and Raymond Moore have estimated the number of home schooled children at 1,000,000 or more (Naisbitt, 1982, p. 159).[1] The inquiry undertaken in this chapter does not support estimates at these levels. Growth is undisputed, however. Based on examination of curricular enrollments, adjusted to account for the large number who do not enroll, it seems likely that some 10,000 to 15,000 school-aged children were schooling at home in the early 1970s. By the fall of 1983, this probably grew to include 60,000 to 125,000 children; by the fall of 1985, to somewhere around 122,000 to 244,000 children; and by the fall of 1988, between 150,000 to 300,000 school-aged children in home schools. Comparisons with two independent estimates in three states confirm the estimate for the fall of 1988. In this chapter I provide a brief picture of the modern home schooling movement, discuss the evidence behind the population estimates, evaluate the importance of confirmation from the state-based estimates, and suggest ways of improving our ability to obtain information on home schoolers.

DEFINITION OF HOME SCHOOLING

For the purposes of this chapter, home instruction or home schooling means instruction and learning, at least some of which is through planned activity, taking place *primarily* at home in a family setting with a parent acting as teacher or supervisor of the activity,[2] and with one or more pupils who are members of the same family and who are doing grade K-12 work. If children are of an age covered by compulsory education laws, this definition is used regardless of whether the home school meets all the requirements of these laws relating to official approval of the program.[3] No definition is fully adequate, but this definition approximates what state compulsory education laws seek to

---

[1] Dr. R Moore adds membership in home schooling associations, without eliminating duplication and without eliminating those who are not actively home schooling; he also apparently makes projections based on size of audience attending his seminars and other home school gatherings (Moore, 1983).
school gatherings (Moore, 1983).

[2] This distinguishes it from home instruction programs based in schools, which use the home program as a supplement.

[3] Whether the home school in fact will satisfy state law depends on the degree of regulation in the state. States with the poorest compliance would be Michigan and Iowa, as there parents must be certified teachers. Few are.

cover (outlined in the Appendix) and what parents mean when they say they are engaged in home schooling.[4]

This definition also encompasses a large variety of teaching and learning arrangements. Some families follow formal lesson plans; some adhere to the philosophy of the late John Holt, a teacher, writer, and early home school advocate, and allow the child to set the pace, even if this means a long wait before the child expresses an interest in anything. Many enroll in correspondence schools; some attend a school, on campus, part time. Many others prefer to design their own curriculum. Many also form networks and arrange for their children to meet on a regular schedule for group activities. A few "part-time" schools, or tutoring services, have been formed for the express purpose of serving home schoolers, who attend classes in specific subjects and take the rest of their instruction at home.

Legal status and type of program do not necessarily mean the same thing. It would be possible, for example, for a family to enroll in a public school in California to achieve legal status, and in a home school correspondence program in Baltimore. Or a family may enroll in an existing private school only to obtain shelter from legal requirements, rather than to use the resources of the school.

OVERVIEW OF THE KNOWN HOME SCHOOL MOVEMENT

About three decades ago, home schoolers were largely limited to those who were geographically isolated, traveling or stationed abroad, and those who undertook home schooling because of religious tradition: Mormons who operate "kitchen schools" for a few neighborhood children aged 5 to 7; Seventh-Day Adventists, many of whom believe that younger children should remain at home; the Amish, who often remove their children from school after grade 8. Gradually, programs instituted to serve the geographically isolated—most notably the program operated by the state of Alaska and correspondence schools serving children of missionaries—began to serve individuals within a conve-

---

[4] This chapter focuses on children from kindergarten through grade 12, although compulsory education requirements, which vary state to state, tend to focus on children aged 7 through 16. However, most children begin formal education earlier and remain longer, and home-schooled children are no exception. For home schooling families, the failure of compulsory requirements to cover the full period from K–12 simply means a respite from state regulations at the start and the end of the home program.

nient distance to a school building.[5] Today most home schooling families could easily send their children to public or private school. The largest growth in home schooling appears to be among devout Christian parents who are unhappy with the secular nature of the other schools. They are mostly Protestant, but at least two Catholic schools now provide support to home schoolers.[6] According to some of the correspondence schools, Jehovah's Witnesses and Bahais are also interested in home school.

Contemporary Studies of Known Groups of Home Schoolers

It is possible to describe known groups within the home school population, even if it is not possible to claim that any of these reflect the entire home school population. Researchers have sampled and surveyed known populations—those who join an association, subscribe to a periodical for home schoolers, register with state or local officials, or use a curriculum from a supplier of home school curriculum—although they have not systematically examined all known populations. Even a systematic study of multiple groups must deal with the possibility that some home schoolers simply do not join, register, or purchase services or curricula and so escape the researchers altogether.

A review of the research on known populations will assist in determining the extent to which each new study has a comparable population to other studies, and, like pieces of a puzzle, will help build a more complete picture of the home school movement. Thus, this chapter briefly summarizes some of the characteristics of home schoolers, drawing from studies based upon relatively larger samples—those with a sample of 200 or more families and with responses of 100 or more. This includes studies by Wade Gladin (1987),[7] Maralee May-

---

[5] The State of Alaska serves any Alaskan child, on request of the family, regardless of location. Over half are in the Anchorage area. Geographical distance from schools does not seem to be the driving factor for Alaskans. A number of the organizations listed in Table 1.1 began by serving missionary families, such as Home Study International and the International Institute.

[6] They are Our Lady of Victory in California, and Seton School in Virginia; both have a substantial home school enrollment. See Table 1.1.

[7] Gladin surveyed families on the Bob Jones University Press (BJUP) home school mailing list, in May 1986. He sampled 6% of the families, or 416 addresses, in the 11 most active home schooling states. Of these, 403 were usable. He obtained a return of 252 questionnaires of which 9 were incomplete and were discarded, leaving him with 243 usable questionnaires. Not all families answered all questions, however (Gladin, 1987).

berry (1988a, 1988b),[8] the Washington Department of Public Instruction (1985),[9] the Home School Legal Defense Association (Scogin, 1989),[10] Sonia K. Gustafson (1987),[11] Jon Wartes (1989a, 1988b),[12] and a few other special-purpose efforts. Each of these studies draws from different subpopulations of home schoolers, but they yield similar results on many characteristics, permitting greater confidence in our generalizations about home schoolers.

Demographic Characteristics

An overview of these studies indicate that the typical home schooling family is white,[13] a two-parent family,[14] likely to be somewhat more

---

[8] Mayberry surveyed Oregon families in 1987–88. In March of 1988, she reported responses from 435 families (Mayberry, 1988a); in November of 1988, she reported a 35% return from 1600 sampled families ($n = 560$) (Mayberry, 1988b). She does not explain the discrepancy. The dates appear to indicate it was the same study; possibly she drew a supplemental sample. She also does not explain how she constructed the list of 1600, but context suggests she used either the home school association list or the official registration lists. To obtain a more representative sample, she would have used both.

[9] In 1984–85 the state of Washington conducted an experimental home-schooling program (at a time when home schooling was officially illegal in that state). The state offered to recognize a home school as a legal school if it was supervised by a certified teacher. In this way the state was able to identify 500 home-schooled students. The state obtained completed questionnaires from 313 "parent/tutors" teaching these 500 children. The response rate was 100% (Washington State Superintendent of Public Instruction, 1985).

[10] HSLDA can claim a 100% response rate, as it requires all members to complete a membership form annually. HSLDA drew a 10% sample from its membership applications for analysis. This yielded information on 300 families, or 598 parents. Two families were singled-parent families and eliminated from analysis of parental educational background (Scogin, 1986).

[11] Gustafson surveyed a sample of 257 families who consented to publication of their names and addresses in *Growing Without Schooling* (December 1, 1985). While all samples contain biases, this sample has an unusual one that will affect questions relating to duration and commitment to home schooling. Families on the list hold themselves out as "old timers" who are willing to help newcomers. Gustafson reports a response rate of 60%, or 147 returns, or which 143 were useable (Gustafson, 1987).

[12] In 1986, Wartes sampled 219 home-school parents registered and in apparent compliance with Washington's compulsory education law. Test scores were obtained directly from one testing service, with a 100% return ($n = 426$) (Wartes, 1987). In 1987, he repeated the procedure, obtaining test scores from six testing services, with a 100% return ($n = 873$). For 1987, he does not report the number that returned questionnaires, but it appears to be at least 287 (the number reporting level of structure and hours per week of schooling) did so (Wartes, 1988a, 1988b).

[13] A surprising number of reports fail to provide racial data. Those that do are reported in the text. The conclusion about the dominance of Caucasians can be confirmed by visually scanning crowds attending home school conventions and jamborees, however.

[14] Wartes, 1988b, p. 44 (93%); Scogin, 1986 (99%).

affluent and of a somewhat higher education attainment than families nationally, and Protestant. In this typical family, religion is likely to be the most important motivation for home schooling but it is rarely the only motivation. There are usually two children of school age who are being home schooled, and a third child, usually a pre-school-aged child, in the family. The typical mother takes the largest share of the teaching responsibility. The typical family utilizes community and other resources, such as other home schoolers, a church, a local school, the local library, and/or a distant school or organization offering material or services for home schoolers.

In the survey by the Washington Department of Public Instruction (1985), 74% of the parents were Caucasian; 14% were Hispanic; and a few were native American (five parents), black (four parents), or Asian (one parent). Eighty-five percent of the parents reported incomes below $30,000 (1984–85 dollars). Seven percent (23 parent/teachers) did not have a high school degree; four of these reported only a grade school education. Almost one-fourth held a high school diploma; a few more had General Equivalency Diplomas; 41% reported some college; 16% held bachelor's degrees; 4% held graduate degrees.

All the other studies reviewed suggested higher income and education levels, including a later sample of the same population. In 1986, Wartes analyzed Washington home schoolers and found a higher proportion of Caucasians (96%); a higher education level (26% with a bachelor's degree); and apparently a higher income level.[15] According to Gladin's survey of the mailing list of home schoolers kept by Bob Jones University Press (BJUP), about 50% of the families indicated an income above $30,000; the average income was $30,972; 85% reported an income below $40,000. In Gladin's sample, 52% of fathers and 38% of mothers had completed four or more years of college; 26% of fathers and 10% of mothers had completed graduate studies (Gladin, 1987).

Mayberry reported 3% of her sample of Oregon parents did not complete high school (unfortunately, she did not specify whether this meant both parents or the most active parent); 16% completed high school; 62% had some college or completed college; and 19% had some graduate school training or a graduate degree. When she compared this to the distribution in the state of Oregon, she concluded that home schoolers were, on average, better educated than their fellow state citizens. She found higher income levels as well; with 9% earning under

---

[15] Wartes, using different income coherts, reports 93% earning more than $25,000 per year (Wartes, 1988b, pp. 44–45).

$10,000; 26% earning from $10,000 to 19,000; 45% earning $35,000 to 49,000 (Mayberry, 1988b).[16]

Fifty-eight percent of the "old timers" on a list compiled by Holt's organization, reported earning less than $30,000; 59% of mothers and 72% of fathers had completed college or graduate school; and an additional 33% of mothers and 23% of fathers reported some college (Gustafson, 1988).[17]

The variations in these studies could be due to several factors. Populations studied by Gladin, Scogin, and Gustafson are willing to undergo an expense (payment of dues or purchase of books) and so may be more affluent. Or the earlier Washington group may be more broadly constructed, or Washington parents at that time may have been less affluent.

Religious affiliation appears to vary widely depending on the subpopulation. However, most are affiliated with Protestant groups. The range may be noted by examining Gladin's and Gustafson's two very different groups. Gladin, who surveyed individuals on the BJUP list (a Protestant book seller), knowing his population's religious orientation, did not ask affiliation in traditional research categories, but asked if parents labeled themselves evangelical, fundamental, charismatic, or "other." Only 7% chose "other."[18] The experienced home schoolers on the Holt list had the lowest level of religious affiliation, but 66% indicated an affiliation. The largest of these were "mainline Protestant" (Lutheran, Baptist, Methodist, Episcopalian, Presbyterian, etc.); 22% were in other churches, including Mormons, Jehovah's Witnesses, and lesser known groups, identified, for example, as "Self-Realization Fellowships" and "Reformed Congregation of the Goddess." Finally, 4% said they were part of a "Spiritual-Unity" movement.

Conclusions about number of children in a family can be based on enrollment data from the larger correspondence schools and from state registration data. Christian Liberty Academy, the largest of the correspondence organizations, has an average of 1.8 children enrolled in their program for each family (but no data on children enrolled else-

---

[16] She reports 42% finished college and 37.3% reported some graduate school work in her earlier piece. Although she does not so state, it seems most likely that this was a preliminary report and did not include her entire sample (Mayberry, 1988a).

[17] A random sample of members of the Home School Legal Defense Association also indicates that in 1986 parents in this group had an average higher education attainment; 1.5% reported "some high school;" 24.92% graduated from high school; 26.09% had "some college;" 36% received a bachelor's or comparable degree; and 10% a graduate degree (Scogin, 1986). She did not survey income.

[18] 37.3% said evangelical; 35% said fundamental; 20.1% said charismatic. Note some parents marked more than one.

where or on preschool siblings). Families returning a Florida department of education questionnaire average 1.6 children in each home
school program (L. Dukes, Florida State Department of Education,
personal communication, December 2, 1988). Wisconsin (in the 1987–
88 school year) registered 3,624 home schooled children, in 1,921
families—1.9 home-schooled children per family (M. Berg, Wisconsin
Department of Public Instruction, personal communication, December
16, 1988).

There is often a third, younger child in the family. The Gladin survey indicated two home-schooled children per family, with a third
(usually younger) child present in the family (Gladin, 1987, p. 122).[19]
Wartes also found family size was between two and three. Gustafson
reports 2.2 children per family.

Reasons for Home Schooling

Religion appears to be an important reason for home schooling. Not
only do parents indicate this is so in response to a direct question,[20]
but this reponse is consistent with other attributes of these families.
Church attendance is high.[21] Gladin (1987, p. 108) found, among families with a child in a school prior to turning to home schooling (about
two-thirds of the total), half or more had previously chosen a private
Christian school.[22] In addition, he found "minister" was the most fre-

---

[19] Gladin did not have a question about number of children in the home school, but
he did ask about the enthusiasm level that each child has about home schooling, by
grade level. This question elicited responses for 464 home-schooled children in 239 home
schooling families. Note that the average family in this survey had 2.78 children (obtained in response to a question about age of children in family) (Gladin, 1987, p. 96).

[20] In a sample of home-schooling parents on the mailing list of Bob Jones University
Press, 197 of 242 respondents said it was "very important" to home school" to fulfill my
God-given responsibility" and 143 of 243 said it was "very important" "to provide more
religious instruction" (Gladin, 1987, Table 26, p. 128). Mayberry found 89% of her sample said "religious commitment" was "very important" compared to 43% on a national
NORC survey (Mayberry 1988a, p. 3; 1988b, p 35). The largest number of 219 home-
school parents registered in the state of Washington ranked "Religion or philosophy"
highest (21.5%) when restricted to just three choices on a list of 22 reasons for home
schooling (Wartes 1988b, p. 46).

[21] In the BJUP sample, the average family attends religious services two or three
times weekly (Gladin, 1987, p. 101). Mayberry reports church attendance of "every week
or more often" for 73% of her respondents, compared to 28% of respondents to a NORC
survey (Mayberry, November 1988b, p. 35). Wartes reports religion or philosophy to be
a dominant reason for home schooling for Washington parents (Wartes, 1987).

[22] Of the total, 34.7% chose home schooling before the child had attended any school;
35.6% after some experience with a Christian school; 28.5% after experience with a public school; and 2.3% following experience with some other private school. Compare with
the group studied by Wartes (November, 1988a), where, among those previously in
school, 54% had been in public schools.

quent occupation response (14%) for fathers. In the survey of Washington parents by Wartes (1988a, 1988b), which limited parents to three choices out of 22, the largest number named "religion or philosophy" (21.5%). Another subset of home schoolers, those interested in the philosophy of John Holt, do not usually home-school for religious reasons.[23]

A majority of Gladin's parents also ranked as "very important" several other reasons: "to have more control over what my children learn," "to reduce the effect of peer pressure," "to improve the quality of our family life; "to be able to spend more time with my children."[24] The parents in Wartes' study next ranked "avoid peer pressure" (16.2%); "greater parent-child contact" (14.5%); and "enables better self concept" (13.2%) (Wartes, 1988b, p. 46).

Teachers and Teaching

The home program varies greatly from family to family. Typically the pupil or pupils are siblings, with one teacher, who is usually the mother. According to the Washington poll, 89% of the parent/tutors were female and almost all parents (95.8%) taught only their own children. Three of the parents said that they schooled children in addition to their own; five said that they tutored other children with assistance from the parents of those youngsters; nine said that neighborhood children sometimes joined them on projects. A majority (56%) estimated that they spent from 20 to 30 hours per week in directed activities with their children; 24% spent more than 30 hours; 13% spent between 15 and 20 hours; a few (6%) spent less than 15 hours.

In Gladin's survey, mothers were virtually always the primary teacher.[25] Their home school day averaged 6.06 hours, 4.97 of which were for instruction, independent study by students, or work in a fam-

---

[23] A survey of experienced home schoolers on the Holt Associates published list, a group expected to be biased in favor of Holt's philosophy of home schooling, revealed that 34% had no religious affiliation. This group rated importance of explicit religious instruction fifth out of seven reasons for home schooling (Gustafson, 1988, p. 7).

[24] This was 186 of 243, 173 of 243, 138 of 241, and 121 of 243 respondents, respectively (Gladin, 1987, table 26, p. 128). "Avoid peer pressure" was rated highest by 16.2%; greater parent-child contact by 14.5%, and "enables better self concept" by 13.2% of the parents (Wartes, November 1988a, p. 46).

[25] 90% of families reported the mother was the teacher; 9.2% said both parents were teachers; and only father (.4%) was the sole teacher. Moreover, when fathers taught, it was less than 10% of the time (Gladin, Table 14, p. 110).

ily cottage industry.[26] This probably translates to 25 hours of directed activities per week, about the same as the Washington survey.

Teaching Styles

Interviews with individual families indicate that some families use a very traditional approach, including schedules and lesson plans that look exactly like those used in large-group instruction. Research by Gary Knowles indicates that, on the whole, the home schools imitate the methods of classroom teachers who taught the parents when they were children. On the other hand, some families strongly believe in allowing the children to set the pace and direction of home learning and seek a very informal setting. Mary Anne Pitman's anthropological studies are of precisely this kind of family. Some families move from structured to unstructured programs as the children become more self-directed (Van Galen, 1988). Many families try to arrange for some activities with other children and adults in the larger community. Many rely on scouting and church groups for this purpose. Many coordinate field trips with other home schoolers. Some make regular trips to some special place, such as a home for the aged.

Support Networks

There is much evidence that home schoolers like to form local support networks. Sometimes these networks help families get started. For example, the Great Commission Academy, in Laurel, Maryland, formed for the express purpose of assisting parents in home schools, serves over 100 families, and about 200 children, most in grades 1–6 (D. Smith, personal Communication, November 14, 1988). It has helped 22 churches establish similar umbrella organizations. This organization developed materials for parents at a pastor's conference; they do not develop materials for children, but help parents design individualized curriculum using A Beka, Bob Jones, Alpha Omega, and other publishers.

The Materials

An examination of the curricular packages reinforce the conclusion that home schools follow no standard pattern. The materials of the

---

[26]1.09 hours was for teacher preparation. The breakdown of the 4.97 student hours was 2.58 instruction; 1.77 independent study; .62 cottage industry (Gladin, 1987, Table 15, p. 111). Most families did not have a cottage industry. Among those that did, most spent one hour a day on it. A few (5) spent 4 hours per day on it. As Gladin presents totals for all families, it is not possible to ascertain whether this group had a longer school day or not.

School of Home Learning in Escondido, California, display the motto, "Question authority." The program of Basic Education implies a strong message to the contrary. On small California group relies almost exclusively on the World Book Encyclopedia, supplemented by activities and projects.

The Calvert School, oldest of the organizations enrolling home-schooled children (begun experimentally in 1906 and officially in 1908), uses the same materials in its home program as on its Baltimore campus. These materials are based on those developed by the school's first headmaster, Virgil Hillyer, who adhered to such "radical" (for his day) ideas as teaching reading before teaching the alphabet and learning without textbooks. Calvert now uses a comprehensive set of workbooks, supplemented with other readings, including a healthy dose of the classics. The materials may be purchased for use with or without the services of a correspondent teacher.

Alaska originally modeled its program after Calvert's, but it has since added some significant modifications. In particular, the correspondence teachers, based in Juneau, visit their students in person from time to time and are in frequent contact by telephone. (Alaska has a grant from the U.S. Department of Education to provide technical assistance to public or private institutions that wish to replicate its program.) Family Centered Learning Alternatives, in the state of Washington, also maintains personal contact with the children; a certified teacher assists in designing an individual program for each child, meets with each family at least weekly, advises parents on their role as primary tutors, and helps arrange group activities for children from several families. The Hewitt Child Development Center and the Evangelistic & Faith Enterprises of America both provide special assistance to families with learning-disabled children.

The largest of the religiously based organizations appears to be Christian Liberty Academy, which provides home schoolers with an eclectic, individualized package of textbooks and workbooks. The package includes older textbooks, the McGuffey Readers, books from A Beka Publications, and Rod and Staff Publishers (a Mennonite group). Most of their families send tests and other materials to Christian Liberty Academy for evaluation and grading by teachers and other professionals.

Outcomes

Academic and social outcomes are reviewed elsewhere in this book, and indicate that home-schooled children do well on tests. One tentative finding—that student achievement in a home school has little to do with the level of education of the parent doing most of the teaching—is worth noting, because it is contrary to conventional wisdom. The finding is partially supported by both Wartes (1988a, 1988b) and David Neal Quine (1988). These findings are also consistent with tutoring studies that indicate the education level of a tutor has little to do with achievement of a child (Ellson, 1986; Gordon, 1983; Weaver, 1980). Further study of such effects is warranted for it could inform school policy relating to the use of teachers' aides and older students.

THE NUMBER OF HOME-SCHOOLED CHILDREN

The number of home-schooled children is the subject of much debate. As already noted, John Naisbitt (1982, p. 159), a futurist, and Raymond Moore (1983), a home school advocate, have estimated that the number had grown to 1,000,000 or more by the early 1980s. John Holt questioned such estimates during his lifetime, providing a long list of problems with the higher estimates and suggesting estimates that are comparable to those arrived at in this chapter.[27] Based on examination of curricular enrollments, adjusted to account for the large number who do not enroll, it seems likely that roughly 10,000 to 15,000 school-aged children were schooling at home in the early 1970s; 60,000 to 125,000 by fall, 1983; 122,000 to 244,000 by fall, 1985; and 150,000 to 300,000 by fall 1988. Options for arriving at such estimates are discussed below.

A Census or A Survey

A census. The best way to determine the number of home schoolers would be a question on a census. Because home schoolers are, by definition, often at home, a door-to-door census effort would find them.[28]

---

[27] Holt published the correspondence between himself and Ray Moore in (Holt, 1983). At that time Moore estimated 500,000 children and Holt estimated between 10,000 and 15,000 families (which probably would involved between 20,000 and 30,000 home-schooled children, as defined in this chapter). Among other things, Holt pointed out that Moore was using an expansive definition of home schooled children—one not used by state officials, for example—and based his estimate on attendance at meetings without ascertaining whether parents attending were merely seriously interested in home schooling or actually doing it.

[28] Problems of counting the homeless, migrants, and other less stable populations do not apply here (see Coughlin, 1988).

The 1990 Federal Census, which must balance many competing demands, will sample 20% of all households for education status, asking whether family members are in public or private school, or not in school.[29] Home schoolers might choose any one of these three possible responses, but seem more likely to say "private school." Because only a fraction of all those surveyed receive these questions, sampling error must also be taken into account.

Federal population surveys. Between-census efforts on the part of the United States Government to provide information on school-aged children by type of school attended are also not very useful for estimating home-schooled children. There are two major efforts to assess the K–12 school population. The Current Population Survey (CPS), administered by the Bureau of the Census, samples about 60,000 households every October and obtains information about the education status of school-aged children from preschool to 12th grade (regardless of age). Because CPS surveys households rather than schools, it should find home schoolers, but the question about schooling is similar to the question in the Census, and sufficiently ambiguous (from a home schooler's point of view) to make it impossible to say exactly what the CPS figures mean. Interviews with home school parents, including some who have participated in the CPS survey, indicate that they will usually say their children are in "private school."[30] A few, those who are enrolled in an independent study program with a local public school, would reasonably answer "public school." This kind of response might be especially likely to occur in California, where such relationships are encouraged by state regulations. Sample size also is a consideration. If a CPS survey produced an estimate of 300,000 home-schooled children in the country (the outer range of the estimate made in this chapter) one could conclude only that one had a 95% chance that there were between 250,000 to 350,000 home-schooled children in the country—yielding a result not much more precise than that made in this chapter. Although the survey would allow use of standard statistical procedures, the expense may not warrant the effort.

---

[29] It takes immense political effort to change the Census questions. Moreover, there has been no real pressure to do so. This may be changing. By 1988, in response to a question from the speaker's podium about being counted in official government efforts, about 2000 home-schooling parents in the state of Washington responded with a resounding "yes."

[30] Based on a show of hands at large audiences, I have found that about 90% of home schoolers will tell an official surveyor that their children are in private school. Following such meetings I have heard from five families who were actually in the survey; one family insisted that their children were "not in school" despite perceived pressure from the surveyor to make a different response.

Three Independent Networks for Estimating the Number of Home-schooled Children

Short of these more conventional methods of estimating a population, there are at least three independent sources of information on the home-schooled population. All provide less precise data, but reliance on any of them would be less expensive than a census or a survey. The first consists of home school associations, at least one of which exists in each state.[31] Memberships and attendance at meetings provide some clue to number, but these should be adjusted to eliminate overlap and those who are not homeschooling. Generally, this means an adjustment downward to account for families that (a) join more than one association, (b) affiliate with such associations although they are not home schooling (e.g., past home schoolers, and those who plan to do so), and (c) are home-schooling prekindergarten children (of which there are many[32]) who join the association. Conversely, the number must be adjusted upward to account for home-schooling families who do not affiliate.

The second independent network consists of state departments of education. Virtually[33] all state compulsory education laws have some minimal reporting requirement to state or local authorities. Official state records will be realistic only to the extent that states successfully obtain compliance with their reporting requirements. Such data must be adjusted upward to account for those who do not register. The Gladin survey confirms substantial noncompliance with registration requirements for the 11 states studied (those with the largest number of families who had at one time or another purchased material from BJUP). In response to a question about their "relationship with civil authorities," 38.7% said civil authorities "do not know we have a school" (Gladin, 1987, p. 117)[34] One of the 11 states, Texas, was at the time in the process of litigation over home schooling and trying to promulgate new statewide regulations; public relations with home schoolers was low. Possibly, today, fewer parents would be "in hiding"

---

[31] A list is available from Holt Associates.

[32] See Gustafson (1988, p. 5). A substantial number of her respondents indicated they had been "home schooling" since "birth." Scanning the list of experienced home-schooling families maintained by Holt Associates (the list she used) reveals a number of families with preschool children only. I also found a large number of parents affiliated with the Washington Home School Association counted preschool children as "home schooled."

[33] Illinois does not have such a provision in its law, but it has a voluntary reporting requirement for private schools. Home schools are classified as private schools in Illinois.

[34] Another 32.4% said, "They do not bother us," 25.6% said "They have been cooperative with us"; and 3.4% said "They have given us a hard time" (Gladin, 1987, p. 117).

from the state, and this statistic may not hold true. Nonetheless, states are still changing their regulations, sometimes making them more rigorous, and home schoolers still join the Home School Legal Defense Association (HSLDA) in growing numbers. (HSLDA provides prepaid legal services if home schoolers face a challenge to their program; in short, its members are nervous about state regulatory intentions.) It is expected that the estimate based on state official reports will continue to be smaller than estimates based on other networks.

A third network consists of schools and education organizations providing curricula and services to home-schooled children. There will be overlap among the clientele of many of these organizations, but there is one group where all familiar with the situation believe no overlap exists: Some of these organizations provide a complete,[35] graded,[36] year-long curriculum package for each child[37] and they "enroll" the child, meaning that they keeps records of the name of the child, address, courses taken, grades, test scores, and/or similar data.[38] In most cases the provider also offers teaching and consultant services by correspondence. Usually a correspondence teacher gives assignments, grades papers, and comments on the child's work, while the parent acts as the on-site teacher. In some cases, the curriculum provider also offers special training to the parents. Other families purchase the correspondence package without the services, but are nonetheless "enrolled" in the sense that the provider keeps a record of the child's name and address, and includes the child in newsletters and similar group efforts.[39] The number of children who are enrolled in this manner can provide a starting point for a nation-wide estimate of home schooled children.

---

[35] "Complete" means it has English or language arts, history or social studies, math, and science.

[36] "Graded" means that it is sequential to other packages in the series and generally can be recommended to specific age groups.

[37] The base does not include lists of home schoolers who have purchased books or workbooks from a publisher or distributor who does *not* sell this material as part of a complete, graded, year-long package, even if a family could put together such a package from the publisher's list. Most notably, Bob Jones University Press, A Beka Publications, Alpha Omega Publications—all popular among home schoolers—are excluded from the base. Also excluded are those who sell workbooks for a single subject. Bible curricula and phonics seem popular in this group.

[38] The Home School Legal Defense Association has examined its membership files, which include information on use of a curricular package, and found that families list only one organization in response to their question.

[39] Table 1.1, lists the suppliers of these curriculum packages. Most actually "enroll" the child—keeping records on the child as would a private school. Most notably, Calvert offers the package without teaching services, but it continues to include the child on its rolls for purposes of newsletters and similar matters.

Table 1.1.   Estimate of Number K—8 Children in Home Instruction

Distribution of Complete Graded, Yearlong Curricula	1985	1988
A Beka (In 1985, Pensacola Christian School), Pensacola, FL	1,870*	4110*
Abbott Loop Christian Center, Anchorage, AK	67	83
Accelerated Christian Education (ACE) (see Basic Education)		
Advanced Training Institute of America, Oak Brook, IL	750**	3,000
Alaska State Department of Education, Juneau, AK	800	600*
American Christian Academy, Colleyville, TX (was closed by 1988)	700	0
Basic Education (formerly ACE), Dallas/Fort Worth,***	1,800	2,600
Calvert School, Baltimore, MD (1988 number estimated)	4,168	6000
Christian Liberty Academy, Arlington Heights, IL	17,000***	18,100*
Christian Light Education, full service plan, Harrisburg, VA	450**	500
Clonlara School, Ann Arbor, MI****	1,560*	1,666*
Evangelistic & Faith Enterprises of America, Inc. Oliver Springs, TN	300	500
Hewitt-Moore Child Development Center, Washougal, WA (Now Hewitt CDC)	4,000	4,750
Home Study International, Takoma Park, MD	1,509	750
International Institute, Park Ridge, IL	1,000	1,000*****
Living Heritage Academy (See Basic Education)		
Marquette Manor Baptist Academy, Downers Grove, IL		90
McGuffey Academy, Milford, MI		128
National Academy of Christian Education, Reynoldberg, OH	1,050	700*
Oak Meadow Education Services, Blacksburg, VA & Ojai, CA	2,500* **	2,250
Our Lady of Victory, Mission Hills, CA	600	700*
Pensacola Christian School (See A Beka)		
Seton School Home Study, Front Royal, VA	500	1,200
Summit Christian Academy, Dallas, TX	800**	450*
Total—Home School Curriculum Distribution	41,424	49,177

Table continued on next page

The starting point requires identification of members of this group of service providers. Fortunately, as discussed below, the larger organizations are relatively easy to find. They are, after all, actively searching for their clientele. Reports from these organizations appear to be a relatively reliable indication of the number of home schoolers who use such services.[40] These reports are shown in Table 1.1, and they indicate almost 50,000 children, K–8 "enrolled" or receiving a current,

---

[40] There are always some problems in accuracy of bookkeeping and reporting, but efforts have been made to doublecheck data where discrepancies appear. The means of identifying the providers is discussed below.

Table 1.1. Continued

Rough Estimate of Population based on Distribution	EST.	EST.
Less rough estimate of foreign nationals obtaining curricula (see text)	4,000	4,000
Plus rough estimate of numbers of curricula packages reused (see text)	14,000	16,000
Subtotal, based on curricular package distribution	51,474	61,177
Plus rough estimate of number whose parents prepare own curriculum (see text)	41,000– 153,000	61,000– 183,000
Total Rough Estimate, K—8	102,424– 204,000	122,177– 244,000
Plus rough estimate of High School—aged students	20,000– 40,000	25,000– 50,000
TOTAL ROUGH ESTIMATE, K—12	122,000– 244,000	147,000– 294,000

* Total enrollment given; K–8 proportion estimated by the curriculum provider.

** Figures for 1985–86 are corrected numbers, obtained on 1988 interviews.

*** Basic Education also distributes 225,000 K–8 packets (54 are required for a full year) to home schools, other schools, and "tutorial centers" (six or more children, two or more families). These are not counted here.

****Clonlara recommends materials to enrolled children; families may purchase items from Clonlara or elsewhere.

*****International Institute did not respond to requests for information in 1988; 1986 enrollment shown.

Note: These providers usually enroll children, keep records, assist in testing, grade papers, and grant degrees. Most will also make the curricular package available without these services. Both enrollments and children receiving a full curriculum without services are counted.

year-long, graded and complete home-schooling curriculum in the Fall of 1988.

This, however, is the tip of the iceberg. Many other home schoolers design their own program, selecting specific books and materials from one or more sources. As already noted, some enroll in a private school and use that school's curriculum (or one of the curricula listed in Table 1.1). The reports from providers is only a starting point. As noted below, two independent polls guide the estimate of the remainder of the population. It may also be necessary to adjust the estimate upward to account for parents who reuse a curricular package without enrolling a younger child.[41]

---

[41] This depends on whether parents who say they use a "correspondence" program say this even when they use "hand-me-down" curricular materials for an unenrolled child.

Minor problems include identifying and classifying organizations as suppliers of a complete, graded, year-long curricular package,[42] and obtaining correct data.[43] Theoretically, a family could use two such packages, picking material from both, although price will discourage such arrangements; moreover, most of the children are "enrolled" and receiving services. In addition, the estimate of foreign nationals is very rough, but in general this number seems to be small.[44] Table 1.1 makes some adjustment for these minor problems.

Deriving the Estimate Based On Curricula Distribution

The estimate provided in this chapter relies on the last source. I first compiled lists of providers of complete, graded curriculum packages (whether sold as a package alone or with correspondence services to child or parent). This definition was chosen to approximate an enrollment of a child. The list was derived over time from over six independent sources.[45] A master list was made, duplication eliminated, and all candidates on the list were contacted to determine if they met the definition for a provider of a complete package. It was important to distinguish between organizations providing home-school curricula and publishers of curricular materials in general who have success-

---

[42] See the discussion of the BJUP "package" on p. 26. I probably have failed to identify all sources of curricular materials for home schoolers. In 1983–84 I missed about 20 suppliers, 6 of which sold over 1,000 packages each. In 1985–86 I missed one, although I had contacted it, but had received no response. Thus, I failed to count the 1,700 curricular packages it sold in the 1985–86 school year. Subsequently, I found four other suppliers identified as "biggies" in Mary Pride's book, *The Big Book of Home Learning*. Balancing these errors, I incorrectly included Alpha Omega as a supplier of a complete curricular package. Corrected numbers appear in Table 1.1.

[43] For example, I suspect that two of the smaller organizations who told me that they had no children actually have some, but were fearful of reporting it. However, at this point almost all of the organizations listed seem very pleased to provide information.

[44] The organizations with a substantial overseas constituency are few—Basic Education, Calvert, Clonlara, Home Study International, International Institute. The latter two were originally organized to serve missionary families, but overseas shipments now account for only about 10% of their total. Basic Education, although newer, has the largest overseas shipment, and sends about 18% of its packages overseas. Some of these may be American nationals, however.

[45] The initial list depended on (a) Pride, 1987, (b) advertisements in periodicals aimed at home schoolers, such as *Teaching Home*, (c) the list of suppliers compiled by Holt Associates, (d) examination of surveys (such as Gladin's) which request parents to name the correspondence course they use if any, and (e) word of mouth. In addition, after I began publishing results, individuals often provided me with names of organizations that they thought should be counted. Many were eliminated because they did not meet definitional standards established in the research.

fully reached the home-school market. For example, one individual was of the opinion that I should include BJUP because they supply "curricular packages." BJUP tells me, however, that they have no "package" but a large list from which a parent could create an individualized package. As another example, KONOS character curriculum regards itself as a complete "core" curriculum and believes that a family using this curriculum would be highly unlikely to use any other complete curriculum package. However, it does not include math and science, so it does not fit the definition in this chapter of a complete curriculum and is not used as part of the base in Table 1.1. Through the use of in-depth telephone interviews,[46] with a 100% response in 1985 and a 96% response in 1988,[47] and after collecting and examining advertising brochures and sample packages, I believe that I have correctly identified those supplying a complete, graded package.

Based on interviews with those familiar with the movement and on two surveys conducted in 1985 and 1986, it appears that 50–75% of all parents who engage in home schooling design their own curricula rather than use the services or materials of these institutions.[48] The two surveys do not present perfect statistics. They draw from subpopulations that may not be representative of all home schools. Second, the choice of curriculum may change over time for home-schooling families. Finally, the two surveys were not specifically designed for this

---

[46] See Rosenblum (1987). The first effort at collecting data in 1983 was a failure; a scripted set of questions was used, and many respondents declined to give information. In 1983, I combined what Rosenblum would call "personal/professional" talk. A list of questions was presented on the nature of curricular materials and services available, and on enrollments. The unscripted "personal" talk was actually professional, in that it concerned home schooling, either an exchange of information on research or "stories" about exceptional children or experiences. This kept the interview "fresh" and often yielded valuable insights into the topic.

[47] One provider reached in 1985 is still in business, but did not respond to telephone messages or mailed requests. I used the 1985 data for them, as indicated in Table 1.1.

[48] In a Washington poll of 100 teachers supervising home-instruction programs, 41% said parent/tutors "usually/always" selected curricular materials from a publisher, and 47% said they "never/sometimes" did so. (Washington State Superintendent of Public Instruction, 1985) Given the nature of the question, it seems likely that these teachers included parents who pick and choose materials from a large publisher such as Alpha Omega or Bob Jones University Press (BJUP), even if there is no "package."

In 1986, the Home School Legal Defense Association (the HSLDA) randomly sampled 300 of its membership files (about 3,000 total) and found that 72.33% of its members said they used a "parent-planned combination" curriculum and that 27.67% said they used a "correspondence course." The HSLDA question seems more closely to approximate the question that should be asked. The HSLDA families may be of a higher income and education status than the average home schooling family; they are in fact of higher income and education status than the families in the Washington survey (Scoggin, 1986).

purpose, and they ask different questions. It goes without saying that there was no pretesting of the questions for the purpose of this chapter.

I did not attempt to obtain data for high school curricular sales.[49] Many adults are enrolled in these high school programs, and I was doubtful of my ability to obtain a good estimate of the number of school-aged children enrolled with this group. Thus, I also estimated the size of the enrollment of school-aged students at the high school level, based upon proportions of such children in correspondence programs that knew their constituency was all of school age, such as the state of Alaska's program.

The estimate of numbers of children using "hand-me-downs" or photocopies of curricular materials requires more research. Based upon a show of hands at a home school conference in Washington State (with about 2,000 individuals present) one would conclude that everyone who uses a package plans to reuse it. However, since the correspondence schools average nearly two children per family—about the same as the number of registered children per family in most states—there is evidence that these packages are not being reused.

In the early 1970s, John Holt estimated that there were from 10,000 to 15,000 home schooling *families* (about 20,000 to 30,000 children) (Holt, 1983b). His estimate was confirmed by retroactively obtaining enrollments from the handful of educational institutions that have been around since the early 1970s, and who provided complete curricular packages to a substantial number of children (over 100 K–8 children): The Calvert School, Home Study International, the International Institute, and the State of Alaska. Between 5,000 and 6,000 children in grades K through 8 were enrolled in or receiving curricular materials from these organizations in the early 1970s. Assuming that the proportion of those using these organization then was the same as it is now, between 10,000 and 15,000 children were probably being schooled at home during that period.

In 1983–84, I conducted my first survey of home-school providers, and found over 22,000 children in the K through 8 range receiving a curricular package (Lines, 1985, p. 48). At that time, I guessed that as many as half of the families were developing their own curriculum. This yielded a rough estimate of at least 50,000 K–8 children in home schools. At that time my list of providers was not complete, making the estimate too small.

For the fall of 1985, with improved capacity to locate the providers

---

[49] For example, the North Dakota Independent Study and the University of Nebraska and commercial high school correspondence courses, such as the American School.

of the home school curricular materials, I estimated about 120,000 to 260,000 home-schooled children. After adjusting these figures as discussed above, this would account for about 41,424 children in grades K–8 receiving home school curricula for Fall 1985. After adjusting for overseas shipments to foreign nationals and for families that reuse packages for a younger child, I estimated 51,000 American children were using K-8 home curricula. After accounting for parents who design their own curricula, it appeared that 51,000 to 153,000 additional K-8 children were schooling at home. Finally, with apparently another 12.5% to 20%[50] of home-schooled children in grades 9–12, the total number of school-aged children learning at home seemed to be, roughly, anywhere from 122,000 to 244,000. In the Fall of 1988, I found 49,477 children receiving K–8 curricula. After adjustments discussed above, I estimated about 122,000 to 244,000 total K–8 children, and 147,000 to 294,000 K–12 children in home schooling. Details appear in Table 1.1.[51] While the numbers may seem high, they continue to represent less than 1 percent of the total school-age population and less than 10 percent of the private school population.

Table 1.2 shows organizations that do not fit the definition for Table 1.1, including publishers and consultants. Sometimes individuals involved in home schooling inform me that the organizations named here should be included in my tables. However, the numbers in Table 1.2 cannot be added to themselves or Table 1.1 because of overlap in the lists, and because the lists are cumulative—including names of families that are no longer home schooling. Evidence of overlap can be found in Gladin's survey, as most of his sample (from the BJUP list) reported also purchasing materials from Alpha Omega, A Beka, and others. Those listed in Table 1.2 are estimated at the bottom of Table 1.1, as part of the "rough estimate of number whose parents prepare own curriculum."

---

[50] The high school population is more difficult to estimate. The proportion of high school students varies among the different correspondence programs. High school students also behave differently from students in the K–8 grade age range, in that they may enroll in community college courses and high school correspondence courses originally designed for adults. The state of Wisconsin, the state that probably registers a larger proportion of home schoolers than any other state, and has an outer limit in its compulsory education laws of 18, has registered 452 students in grades 9–12, or 12.5% of the total registered. Christian Liberty Academy, the largest of the correspondence schools, reports about 20% of its enrollment are in grades 9–12.

[51] There are differences in the 1985–86 dates and my previously published work (Lines, 1987) for 1985–86 based upon information gathered in 1988 and on a shift to a tight definition of what should be included in Table 1.1. Previously I included all those who offered a complete curriculum *or* consulted on a complete curriculum *or* enrollment.

Table 1.2a.   Sources of Materials and Support for Families not Relying on Complete Curricular Package—Partial Listing

School Publishers/Distributors/Specialized Curriculum/ Consultants—Partial List	1988
Alpha Omega Publications, Tempe, AR	15,000 families
Basic Education, Dallas-Fort Worth, TX	1,800 families**
Bob Jones University Press, Greensborough, NC	10,000 families
Christian Light Publications, Harrisburg, VA	2,400+ families***
Educators Publishing Service, Cambridge, MA	19,000 families
KONOS, Richardson, TX*	10,000 families
Learning at Home, Honaunau, HI	4,500 families
Lifeway Curriculum, Wheaton, IL*	"thousands"
Mott Media, Milford, MI	18,000 families
Rod & Staff Publications, Crockett, KY	15,000 families
Teaching Home Magazine	100,000 families
Weaver Curriculum, Riverside, CA	10,000 families

Notes: Figures cannot be added together or to Table 1.1 because of evidence of overlap in lists. Lists are usually cumulative, and will include families who are no longer home schooling.

*Alta Vista, Konos, and Lifeway do not offer complete curriculum, as defined here, because they lack math, science, history or social studies, or English or language arts, and parents would be expected to supplement for these subjects.

**This is an estimate based on curricular sales of individual packages. It does not overlap with the entry for Basic Education in Table 1.1.

***The children enrolled in the "full services" plan for Christian Light Publications, shown in Table 1.1, do not overlap with this group receiving materials and services.

Source: Interview with Beth Bauler, Alpha Omega, November 6, 1988; Gladin, 87 (for BJUP, as of May, 1986); letter from Paul E. Reed, Christian Light Publications, January 3, 1989; letter from Robert G. Hall, Educators Publishing Service, December 28, 1988; Interview with Wade Hulcey, KONOS, November 25, 1988; interview, Ann Pervinkler, December 16, 1988 (they have another list of 30,000 of families that have made inquiries); interview, July Innes, Mott Media, December 14, 1988 (figure includes inquiries); interview, telephone receptionist, December 19, 1988 (figure is estimated; the total list of home schoolers making inquiries is 30, 000, and half of these are estimated to be home school purchasers); interview with Mary Pride, member of the board of Teaching Home, November 1, 1988; or corresponding interviews listed for Table 1.1.

TESTING THE ESTIMATES

To test the estimate, I derived state-based estimates and compared them with estimates from two independent sources for three states.[52] To scale down the national estimate based on enrollments in Table 1.1, I used address lists from Christian Liberty Academy (CLA), BJUP, and

---

[52] See Denzin's comments on triangulation of data collection. While he recommends triangulation to help assess cause and effect relationships, it can also help determine validity of data sources (Denzin, 1978).

Table 1.2b.   Sources of Materials and Support for Families not Relying on Complete Curricular Package—Partial Listing

Examples of Schools With K-8 Home School Enrollments (no curriculum package produced)	1985
American Heritage Christian Academy, Sacramento, CA	150
Baldwin Park Christian School, Baldwin Park, CA	75
Discovery Christian School, Concord, CA	240
Family Centered Learning Alternatives, Arlington, WA (259 K–12)	150
Pilgrim Schools, Porterville and three other sites in CA	200
Pilgrim Christian School, Maywood, CA*	80
Santa Fe Community School, Santa Fe, NM	200
School of Home Learning, Escondido, CA	80
Sycamore Tree, Costa Mesa, CA	175**
15 schools with fewer than 50 children in 1985–86 (includes the Corvallis Open School Extended Program, Corvallis, OR, Creative Christian Education Service, Angwin, CA, Discovery Christrian Schools, Concord, CA, the Learning Connection, Grants Pass, OR.)	123

Note: Figures can be added to each other, but should not be added to Table 1.1. Parents enrolling in a school do not normally indicate the school as a "correspondence course" and their numbers will therefore be estimated in on the line for "parents who prepare own curriculum." Other schools that may qualify but have not responded to requests for enrollments include Abilities Research Associates, Anaheim, CA; Associated Christian Schools, Indianapolis, IN; Quest Academy, Phoenix, AR.

*Although they redistribute the ACE (Basic Education) curriculum, they believe their parents would say that they are using a parent designed curriculum. Interview, Mr. Arthurs, December 16, 1988. Note they now have about 95 K–8 children.

**They now have 400 to 500 K–12 children in the home program. Interview with Sandy Gogol, December 19, 1988.

Growing Without Schooling (GWS) to determine state-by-state locations of addresses of known home schoolers in their networks.[53] Table 1.3 provides detail on the location of approximately two thirds of the home school addresses in the nation found on each of these lists. The table demonstrates several things. First, it indicates that home schoolers are not evenly distributed throughout the United States,[54] and

[53] The BJUP list was described in Gladin and is from 1986. It consisted of addresses of families who said, in response to a form, that they were home schooling. The CLA list was provided by CLA for analysis in this chapter, and represents families who were enrolled with CLA (correspondence or curriculum and testing only) as of November 10, 1988. The GWS list consists of families who are "old-timers" and willing to offer assistance to other families interested in home schooling, and was current as of December, 1988.

[54] They may also be unevenly distributed within states. Mayberry notes that home schools in Oregon tend to be found in smaller cities or rural areas (Mayberry, 1988a). Gladdin found that, for his 11-state area, 51.3% were in suburban areas, 36.7% in rural areas, and 12% in urban areas.

Table 1.3. Distribution of Home Schooled Children in Most Active States in Three Separate Populations; and Distribution of Children 5—17 Nationwide

(in descending order, according to state population)

population	BJUP	%	CLA	%	GWS	%	USA	%
California	1,658	16.6	855	6.3	168	14.3	4,878	10.8
Texas	1,224	12.2	1117	8.2	44	3.7	3,435	7.6
New York			764	5.6	62	5.3	3,145	7.0
Illinois	380	3.8	1224	8.9	45	3.8	2,187	4.8
Ohio	408	4.1	380	2.8	35	3.0	2,075	4.6
Pennsylvania			412	3.0	76	6.5	2,074	4.6
Florida	422	4.2	628	4.6	37	3.1	1,848	4.1
Michigan	498	5.0	541	4.0	38	3.2	1,809	4.0
Georgia	554	5.5	334	2.4			1,245	2.8
Indiana	418	4.2	477	3.5			1,084	2.4
Virginia			503	3.7	33	2.8	1,030	2.3
Massachusetts					89	7.6	960	2.1
Missouri			329	2.4	30	2.6	939	2.1
Wisconsin			466	3.4	33	2.8	914	2.0
Washington	433	4.3	559	4.1	39	3.3	817	1.8
Minnesota			328	2.4			786	1.7
Oklahoma	474	4.7					632	1.4
Arizona					30	2.6	629	1.4
Oregon	381	3.8	392	2.9	37	3.1	494	1.1
Subtotal, active states	6,850	68.4	9,310	68.2	796	67.7	30,977	68.6
Total USA	10,000		13,676		1,175		45,143	

(thousands)

Note: If there is no entry, the home schooled population for that cell was small enough to place the state in the bottom third for the population charted in a particular column.

Source: Column 1 is for Spring, 1985, and is from Gladin, p. 87. Column 2 is for fall of 1988, and is based on a computer analysis done by Christian Liberty Academy and made available to the author. Column 3 is based on the December 1988 directory of Growing Without Schooling (Holt Associates), a directory of only those on the Holt list who are willing to list their names in a published directory. Column 4, national population, is for resident children age 5—17, taken from preliminary estimates as of July 1, 1986, based on the fall population survey. National Center for Education Statistics, Digest of Education Statistics 1988, Washington D.C., Table 15, p. 23.

seem to be more populous in the West and South, and less so in the East. Second Table 1.3 shows that subgroups of home schoolers are not identical with respect to state distribution. The BJUP list, for example, indicates a much larger number of home schoolers in California than do the other lists. As noted at the outset, most lists will have a bias, and while one can make some intuitive guesses about these biases, nothing precise can be known. Those familiar with BJUP have suggested that Californians, including conservative Christian Californians, are more independent; the BJUP list allows a home school to shop among a wide selection of publications and build an individual program, and so may appeal to Californians more than, for example, Texans. This would also account for above-average representation of Californians on the GWS list, which presumably attracts individuals who agree with the philosophy of the late John Holt. Finally, and not surprisingly, the table demonstrates that a state's home-schooled population is roughly proportional to the population of all school-aged children.

Wisconsin was chosen for comparison because it has the best chance of full compliance with state registration requirements, according to Christopher Klicka, an attorney and executive director of the Home School Legal Defense Association (personal communication, December 1, 1988). Wisconsin's requirements are fairly simple and less threatening to home schoolers than those of most other states. Wisconsin home school leaders agree that compliance with registration requirements is excellent and they rely on the state data (L. Kaseman, Wisconsin Parents Association, personal communication, December 19, 1988). In the fall of 1988 Wisconsin registered 3,946 children (M. Berg, Private School Laison, Wisconsin Department of Public Instruction, personal correspondence, November 23, 1988).[55] If the CLA mailing list is representative of the universe and if there are about 150,000 to 300,000 of home-schooled children in the nation, as suggested in Table 1.1, then Wisconsin would have about 5,100 to 10,200 home-schooled children in the fall of 1988. If the published list in *Growing Without Schooling* is representative, Wisconsin would have about 4,200 to 8,400 children. The BJUP list suggests even fewer. All in all, the official registration of about 4,000 seems consistent with the lower range of estimates in Table 1.1. If there are any unregistered home-schooled children in the state, and this seems likely, the estimates would come even closer. An estimate of a million, a figure some (Naisbitt, 1982, p. 159; R. Moore, personal communication) have forwarded,[56] would suggest 34,000 in

---

[55] The number of families was 2,032.
[56] See note 1.

Wisconsin—clearly too high. Even an estimate of 500,000 nationwide seems to high.

Washington state also offers a good opportunity to compare official state estimates with other estimates. The state has a relatively simple decentralized registration requirement that is monitored by state officials. From Table 1.3, it would appear that Washington may have a little more than 4% of all home schoolers in the nation. If so, Table 1.1 predicts 6,000 to 12,000 K–12 children to be located in Washington. In the fall of 1988 there were 4,045 home-schooled children registered with the state, which requires registration for children from age 8 through 17, in 1987–88. To be comparable, the state data must be adjusted upward to account for children under age 8 who are of school age, to an estimated 5,500 (B. Mertens, Washington State private school liaison, personal communication, December 5, 1988).[57] If about half the families comply with registration requirements, as is suggested by one poll (Gladin, 1987, p. 117),[58] the registration data would suggest over 9,000 children, K–8 in Washington, and is consistent with the middle range of the estimate based on curricular sales. The two major associations in Washington estimate that there are 15,000 to 20,000 children in families where parents are teaching or plan to teach a child at home (S. Hall, personal communication, December 21, 1988; K. McCurdy, personal communication, December 20, 1988).[59] This number apparently includes a substantial number of preschool children,[60] and should be adjusted downward to perhaps 12,000 to 16,000. Adjusted, it is somewhat above the upper range of the estimate based on curricular sales. In contrast, an estimate of a million children would suggest 40,000 in Washington state—too high when compared to any of the three estimates examined here.

In the school year 1988–89, Florida received a "notice of intent"

---

[57] The state does not have authority to require registration prior to age 8 but some families register the younger children anyway. However, there are more younger than older children in home schooling. The 5,500 estimate assumes about 25% of the K–2 group is not registered.

[58] In the BJUP survey, 61.4% indicated that the authorities knew about their school (Gladin, 1987, p. 117). Washington was one of 11 states in his sample.

[59] Based on attendance at statewide conventions, a survey asking for number of children in the family, and an estimate of those who do not attend conventions, the chairman of the Washington Home Schoolers Organization estimated 15,000 to 20,000 such children. Interview with Sandy Hall, chair, Washington Home schoolers Organization, December 21, 1988. Kathleen McCurdy, the executive director of the Family Learning Organization of Washington State, the major organization in the eastern part of the state, estimates 20,000 based on newsletter subscriptions, conference attendance, and other contacts. The number includes children below age 8. Letter of December 20, 1988.

[60] Sandy Hall has estimated that 60% of the home-schooled children in her local support group of about 100 members are younger than age 8, the age of compulsory education in Washington. Interview, 1988.

from 2,888 families, reporting intentions to home school about 4,000 children (L. Dukes, Florida State Department of Education, personal communication, December 2, 1988).[61] The Florida home school association takes state registration and increases it to account for those who do not register. This yields an estimate of 8,664 families and about 13,900 children (R. Lynd, personal communication, December 14, 1988).[62] Table 1.3 suggests that Florida has from 3–4.6% of the home schoolers in the country, or from 9,000–13,800 children, at the very most. The outer range of the estimate in Table 1.1 is consistent with the association estimate. An estimated 500,000 or a million home-schooled children in the country would suggest from 15,000 to 43,000 in Florida—too high compared to this local estimate.

These comparisons confirm the estimate of 200,000 to 300,000 and suggest that estimates of 1,000,000 and even 500,000 are too high.

Discussion of How to Use the Estimate

Even with this corroborating data from three states, the estimate is rough, with weaknesses in the later steps. Thus, it must be used with care. It provides one model of how to make a better estimate. It permits one to say that there is a home school movement (a fact that some educators and puplic officials doubted prior to this kind of documentation) and that it is growing. The estimate helps those attempting to decide whether it would be worthwhile to include a home-school question in a census or survey, and to determine sample size. Educators should not use the estimate to make quantitative predictions about school enrollments or cost of programs where home school population may be a factor.

SUGGESTIONS FOR FUTURE DATA COLLECTION AND RESEARCH

Until states win the confidence and cooperation of home schoolers, researchers will have to pursue innovative and imaginative techniques for studying the population. No research finding can be regarded as

---

[61] The state has details on a smaller group, however: Only 1,572 (representing 2,550 children) returned a state questionnaire on their programs. Note over two/three of the children were age 5 through 11; 87 were 16 and over. Note older children are not subject to compulsory education requirements.

[62] This is based on surveys at book fairs and other meetings, which indicate that about one-third of the families give the state a notice of intent to home-school. Lynd rounds up to 9,000, but I have used the actual "notice-of-intent" figure and multiplied it by 3. The estimate of children is based on a ratio of 1.6 children per family among those who returned a state questionnaire. This is lower than the number of children per family on other lists.

representative. Surveying existing publishers or school lists assumes a family is willing to pay for supplies or memberships. Surveying those who register with their state may locate only those who are more confident about their programs. Surveys of home school associations assume families who join are the same as those who don't. Ideally, researchers will draw their sample from several sources. If this is not an option, researchers examining just one source could at least note the way in which their particular subset of home schoolers differ from all other known groups of home schoolers. Questions about income of both parents, education of both parents, race and religious affiliation, who does the primary teaching, hours of intentional guided instruction, hours of unguided work, and reasons for home schooling all will assist in comparing studies of different subgroups of home schoolers. It would be obviously useful if future researchers would use the same questions as used in the larger studies, and report data in the same clusters as used by Census and CPS.

One of the most challenging aspects of home-school research relates to the difficulty in identifying the universe of home schoolers. Based on the research here, it appears that the home-schooling population is still too small to make it worthwhile for the federal government to include a home school question in its surveys. If the movement continues to grow, however, home shoolers could comprise about 1% of the total school-aged population and 10% of the private school population by the close of the century. In states where the home-school population is disproportionately large (as seems to be the case in Oregon and Washington[63]), they may comprise as much as 1 to 2% of the state's total school-aged population, and 20 to 30% of the private school population. In California, official reports suggest that over one-third of the total private *schools* are home schools.[64] (Note, this represents numbers of home schools and private schools, not children.) Some states may wish to conduct surveys of their own. States which do not wish to undergo this expense might want to make a preliminary assessment using a method comparable to the one described in this chapter.

This chapter has outlined ways to estimate the home-schooled population, by using one source as a starting point, and using surveys of home schoolers drawn from a second data source to adjust the estimate. What starting point is best depends on the circumstances in any given

---

[63] See Table 1.3.

[64] The official reporting form does not ask if a private school is restricted to a single family. However over one-third of the private schools in California have four or fewer pupils. Since there are other legal and "illegal" ways to home-school in California, the raw number does not help to determine the number of home schoolers in the state.

area. In states with "no hassle" registration and good relations with home schoolers, state registration figures would be acceptable as such a starting point. The estimate should be adjusted to account for those who do not register; surveys of families using libraries during school hours might be one way of locating these nonregistering families. In states with no confidence in their registration figures, the home-school association might provide the starting point, but these numbers must also be adjusted, as outlined above. Where neither of these sources are helpful, the state may wish to collect data for its state from curriculum suppliers nationwide. Not all suppliers will be able to provide state-based figures, however.

In order to obtain better information for making these types of estimate, it would be useful for researchers who are conducting surveys of known home school populations to ask certain key questions that allow them to tie their population to other home school populations. One such question would include information on whether or not a family is enrolled or obtaining a complete curricular package in the specific correspondence schools listed in Table 1.1. This question permits researchers to estimate the proportion of the total population that are receiving the curricular packages represented in Table 1.1, and to use the estimates in Table 1.1 as a base. This question should ask the family specifically to identify the source of the curriculm in order to confirm that the family and the researcher agree on the definition of "curricular package," and to corroborate the assumption that families that use these curricula use only one per child. A related question would discover how many families would allow appraisal of the full population based on distribution of complete, graded curricular packages. Another set of questions allowing assessment of the population would discover whether the home-school family has registered with the state (to permit researchers to estimate the state population, using the state registration data as a base); whether the family affiliated with a home-school association (to allow an estimate based on membership data); whether the child, although home-schooled, is enrolled in a public or private school (to permit estimates based on surveys of schools). Some of these provide a better base than others. For example, if only about 10% of home-schooled children enroll in a campus-based school,[65] private school enrollment will not provide as substantial a base as regis-

---

[65] According to the Home School Legal Defense Association (HSLDA), 11% of its membership enroll the child in a local, private school. They regard this as exclusive of the enrollments in the correspondence school programs listed in Table 1.1. Note HSLDA does not accept members who have the child pursue independent study while enrolled in a public school, a popular practice among home schoolers in California, and the only method recognized as legal by New Hampshire officials.

tration figures or use of a curriculm. It might also be useful to repeat the Census question, to assist in interpreting the results of the forthcoming Census.

It would be useful to elicit information from families on the month in which home schooling starts each year, in order to confirm the assumption that most parents begin home schooling in late August or September and to assist in timing surveys. A question about library use might provide a key to understanding home schoolers. Such a question would help in comparing home schoolers in different surveys.[66] It could also assist in determining the merits of a survey of *library users* during school hours.

Yet untried, a survey of library users might yield an interesting population of home schoolers. Gladin found widespread library use in his sample: 217 of 241 families said they used a library at least once per month. Gustafson also reported a "large number" of parents who indicated frequent library use, in response to an open-ended question asking for an explanation of their assessment of advantages/disadvantages of home schooling. If other studies affirm this high incidence of library use in a variety of known home-school populations, the broadest-based study of home schoolers would include a library-based survey, in cooperation with all libraries in an area for a period of at least one month.[67] It would be appropriate to station a researcher at the children's and teenage section during school hours, and to offer reading materials as an enticement to participate. A library-based survey has additional advantages as it would also permit interviews with children.[68]

Given the importance to educators in understanding teaching and learning, those who examine academic achievement should attempt to include analysis of the relation between achievement and other factors. They should examine income and education of fathers and mothers separately, pupil–teacher ratios, teaching styles, and other possible factors that might influence academic outcome—for both control and experimental groups.

Finally, it would be useful to think through which questions are really important. Research already conducted is rich in suggesting what is important to parents, and much of this can guide future re-

---

[66] I would very much appreciate it if any researcher following these suggestions would contact me and share the findings.

[67] Librarians have expressed an interest in home schoolers and are often aware of their use. It seems likely that cooperation from libraries is possible in such a research effort.

[68] Wright (1988) and this author both have noted the absence of data based on interviews of children.

search. Academic outcome, for example, is not as highly rated as religion and a belief that home schooling will produce children that adopt religious and ethical values of their parents. A longitudinal study of home-schooled children and a control group, and the extent to which children's religious and other beliefs match their parents, would be highly informative to parents who turn to home schooling for this reason. It seems appropriate to examine such things as incidence of drug use, smoking, and drinking as well.

It would also be useful to interview public officials about their concerns for home-schooled children, and to conduct research that address these concerns, including research that suggests ways in which parents can adjust home schooling to mitigate any adverse results. This probably will mean more rigorous research on academic and social outcomes. Such research should be careful to note differences between families in compliance with state laws and families that are not in compliance, for it makes no sense as a matter of policy to change the legal requirements for those in compliance if concern is based only on data for those not in compliance.[69]

Finally, future research on home schooling must be interdisciplinary. If parents home school for religious reasons and public educators fear that the children are not well-adjusted socially—then careful constitutional analysis would be in order before policy decisions are made based upon even the soundest research, even if there is empirical data that home-schooled children do not meet academic expectations.

REFERENCES

Alaska Department of Education. (1986). *Results from 1981 CAT [for Centralized Correspondence Study]*. Juneau, AK: Author.

Alaska Department of Education. (1985, Spring). *SRA survey of basic skills, Alaska statewide assessment*. Juneau, AK. Author.

Alaska Department of Education. (1984). *Summary of SRA testing for Centralized Correspondence Study*. Juneau, AK.

Benson, P. L., & Dorothy, L. W. (forthcoming). *Private schools in the United States: A statistical profile*. Minneapolis: Search Institute.

Bray, J., & Lines, P. (1983). *What is a school?* (No. LEC-83-17). Denver, CO: Education Commission of the States.

Coughlin, E. K. (1988, October 19). Studying homelessness: The difficulty of tracking a transient population. *Chronicle of Higher Education, 35*(8), A7, A12.

Denzin, N. K. (1978). *The research act: A theoretical introduction to sociological methods* (2nd ed.). Chicago: Aldine.

---

[69] This point is stressed by Wartes (1988a, 1988b).

Ellson, E. (1986, November). Improving productivity in teaching. *Phi Delta Kappan, 68*(3), 111–124.

Frost, E. A., & Morris, R. C. (1988, Summer). Does home-schooling work? Some insights for academic success. *Contemporary Education, 59*(4), 223–227.

Gladin, W. E. (1987). *Home education: Characteristics of its families and schools.* Doctoral thesis, Bob Jones University, Greensborough, SC.

Gordon, E. E. (1983). Home tutoring programs gain respectability. *Phi Delta Kappan, 64*(6), 395–398.

Gustafson, S. K. (1988). A study of home schooling: Parental motivations and goals. Senior thesis, Princeton University, Princeton, NJ. (Published in *Home School Researcher, 4(2),* 4–12, 1987.)

Holt, J. (1983a). Schools and home schools: A fruitful partnership. *Phi Delta Kappan, 64*(6), 391–394.

Holt, J. (1983b). Letter to Ray Moore, how many are we? *Growing Without Schooling,* No. 32, 14–16.

Holt, J. (1981). *Teach your own: A hopeful path for education.* New York: Delacorte-Lawrence.

Knowles, J. G. (1988). Parents' rationales and teaching methods for home schooling: The role of biography. *Education and Urban Society, 21*(1), 69–84.

Lines, P. M. (forthcoming). *Home instruction: Characteristics of and an estimate of the number of children* (Working Paper). Washington DC: Office of Research, U.S. Department of Education.

Lines, P. M. (1987, March). An overview of home instruction. *Phi Delta Kappan 68(7),* 510–517. (Reprinted in *Kaleidoscope 1,* edited by Freshman English Committee, pp. 199–206. Lexington, MA: Ginn Press, 1987.)

Lines, P. M. (1985). *Compulsory education laws and their impact on public and private education.* Denver, CO: Education Commission of the States.

Mayberry, M. (1988a). The 1987–88 Oregon home school survey: An overview of the findings. *Home School Researcher, 4*(1), 1–9.

Mayberry, M. (1988b). Characteristics and attitudes of families who home school. *Education and Urban Society, 21*(1), 32–41.

Moore, R. (1983). Letter to John Holt, how many are we? *Growing Without Schooling,* No. 32, 14–16.

Naisbitt, J. (1982). *Megatrends.* New York: Warner Books Inc.

Pride, M. (1986). *The big book of home learning.* Westchester, IL: Crossways Books.

Quine, D. N. (1987). *Reasoning abilities of home-educated children.* Unpublished paper, Pathways School, Richardson, TX.

Quine, D. N., & Marek, E. A. (1988). Reasoning abilities of home-educated children. *Home School Researcher, 4*(3), 1–6.

Ray, B. D. (1988a). The kitchen classroom: Is home schooling making the grade. *Christianity Today,* pp. 23–26.

Ray, B. D. (1988b). Home schools: A synthesis of research on characteristics and learner outcomes. *Education and Urban Society, 21*(1), 16–81.

Rosenblum, K. E. (1987). The in-depth interview: Between science and sociability. *Sociologicial Forum, 2*(2), 388 400.

Scogin, L. A. (1986). *Home school survey.* Unpublished report, Home School Legal Defense Association, Washington, DC.

Shepherd, M. S. (1986). *The home schooling movement: An emerging conflict in American education.* Unpublished doctoral dissertation, East Texas State University, Waco, TX.

Van Galen, J. (1988). Ideology, curriculum, and pedagogy in home education. *Education and Urban Society, 21*(1), 52–68.

Wartes, J. (1988a). The Washington home school project: Quantitative measures for informing policy decisions. *Education and Urban Society, 21*(1), 42–51.

Wartes, J. (1988b). *Report from the 1987 Washington homeschool testing.* Woodinville, WA: Washington Homeschool Research Project.

Washington State Superintendent of Public Instruction. (1985). *Washington state's experimental program using the parent as tutor under the supervision of a Washington state certified teacher.* Olympia, WA: Author.

Weaver, R. et al. (1980). Home tutorials vs. the public school in Los Angeles. *Phi Delta Kappan, 61*(4).

Wright, C. (1988). Home school research: Critique and suggestions for the future. *Education and Urban Society, 21*(1), 96–113.

Chapter 2
The Academic Achievement and Affective Development of Home-Schooled Children

Brian D. Ray
National Home Education Research Institute
Seattle, WA

Jon Wartes
Bothell High School
Bothell, WA

INTRODUCTION

Parents who teach their children at home often cite improved academic achievement as a reason for educating their own children. However, parents who teach their children at home usually do not have formal training in pedagogy, curriculum design, or learning and development, and many do not even have a college degree. These same parents also often cite improved socialization as a reason for educating their own children. However, it seems that the home education environment might offer a drastically confined experience of societal subgroups and of interaction with other individuals. Therefore, it is understandable that serious doubt exists as to whether parents teaching their children in the confines of their homes can be pedagogically successful at transmitting to their children the highly prized curricula of American schooling. Those curricula were recently reanalyzed by Shulman (1986) who proposed two major agendas of education. One

43

agenda is the academic task, the classroom content. The other agenda is the hidden curriculum, socializing generations of children through the workings of the classroom community. Our purpose in this chapter is to address aspects of both agendas. More specifically, we will attempt to answer the question: "How do the academic achievement and affective development of children who are being taught at home compare to the achievement and affective development of those involved in traditional schooling?"

ACADEMIC ACHIEVEMENT

It is especially pertinent to consider the academic achievement of the home-educated since learner outcomes of the traditional schools has been under such ardent attack and analysis during this decade (e.g., Bloom, 1987; Hirsch, 1987; The National Commission on Excellence in Education, 1983; The United States Department of Education, 1984; Wayson, Mitchell, Pinnell, & Landis, 1988). Several studies have also examined the academic achievement of home-schooled students. Some of the research included achievement as the primary target of investigation while others reported achievement scores somewhat as an addendum to the body of the report. We will first consider a study with which we, the authors, are very familiar.

The Washington Homeschool Research Project

One of us, Wartes, has been a part of the Washington Homeschool Research Project in the State of Washington since 1985. The project has aimed at gathering extensive achievement data from home schoolers throughout the state (Wartes, 1987, 1988a, 1988b, 1989). One aspect of Washington's law is the requirement for an annual assessment of home schoolers using approved standardized tests. Several people around the state have gone into the business of offering testing services in order to meet the demand generated by the law, and a number of home school students are tested by these services. The research method used in the Project's studies simply involved tapping into the test scores of those home schoolers utilizing several of these testing services. Different combinations of eight testing services were used for the 1986, 1987, and 1988 samplings. Each of the services forwarded a set of scores for each home schooler who was tested. Thus, this sampling represented a 100% reporting of scores of those utilizing selected services for each year. Parents of these home schoolers were also asked to fill out a questionnaire dealing with various aspects of the family or their home schooling. All testing services used the Stanford Achievement Test series (SAT). This series consists of the Stanford Early School Achievement Test (2nd ed.) for grade K, the Stanford Achievement Test (7th ed.) for grades 1 to 8, and the Test of Academic Skills (2nd ed.) for grades 9 to 12. The 1986 data utilized 1982 norms while the 1987 and 1988 samplings used 1986 norms.

The population for the three studies by Wartes was those Washington home schoolers who were apparently in conformance with the state law. That is, children who are 8 to under 18 years of age must be tested once per year. This operational definition of the population acknowledges that there are a number of home schoolers who have remained underground. (Although we are often asked for an estimate, there is no known reliable way to determine the percentage of home schoolers who remain underground. See Chapter One for a full discussion of demographic issues related to home schoolers.) Their learning outcomes are not available. The test scores reported here have not been used for comparison with the scores of public-schooled students in the Washington State. There are no state norms available for the SAT; the state uses a different standardized test for its purposes. The reader should note that some of the results in this brief summary involve the combination of test scores from all eight levels of the SAT. This practice assumes that the norming group for each level of the test was similar (which is an assumption that has not been empirically tested). Some data are presented simply in percentiles. Other data were analyzed using linear regression, the t-test, and analysis of variance. An alpha level of .05 was used.

In the 1986 sampling of Washington home schoolers ($n = 424$), the home school students' median score was at the 68th percentile on national norms. The sample size more than doubled ($n = 873$) in 1987 and the median scores were in the 65th to 66th percentile range. The highest scores in 1987 were in the area of science and in the verbal areas of listening, vocabulary, and word reading. The lowest scores were in math computation (42nd percentile) while math application scores were notably stronger (65th percentile). The median scores for the 1988 sample ($n = 726$) was at the 65th percentile. The 1987 pattern for science and mathematics was repeated in 1988. These scores earned by home schoolers suggest that they are, as a group, doing well. Thus, fears that home-schooled children in Washington are at an academic disadvantage are not confirmed.

Relationships between achievement and several other variables were analyzed with respect to the 1987 sampling (Wartes, 1988b). First, the relationship between parent education level and test scores of their children was examined. At various grade levels, the students' scores were compared to the education level of the parent who does most of the teaching, to the other parent, and to the parents combined. Nine of the comparisons (three for the main teacher) produced statistically significant correlations of weak-to-moderate magnitude. Fifteen of the correlations were not significant. Second, parent education level was not a strong predictor of test scores. It is interesting to note in this sample that children of parents who have only a 12th-grade education are, as a group, scoring somewhat above the national norm. Another finding was that children who had no contact at all with a certified teacher scored, as a group, at the 70th percentile on national norms ($n = 200$). Third, the data suggest that there is virtually no relationship between level of structure or hours of formal schooling and academic outcomes ($n = 287$). A fourth finding was that there was no relationship between achievement and the number of consecutive years the student had been home schooled ($n = 268$). Fifth, there was no relationship between academic outcomes and the grade level of the home school student within the K to 9 range ($n = 278$). The data for grades 10 to 12 were not subjected to statistical analysis due to the small sample size, but the 28 students in this grade range had a mean score at the 72nd percentile on national norms. The data also suggested no relationship between family income level and achievement ($n = 271$). Seventh, this sampling (using a secular measure of achievement, the SAT) provided no evidence supporting a relationship between the degree of religious content in the home education and achievement test scores in general ($n = 278$), nor in science ($n = 201$) or social science scores ($n = 206$). Religious content was measured using one 7-point item responded to by the parents. The data just summarized are the most complete and organized in the state of Washington. With the limitations of the study in mind (which will be discussed in more detail in this chapter), the data are an accurate representation of home school students' performance on achievement tests.

More Studies of Academic Achievement

The preceding two studies offer the most detailed and extensive examinations of the academic achievement of home-schooled children, but several other studies offer related data. Rakestraw (1987, 1988) compared the SAT scores of 6- to 12-year-old ($n = 84$) home-schooled children in Alabama to their Alabama public-schooled peers. Several criteria (e.g., age and no attendance at public school the current school year) were established for selecting the home school student subjects

($n = 84$). The researcher trained assistants to administer the SAT at five testing locations, and parents were not allowed to interfere with the testing process. The researcher set alpha at .01. There were no significant differences between the home-schooled and public-schooled subjects in the areas of reading, listening, and mathematics for grades 1, 4, and 5 and no significant difference in mathematics scores for grade 2. However, the home-schooled second-grade students score significantly better than the public-schooled students in reading and listening. Rakestraw considered two other hypotheses closely relevant to this chapter. First, she found no significant differences in achievement among home-schooled children when grouped according to the educational background of the parent–teacher. Second, there was no significant difference in the achievement of home-schooled children in grades 1 and 2 when grouped according to whether the parent–teacher was or had ever been a state-certificated teacher. There were insufficient data to test this hypothesis for grades 3 through 6.

Delahooke (1986), working in California, compared the intelligence and achievement (and social/emotional adjustment, to be discussed later) of 9-year-olds who were home schooled ($n = 28$) and those enrolled in religiously affiliated private schools ($n = 32$) as a part of her preexperimental, causal comparative-type study. She used the Wechsler Intelligence Scale for Children-Revised and the Wide Range Achievement Test-Revised (for reading, spelling, and arithmetic) as instruments. All subjects were individually tested in their homes by the researcher or the trained research assistant. Intelligence scores for both groups were in the above-average range while the achievement test scores for both groups were in the average range and not significantly different from one another, $F(1, 57) = 12.13$, $p < .001$.

Scogin (1986) conducted a random sampling survey of 300 families from the membership list of Home School Legal Defense Association (which is a national advocacy organization well-known among the home schooling community). There were 591 total children in these families. The parents reported the standardized test scores of "after homeschooling results" for 241 of the students (who were apparently in grades K to 12). Scogin did not explain how or by whom the children were tested. In reading, 9% were below grade level, 18% were at grade level to 11 months above, and 73% were one year or more above grade level. In math, the corresponding figures were 21% below level, 29% at level, and 50% above level.

Linden (1983) surveyed home-school families in Texas and presented some California Achievement Tests scores (i.e., reading, mathematics, and language) that were reported by the parents. It was explained that most of the tests were administered by the parents and then forwarded to the test suppliers for scoring. The 16 students ranged from grade 1.9 to 11.6, and the averages of their three scores were on the average 1.04 grades above their actual grade level.

The Hewitt Research Foundation (1985) reported that in a court case involving home schooling, "North Dakota home schoolers average about 83 percentile points on their standardized tests" (p. 5), 22 percentiles higher than the rest of North Dakota school youth (see also Hewitt Research Foundation, 1986a). Hewitt Research Foundation (1986b) also reported that a random sampling of students who use Hewitt's home-schooling curriculum averaged between the 78th and 80th percentile on a standardized test. Students who had been with Hewitt longer scored higher (which conflicts with the findings of Wartes [1988]). The Hewitt Research Foundation did not explain which tests were used nor how or by whom they were administered.

Reynolds (1985) conducted a case study of three home-schooling families. Among other findings, he reported the scores of the five children who had been administered standardized tests. The average (for 69 scores reported) score was at the 86th percentile level. Some of the tests were administered by parents and some were administered by local public schools.

On the other hand, Schemmer's (1985) case study of five children showed that only two were achieving at or above their grade level expectancy on the Peabody Individual Achievement Test. It was implied that the researcher administered the test. Only three of the five children could be examined for achievement gain over the period of one year; Schemmer concluded that the results were equivocal.

Quine and Marek (1988) recently took another approach by examining the cognitive outcomes of home education in terms of intellectual development (per Inhelder & Piaget, 1958) rather than in terms of achievement test scores. The researchers used performance on Piagetian tasks to compare 11 home-schooled children (aged 72 to 131 months) to 19 peers (matched on age and gender) who were involved in Pathways School. Pathways School was an alternative school that provided two, 2-1/2 hour class sessions per week in the areas of math and science. The instruction in Pathways School was specifically designed to promote intellectual development as described by Inhelder and Piaget. Parents of the solely home-educated students had no formal knowledge of or education in the realm of the Piagetian model or the curriculum used at Pathways School. A pretest-posttest research design was used, and the researchers found that there was no significantly different gain between the solely home-schooled and the Pathways School children. Furthermore, Quine and Marek concluded that both groups in their study were slightly ahead, in terms of intellectual development, of the "somewhat priviledged population" of Piaget's original investigation. The researchers said their findings suggested that home-educated students move into formal thought between the ages of 10 and 11, which is far earlier than for the national averages (i.e., ages 15 to 20).

Our data on academic achievement are expanding due to the fact that a few state departments of education collect the standardized test scores of home-schooled students. We have been able to gather some of these reports from Arkansas, Oregon, and Tennessee. In Arkansas, home-schooled students must score no more than eight months behind their expected grade level on an approved standardized test to remain in the home-schooling environment. The test must be administered by a person designated by the State Board of Education. In 1986 (Arkansas Department of Education, 1986), 81% of the 430 home-schooled students who were tested on standardized achievement tests were successful in meeting requirements of the state. Arkansas' 1987 report (Arkansas Department of Education) stated that over 85% of the 594 home-schooled students who were tested met the state's requirements.

More detailed information was forthcoming from Oregon where the home-educated are to annually take a standardized test approved by the Oregon Department of Education and administered by a qualified person who is not related to the child. The scores are supposed to be reported to the state. The Oregon Department of Education (1986, 1988) has provided two reports on home-schooled students' achievement scores. During late 1986, there were 2,691 children registered as home schoolers. Valid test scores were submitted for 1,121. It is difficult to precisely account for the discrepancy between number registered and number of scores reported. Some may have returned to traditional schools, some may have moved out of state, and some may have not been tested or did not report their scores if they were tested. There were 3,103 registered home-school students during the 1987/88 year and 1,658 scores were reported. Data for the two years are presented in Table 2.1. As can be seen, a large portion of the home school students' scores are very high and the distribution is generally negatively skewed.

Finally, the Tennessee Department of Education (TDE) (personal communication, March 30, 1987) reported to one of us on the spring 1986 test scores of public-schooled and home-schooled students (who are required by law to be tested). The TDE examined the reading and math scores of home-schooled students ($N = 212$) in grades 2, 3, 6, and 8. The home-schooled outscored their public-schooled peers on 7 of the 8 comparisons. The TDE (1988) also reported grade 2 home-school SAT scores for 1986/87. The reading score average was at the 85th percen-

Table 2.1.   Standardized Test Score Percentiles
of Home School Students In Oregon

	Percentage of Home School Test Scores	
Percentile Range	Late 1986	1987/88 Year
91 to 99	23.8	21.4
51 to 90	52.3	51.2
21 to 50	17.5	19.7
1 to 20	6.4	7.7

tile and the math average was at the 91st percentile. The 1987/88 SAT scores in reading and math for grades 2, 5, 7, and 9 ranged from the 53rd percentile to the 88th percentile.

Home schooling within a different ambience has occurred at times in Washington, Alaska, and Western Australia. The government has had a hand in home education in these places for a variety of reasons. The Washington State Superintendent of Public Instruction (1985) planned to evaluate the implementation and success of two State Board of Education-approved "private experimental programs using the parent as tutor under the supervision of a certificated teacher" (p. 1). The students' scores on the SAT were used as the dependent variable. One hundred children in grades K to 8 from a cross-section of communities across the state participated. The children averaged the following percentile scores: reading, 62; language, 56.5; and math, 53. Washington State concluded that the majority of the scores were average or above average.

In the far north is Alaska's Centralized Correspondence Study Program (CCS) that "is a complete K-12 education program delivered to students at home through the mails" (Madden, 1986, p. 3), operated by the Alaska Department of Education (ADE), open to any Alaskan resident who has not completed high school, and paid for by the people of the state (Madden, 1986). A home teacher, usually a parent, teaches the student. The home teacher is under the supervision of an advisory, certificated, teacher who is located in Juneau, Alaska. The ADE (1986) examined the students' scores on the California Achievement Tests (CAT) and on the Alaska Statewide Assessment Tests (ASA) in reading and math. The CAT reading scores for CCS grades 1 to 3 were .58 to 1.31 standard deviations (SD) higher than the norm. Grades 4 to 8 reading scores were .67 to 1.12 SD higher than the norm. Grades 1 to 8 math scores of children taught at home were .42 to 1.13 SD higher than the norm, with the exception of grade five that was .21 SD higher than the norm. The CCS student scores were significantly ($p < .01$)

higher than the theoretical distribution. Research in Alaska has revealed three other important findings:

1. Those students in grades 4 to 8 involved in CCS two years or more scored significantly higher on the CAT than those in it less than two years (t-test, $p < .05$) (.61 SD higher in math and .83 SD higher in reading). This finding corroborates Hewitt Research Foundation (1986b) but conflicts with Wartes (1988b).
2. The scores of grades 4 to 8 students after CCS involvement were significantly greater than before CCS study (t-test, $p < .05$) (.29 SD greater in math, and .43 SD greater in reading).
3. On the Alaska test, CCS students scored higher than the Alaska averages in reading and math (by 14.27% in fourth-grade reading and by 8% in eighth-grade reading; by 7.7% in fourth-grade math and by 6% in eighth-grade math).

Another study in Alaska (ADE, 1984) summarized the Science Research Associates (SRA) test math and reading scores of the CCS students. Not all students were tested, and this may have been due to several reasons that were listed by the ADE (e.g., student/home teacher may not have understood it was required. The results for the 22% of the CCS students who were tested "on-site" (not at home) were as follows:

1. ". . . 9 of the 12 grades fell above the 75th percentile in reading . . ." (ADE, p. 1).
2. 8 of 12 grades ranked above the 60th percentile in language.
3. 9 of the 12 grades ranked above the 60th percentile in math.

When one includes the CCS students tested at home (i.e., 18% of the total), their composite test scores were even higher than those just listed (ADE, 1984). It is impossible to say whether the other 60% of the CCS students scored better or worse than the reported levels.

The Alaska Department of Education (1985) also assessed the CCS home-schooled youths' achievement in the areas of reading, math, language, and science using the SRA and the Alaska test in the spring of 1985. The home-schooled students' scores were, in general, at least equal to and in the majority of cases notably higher than the scores of the traditionally schooled.

It appears that the home schooling of CCS has allowed students to achieve at least as well as their Alaskan peers and better than national norms. Falle (1986) discussed the fact that the ADE is attempting to develop more reliable means of administering standardized tests to home schooled children. Nevertheless, he did not indicate that this reliability issue was a major obstacle to accepting as valid the superior achievement of CCS students.

In Australia, as in Alaska, many students are far from a conventional school. The Isolated Students Matriculation Scheme (ISMS) was developed by the Australian government in order "to develop modern correspondence courses for rural matriculation students" (Western Australia Department of Education [WADE], 1979, p. 3). The treatments in this study of a preexperimental design were involvement in ISMS, in which the majority of school learning was done at home, versus conventional schooling. Forty-six students took the Tertiary Admissions Examination during a two-year period. WADE (1979) reported that according to the ISMS main indicator of success, academic achievement, the performance of those schooled at home was satisfactory.

The preceding studies represent most of what has been done in terms of critical analyses of the academic achievement of home school youth. The available evidence indicates that home school youth of compulsory education age score equal to or better than their conventional school peers on measures of academic achievement. This statement is made while keeping in mind the limitations of the static-group comparison design (Campbell & Stanley, 1963), which was generally the design of the studies discussed in this section. There is no complete assurance that the home and conventional school groups were homogeneous in nature. It is quite clear, however, that the overall phenomenon (the combination of the type of youth involved in home school and the home school "treatment") is not inhibiting the youth from matching or excelling average conventional school achievement.

AFFECTIVE DEVELOPMENT

A very different, and yet interesting and controversial, area deals with the affective development of home school children. As Shulman (1986) said, one of the major goals of American schooling is socializing children. According to our experience, socialization is the effective dimension most frequently (and often passionately) mentioned in discussions or debates concerning home schooling.

In its report on their home-education program, Western Australia (1979) made the qualitative conclusion that "students working by themselves or in small groups are severely handicapped socially. The social interaction experienced at camps [provided by ISMS] is good for all students, but those students attending large schools daily have an obvious advantage in this regard" (p. 19). Likewise, concern for the socialization of home-schooled children was expressed in the "parent as tutor program" in Washington (Washington State Superintendent of Public Instruction, 1985). Tizard and Hughes (1984) studied 4-year-olds at home and in preschools and found that the learning environment at home was generally superior to that in the preschools. Nevertheless, they also mentioned that some of the educational needs of children cannot be met within the home; for example, "how to get on with other children, to be a member of a group, to separate from their families, and to relate to, and communicate with, strange adults" (Tizard & Hughes, 1984, p. 259). Statements such as the preceding are basically appeals to a priori knowledge. Some empirical evidence might be helpful in the discussion.

There are a few inquiries that have closely examined aspects of socialization in home schools. The first study to break into this realm was by Taylor (1986a, 1986b). Like many others (e.g., Carin & Sund, 1985; Travers, 1982) who have emphasized the importance of positive self-concept to effective learning, Taylor interpreted self-concept as a relevant construct in that it "is closely linked with values, social competence, and self-evaluation" (p. 53) as well as achievement. Taylor analyzed the relationship between home schooling and the self-concept of children in grades four through twelve. The investigator used the 80-item, self-report *Piers-Harris Self-Concept Scale* (PHSCS) in his study. The PHSCS is a standardized instrument that was normed to public-schooled children in grades 4 through 12 in a Pennsylvania school district. Taylor used the mailing lists of two major, national home education agencies to randomly select families to participate in the study. He mailed the PHSCS (to be answered by the students at home) and a questionnaire (to be filled out by the parents) to families throughout the United States. Although Taylor does not discuss the matter, the PHSCS was probably not designed to be administered by parents at home. Taylor used the scores of 224 grades 4 through 12 home-schooled youth. He explained that this represented an estimated return rate of 45%. Taylor found that the self-concept of home-schooled students (M = 66.72) was significantly higher for the global scale score than that of public-schooled students (M = 51.84), $t(223)$ = 18.86, $p < .001$, SD = 13.87. The scores of the home-schooled were also significantly higher ($p < .001$) than the public-schooled on all six subscales. Taylor stated, "Insofar as self-concept is a reflector of socialization . . . [references given], the findings of this study would suggest that few home-schooling children are socially deprived" (p. 160, 161). In addition, Taylor pointed out that his findings jibed with those of others who have studied home school families.

Delahooke (1986) (whose methodology was previously described in this chapter) provided the second research foray into the arena of socialization and home-educated children. She employed a preexperimental, causal comparative design to determine how home-schooled (n = 28) and one group (n = 32) (religious and private) of traditional-schooled children compared in terms of social/emotional adjustment and academic achievement (as previously discussed). Delahooke developed a theoretical argument based upon "dual process" theories (i.e., both familial and peer systems have significant roles in the development of a child's social competency). The researcher hypothesized that home-educated children would express fewer aggressive social behaviors and a greater perceived reliance on and support from adults than traditionally-educated children. The Roberts Apperception Test for Children (RATC) was used to measure children's perceptions of common interpersonal situations or social/emotional adjustment. Both groups scored in the "well-adjusted" range of the RATC. Delahooke found no significant differences between the two groups on the Aggression, Reliance on Others, Support-Other (from whom they perceive support), Limit Setting (who sets limits on them), the family arena of the Interpersonal Matrix, or the Support-Child (self-reliant and assertive behaviors) scales on the RATC. Antithetically, significant differences were found in the "nonfamily" categories of the Interpersonal Matrix. The finding suggested to Delahooke that the home-educated had their primary focus in the family arena while the private-schooled had a greater focus on peer interaction. The "private school subjects appeared to be more influenced by or concerned with peers than the home educated group" (p. 85). The researcher also said that the data *may* suggest that private-schooled children were more adept at resolving interpersonal (with other children) problems than those educated at home. Delahooke expanded her data by including some descriptive information related to the social activities of the home-schooled children. There was a higher frequency of participation by the home-schooled than by the private-schooled in play groups (64% vs. 9%), organized sports (39% vs. 34%), church-related activities (100% vs. 84%), and in the "other" category of extracurricular activities (68% vs. 41%). Private-schooled children, on the other hand, more frequently participated in organized clubs (44% vs. 32%).

One of us (Wartes, 1987, described previously) has investigated whether home-schooled children are being socially isolated. Parents responded to items on a questionnaire regarding the activities and social skills of their home-schooled children. Parents reported that their children spend a median of 20 to 29 hours per month for each of (a) participation in organized community activities, (b) contact with age peers, and (c) contact with those of two or more years difference in age outside the immediate family. Parents rated at least 94% of their children as average or above average in each of the following skills: constructively interacting with peers, constructively interacting with adults, displaying leadership ability, and showing a sense of responsibility. The data from this study suggest that home schoolers are not being socially isolated.

Rakestraw (1987, previously described) gathered descriptive data, provided by parents responding to a questionnaire, that corroborate those of Delahooke (1986) and Wartes (1987). Namely, the home-schooled children participated in religious or Sunday school activities (98.3% of the students), interacted with other home-schooled children (90%), interacted with neighborhood children (88.3%), were involved in music activities (50%), sports activities (48.3%), public or private school functions (35%), and neighborhood or community service organizations such as scouts (18.3%).

Montgomery (1989a, 1989b) investigated the extent to which age 10 to 21 home school students were experiencing conditions which foster leadership in children and adolescents. Through her reviews of past research, she found that the main predictor of leadership in adulthood is participation of students in extracurricular activities. After identifying those conditions that comprise the key ingredients in students' leadership development, the researcher developed three sets of interview schedules (i.e., one for home schooling parents, one for home schooling students, and one for a control group of conventionally schooled students). A stratified sample of urban, rural, and suburban families, and of families representing a range of family values and motivations for home schooling was selected and resulted in a sample of 55 parents and 87 students. A random sample of same age/sex students in grades 5 to 12 at a Christian school in the same area was also interviewed. Montgomery explained that these students were similar to the home-schooled on many variables except for the type of schooling. However, she also mentioned that students in the private school had no choice but to participate in a performing group at some point beyond fifth grade, and that the private school students typically participate in extracurricular and outside-of-class activities at higher levels than do those college-bound students in other similar-sized public and private schools in the state of Washington. Table 2.2 shows a comparison of the participation rates of home school students with those of the private school control group in major out-of-home organized group activities that are available to both groups, either at school or in the community or both. There was no significant difference ($\alpha = .05$) in the participation rates of these two groups of students in most activi-

Table 2.2. Home School and Conventional School Students' Participation
Rates in Out-Of-Home Activities

Activity	Percentage of Students Who Participate	
	Home School Students	King's Students
Church youth group/related church activities	83	88
Jobs/paid work	78	80
Sports	55	88*
Summer camp	54	76*
Music lessons/recitals	43	44
Performing groups	28	96*
Scouts/youth clubs/4H	26	28
Nothing (that is voluntary)	2	4

*$p < .05$

ties. Montgomery's findings suggest that the home educated are certainly not isolated from social and group activities with other youth and adults. She has also found that those taught at home appear to have many opportunities (and are taking advantage of them) to participate in extracurricular activities just as do those in traditional schools. She concluded that home schooling may nurture leadership at least as well as do conventional schools.

A creative approach was used by Reynolds (1985) to assess the social development of the 12 home-educated students in his case study. The researcher and the mother-teachers independently rated their children, using a 7-point scale, on the first eight of twelve categories listed in the Boy Scouts of America "Scout Law" (e.g., trustworthy, loyal, helpful, and friendly). There was a high degree of agreement between the mothers and the researcher. The ratings suggested a higher than average level of social development in the eight categories for most of the children.

Similarly, Schemmer (1985) conducted a case study of four families engaged in home education. She observed that all of the children were readily able to communicate with the researcher, made the researcher feel they were glad to participate in the study, and were engaged in groups outside the home that offered opportunities for social contacts with other children.

On the other hand, some home schoolers do mention social isolation as a disadvantage of home schooling. Gustafson (1988) examined 143 questionnaires (representing a 60% response rate) based on a systematic random sample from the directory of one national home school magazine whose ideological underpinnings are in the "unschooling" of John Holt (1981). About 25% of the parents cited social isolation as a disadvantage of home schooling. Comments ranged from lack of group participation in music and drama to the idea that extra effort must be expended to provide social contact for their children.

PSYCHOMOTOR DEVELOPMENT

We would like to apprise the reader that we have found no studies that focus primarily on the psychomotor development of home-schooled children. However, studies such as the preceding and others (e.g., Pitman & Smith, 1988) do not indicate that home-schooled children are being deprived of activities that would enhance their psychomotor development.

DISCUSSION

It is clear that the research findings to date cast a flattering light on the ability of parents to transmit curricula and assist their home-educated children in progressing through the major agendas (Shulman, 1986) of American schooling. The several studies that we have described consistently show the achievement scores of the home-schooled to be equal to or better than the scores of their peers in traditional schools. This seems to be the case whether the parents are teaching without formal assistance from the state or are working within government-sponsored programs. In addition, the findings of one study (Quine & Marek, 1988) suggests that the home-schooled may be developing intellectually at a more rapid rate than those in conventional schools.

The home-schooled also appear to be at no great risk with respect to socialization. The research indicates that their self-concept is high; they are socially/emotionally well-adjusted; they are involved in many activities that are predictors of adult leadership; they are consistently engaged in social activities with peers and adults. With few exceptions (e.g., Gustafson's mention of social isolation), the data suggest that home-schooled children are not socially isolated. Our many years of personal experiences with home schoolers confirms the research findings with respect to socialization. In fact, many home-schooling parents find themselves in a dilemma: They are *home* schoolers, but they are simultaneously presented with a delectable and unrelenting smorgasbord of home-school support group activities, one-morning-per-week play groups, field trips, church activities, community service goals, political action plans, soccer teams and ballet recitals, and 4-H

and scout groups that often lures them away from some of their primary aims. That is, many parents must consciously and assertively
organize their lives so that they and their *home*-educated children are
not swept away by the myriad social endeavors that surround and
beckon them.

Where's the catch? Our review of the research on home schoolers'
academic achievement and socialization appears uncomfortably optimistic. It may appear to some that home schooling is quite superior to
traditional schooling on both accounts. Readers and researchers alike,
therefore, must make a number of careful considerations with respect
to the research findings (Ray, 1986, 1988a, 1988b). First, not a single
true-experimental study has been offered in this area of research. The
fact is that there probably never will be one. It is implausible that
someone would ever be allowed to randomly select 1,000 children in a
large metropolitan area and then randomly assign half to home
schools and the other half to conventional schools. The present reported research is correlative in nature, and the bulk of future research will likely be the same. It is difficult to say with certainty why
the home-schooled are doing so well, compared to the traditionally
schooled, on achievement tests. In fact, one alternate hypothesis is
that the home-schooled would have done even better on achievement
tests if they had attended conventional schools.

Second, many (if not all) of the studies include self-selected samples.
For example, Gustafson (1988) selected families from those subscrib-
ing to a particular home education magazine, and only a percentage
(i.e., 60%) of those who were selected returned the questionnaires.
Scogin (1986) only selected from those involved in a legal defense association, and only some of the parents had children's test scores to report. Even in states where testing of home-schooled students is required by law, either not all are tested or not all of the test scores are
reported. Therefore, the general cautions regarding studies involving
self-selection are appropriate in this case.

Third, judging the effectiveness of home education by comparing its
children with those in conventional schools may be like mixing the
proverbial apples and oranges. For example, the home school classroom usually has a student–teacher ratio of only about three or four
to one; traditional school classrooms typically have 20 or 30 to one. It
is also apparent that home-school parents, the large majority of whom
appear to be basic, biblical Christians, hold a special interest in their
children's development. They are willing to make great personal sacri-
fices for their children's total growth and development—academic, social, and spiritual. Given the parental support and commitment they
experience at home, it may be that these home-educated children

would have done just as well, academically and socially, in conventional schools.

Finally, it may be that the detailed measurement of achievement and socialization is a moot exercise in terms of explaining, promoting, or defending home education. As one of us has pointed out before (Ray, 1988b), perhaps what is also needed is for researchers to question home-school parents carefully to find out more precisely what *their* objectives are for *their* children. Researchers could then follow the youth over a long term to determine whether home education is actually effective in meeting home schoolers' goals.

Despite the preceding cautions regarding the research on home schooling, the facts are gathering, and they suggest that the outcomes of home schooling cannot be easily criticized when compared to those of traditional schooling. Home-schooled students' achievement scores are generally equal to or higher than those of their peers in traditional schools. It also appears that home-schooled students are faring quite well in the area of social development. Although many home schoolers teach their children for proactive reasons and do not want to convey criticism of conventional schools in general or public schools in particular, the apparently positive results of home schooling can be perceived as a critique of traditional schooling. The critique is even stronger when findings include that there is, in a practical sense, an insignificant relationship between the education level of the parent–teacher and the achievement scores of their children (Rakestraw, 1987; Wartes, 1988b). The critique is exacerbated when findings include that, upon close analysis, there is an insignificant relationship between the test scores of home-schooled students and whether the parent–teachers were state-certified teachers (Rakestraw, 1987; Wartes, 1988b). How is it possible that these children are doing so well in environments so very different from those of today's conventional schools?

We end with a couple of thoughts. First, today's conventional or traditional schools may be able to learn from home schools. Holt (1983) once pointed out that the home-schooling movement is "a laboratory for the intensive and long-range study of children's learning and of the ways in which friendly and concerned adults can help them learn. It is a research project, done at no cost, of a kind for which neither the public schools nor the government could afford to pay" (p. 393). Finally, it should not be assumed that what *is* ought to be. That is, we should never be satisfied to say that there is one best educational system (Tyack, 1974) for all children and all families. The data suggest that home schooling can compete with conventional schooling in terms of the major agendas of education, the academic task and the socializing of children (Shulman, 1986). It seems that home education is a solid, viable alternative that should be readily and intelligently presented to the public at large.

REFERENCES

Alaska Department of Education. (1984). *Summary of SRA testing for Centralized Correspondence Study April/May 1984*. Juneau, AK: Author.

Alaska Department of Education. (1985). *SRA survey of basic skills, Alaska Statewide Assessment, Spring of 1985*. Juneau, AK: Author.

Alaska Department of Education. (1986). *Results from 1981 CAT [for CCS]*. Juneau, AK: Author.

Arkansas Department of Education. (1986). *Arkansas Department of Education news release, July 21, 1986*. Little Rock, AR: Author.

Arkansas Department of Education. (1987). *Arkansas Department of Education new release, July 27, 1987*. Little Rock, AR: Author.

Bloom, A. (1987). *The closing of the American mind: How higher eduction has failed democracy and impoverished the souls of today's students*. New York: Simon and Schuster.

Campbell, D. T., & Stanley, J. C. (1963). *Experimental and quasi-experimental designs for research*. Boston, MA: Houghton Mifflin.

Carin, A. A., & Sund, R. B. (1985). *Teaching science through discovery*. Columbus, OH: Charles E. Merrill Publishing Co.

Delahooke, M. M. (1986). *Home educated children's social/emotional adjustment and academic achievement: A comparative study*. Unpublished doctoral dissertation, California School of Professional Psychology, Los Angeles, CA.

Falle, B. (1986). Standardized tests for home study students: Administration and results. *Method: Alaskan Perspectives, 7*, 22–24.

Gustafson, S. K. (1988). A study of home schooling: Parental motivation and goals. *Home School Researcher, 4*(2), 4–12.

Hewitt Research Foundation. (1985). North Dakota trial results pending. *The Parent Educator and Family Report, 3*(2), 5.

Hewitt Research Foundation. (1986a). Study of home schoolers taken to court. *The Parent Educator and Family Report, 4*(1), 2.

Hewitt Research Foundation. (1986b). On home-schooling figures and scores. *The Parent Educator and Family Report, 4*(2), 1,2.

Hirsch, E. D. (1987). *Cultural literacy: What every American needs to know*. Boston, MA: Houghton Mifflin Company.

Holt, J. C. (1981). *Teach your own: A hopeful path for education*. New York: Delacorte.

Holt, J. C. (1983). Schools and home schoolers: A fruitful partnership. *Phi Delta Kappan, 64*, 391–394.

Inhelder, B., & Piaget, J. (1985). *The growth of logical thinking from childhood to adolescence* (A. Parsons & S. Milgram, Trans.). New York: Basic Books.

Linden, N. J. F. (1983). An investigation of alternative education: Home schooling. Doctoral dissertation, East Texas State University. *Dissertation Abstracts International, 44,* 3547A.

Madden, M. M., Ed. (1986). Home study by correspondence. *Method: Alaskan Perspectives, 7*(1) [special issue].

Montgomery, L. (1989a). The effect of home schooling on the leadership skills of home schooled students. *Home School Researcher, 5*(1), 1–10.

Montgomery, L. (1989b). *The effects of homeschooling on the leadership skills of homeschooled students.* Doctoral dissertation, Seattle University, Seattle, WA.

National Commission on Excellence in Education. (1983). *A nation at risk: The imperative for educational reform.* Washington, DC: U. S. Government Printing Office.

Oregon Department of Education. (1986). *December 1, 1986 homeschool data report.* Salem, OR: Author.

Oregon Department of Education. (1988). *March 1, 1988 homeschool data report.* Salem, OR: Author.

Pitman, M. A., & Smith, M. L. (1988, November). *Culture acquisition in an intentional American community: A single case.* Paper presented at the annual meeting of the American Anthropological Association, Phoenix, AZ.

Quine, D. N., & Marek, E. A. (1988). Reasoning abilities of home-educated children. *Home School Researcher, 4*(3), 1–6.

Rakestraw, J. F. (1987). *An analysis of home schooling for elementary school-age children in Alabama.* Doctoral dissertation, University of Alabama, Tuscaloosa, AL.

Rakestraw, J. F. (1988). Home schooling in Alabama. *Home School Researcher, 4*(4), 1–6.

Ray, B. D. (1986). *A comparison of home schooling and conventional schooling: With a focus on leraner outcomes.* Corvallis, OR: Oregon State University. (ERIC Document Reproduction Service No. ED 278 489)

Ray, Brian D. (1988a). Home schools: A synthesis of research on characteristics and learner outcomes. *Education and Urban Society, 21*(1), 16–31.

Ray, B. D. (1988b, August 12). The kitchen classroom: Is home schooling making the grade? *Christianity Today,* pp. 23–26.

Reynolds, P. L. (1985). *How home school families operate on a day-to-day basis: Three case studies.* Unpublished doctoral dissertation, Brigham Young University, Provo, UT.

Schemmer, B. A. S. (1985). *Case studies of four families engaged in home education.* Unpublished doctoral dissertation, Ball State University, Muncie, IN.

Scogin, L. A. (1986). *Home school survey.* (Available from The Home School Legal Defense Association, 731 Walker Rd., Suite E-2, P.O. Box 950, Great Falls, VA 22066)

Shulman, L. S. (1986). Paradigms and research programs in the study of teaching. In M. C. Wittrock (Ed.), *Handbook of research on teaching* (3rd ed.). New York: MacMillan.

Taylor, J. W., V. (1986a). *Self-concept in home-schooling children*. Doctoral dissertation, Andrews University, Berrien Springs, MI.

Taylor, J. W., V. (1986b). Self-concept in home-schooling children. *Home School Researcher, 2*(2), 1–3.

Tennessee Department of Education. (1988). *Tennessee statewide averages, home school student test results, Stanford Achievement Test, grades 2, 5, 7 and 9*. Nashville, TN: Author.

Tizard, B., & Hughes, M. (1984). *Young children learning*. Cambridge, MA: Harvard University Press.

Travers, R. M. W. (1982). *Essentials of learning* (5th ed.). New York: Macmillan.

Tyack, D. B. (1974). *The one best system: A history of American urban education*. Cambridge, MA: Harvard University Press.

United States Department of Education, The. (1984). *The nation responds: Recent efforts to improve education*. Washington, DC: Author.

Wartes, J. (1987). *Washington Homeschool Research Project report from the 1986 homeschool testing and other descriptive information about Washington's homeschoolers*. (Available from Washington Homeschool Research Project, 16109 N.E. 169 Pl., Woodinville, WA 98072)

Wartes, J. (1988a). *Washington Homeschool Research Project report from the 1987 homeschool testing*. (Available from Washington Homeschool Research Project, 16109 N.E. 169 Pl., Woodinville, WA 98072)

Wartes, J. (1988b). *Washington Homeschool Research Project: The relationship of selected input variables to academic achievement among Washington's homeschoolers*. (Available from Washington Homeschool Research Project, 16109 N.E. 169 Pl., Woodinville, WA 98072)

Wartes, J. (1989). *Washington Homeschool Research Project report from the 1988 homeschool testing*. (Available from Washington Homeschool Research Project, 16109 N.E. 169 Pl., Woodinville, WA 98072)

Washington State Superintendent of Public Instruction. (1985). *Washington states's experimental programs using the parent as tutor under the supervision of a Washington State certificated teacher, 1984–1985*. Olympia, WA: Author.

Wayson, W. W., Mitchell, B., Pinnell, G. S., & Landis, D. (1988). *Up from excellence: The impact of the excellence movement on schools*. Bloomington, IN: Phi Delta Kappa Educational Foundation.

Western Australia Department of Education (WADE). (1979). *Innovations in rural education: The Isolated Students Matriculation Scheme in Western Australia and the Chidley Educational Centre*. Western Australia: Author.

Chapter 3
Ideologues and Pedagogues: Parents Who Teach Their Children at Home

Jane A. Van Galen
Youngstown State University

The home schooling movement has generated considerable controversy in recent years as increasing numbers of local and state education officials have been called upon to respond to requests that parents
be allowed to educate their own children. The public debate generated
by such requests has fueled ongoing conflicts over the purposes of formal education in society and has drawn further attention to the ongoing tensions between between the family, the state, and the church
that underlie much of education policy (see Chapter 5).

However, as Tyack and Hansot (1981) have argued, Americans have
no ideology that justifies conflict in public education. Consequently,
when controversial issues such as home education do arise, the primary recourse available to educators is to define the issue as an educational problem to be solved within existing educational institutions.
Such has been the reaction of educators and of the general public to
the movement of parents who chose to teach their children at home,
as efforts to "manage" home schooling commonly center on such de-
vices as the regulation of the children's curriculum or the certification
of the teaching parents.

In this chapter, I discuss home schooling as much more than a pedagogical endeavor. Such a perspective on the movement is timely and
important, for if home schooling is not merely an educational problem,

the educational solutions usually recommended to manage home schooling will fail to address not only the broader concerns of these parents but will also leave unexamined the weaknesses of public education made explicit by the home schooling controversy.

THE STUDY

The goal of the study discussed here was to document the values and beliefs of parents who chose to teach their children at home and to analyze the social context within which those values and beliefs are created and maintained. The chapter discusses why some parents become home schoolers and how the parents' beliefs about family and about education are embedded in broader ideologies that define the families' relations with the broader society.

The study involved participant observation at state, regional, and local meetings of home schoolers in a state in the southeast over a period of 18 months. I met most often with Central Christian Academy, an affiliation of 15 to 20 families in one of the state's larger cities. I also periodically met with a second local group that was organizing in a nearby community.

Beyond my work with these groups, I accompanied home schoolers from across the state as they met with representatives from other education groups to discuss legislation, as they conducted informational meetings in which they explained home schooling to others, and as they attended public functions at which educational or other family concerns were discussed.

I conducted interviews with a total of 23 parents from 16 home-schooling families. This sample of families was selected in several ways. I requested interviews from selected parents affiliated with Central Christian Academy. The study was announced in the state home-schooling newsletter and at several statewide meetings of home educators, and parents often volunteered to be interviewed after these announcements. Finally, I wrote to the families listed in the directory of a nationally circulated home-schooling newsletter *(Growing Without Schooling)* to request interviews. In selecting parents to be interviewed, I considered the parents' economic and educational backgrounds, the length of time the family had been home schooling, and the family's ideological persuasion. I sought parents who were active in state and local home schooling organizations and those who were not affiliated with any formal groups.

The children in half of these families had never attended school; children from the remaining families had been withdrawn from public or private schools. Thirteen of these families described themselves as conservative Christians, and the other three families had no religious affiliation.

Of the 16 mothers who I interviewed, one had a masters' degree and six had bachelors' degrees Five of the mothers had attended college but had not completed a degree and the remaining four had graduated from high school. Six of the fathers in these families had graduate degrees and six others held bachelors degrees. Two had attended college without graduating and one had not completed high school. Four of the fathers held blue-collar jobs in construction or manufacturing. Two owned small businesses. Two of the fathers were unemployed at the time of the study, one was a graduate student, and the remainder worked in a variety of professional and managerial positions.

One of the mothers worked part-time outside of the home for a relative. None of the other mothers was employed outside of the home at the time of the study, and only one of the mothers had worked outside of the home after her children were born.

I interviewed two families in their first year of home schooling and three more at the end of their first year. Four of the remaining families were in the middle of their second year, one had completed two full years of home schooling, and four families were at the end of their third year. One of the families had been teaching at home for five years, and one family had not yet begun formally teaching their five year-old-son.

All the interviews were audiotaped and later transcribed verbatim.

I conducted 10 additional interviews with state and local education officials and others who were involved with monitoring or regulating home schooling in the state. Included in this series of interviews were several meetings with the president and other officers of the state home schooling organization. Additionally, I interviewed both individuals who directed the Governor's Office of Non-Public Education (the state agency responsible for monitoring home schooling in the state) during the course of my study. I also interviewed the assistant state attorney general who had prosecuted several of the home schooling cases that had reached appeals court and a lawyer who had defended several parents who were taken to court. Finally, I interviewed representatives from several public education lobbying groups about their organization's perceptions of home schooling. All of these interviews were also audiotaped and transcribed verbatim.

I collected and analyzed a variety of documents. I read approximately five years of back issues of two nationally circulated home-schooling newsletters: *Growing without Schooling,* edited by the late John Holt, and *The Home Educator and Family Report,* edited by Raymond and Dorothy Moore. I also received the newsletters of the state organization and information packets that the state group provided for parents to give to legislators when lobbying. I subscribed to the newsletter issued by Christian Liberty Academy, a popular supplier of home-schooling curriculum materials. I read approximately 15 books on home schooling or more general educational issues recommended in these newsletters or by the parents I met. I monitored press reports of home schooling in the state and received newsletters from several education lobbying groups that I expected would take a stand on home education if the issue reached the legislature. I also reviewed the files of a lawyer who had defended several home-schooling families that had been taken to court.

From this data, I categorized and analyzed the home schoolers' shared beliefs, practices, and interpretations of events and experiences using Glaser and Stauss' (1967) constant comparitive method.[1]

This chapter specifically examines the broad ideological frameworks within which parents make their decisions about home education. While beliefs about pedagogy are central to this ideology, this analysis focuses particularly on the nonpedagogical issues that are at the core of the home-schooling movement.

RESULTS

Although parents decide to teach their own children for a variety of reasons, the values and beliefs of the parents in this study fall broadly into two categories. For the purposes of this analysis, I have categorized these parents as either "Ideologues" or "pedagogues."

These categories are by no means discrete. Categorization of the parents within either group, however, is based upon the rhetoric that the parents use to explain why they are home schooling and upon the values and beliefs implicit in the parents' interpretation of their role in society and in their descriptions of how they structure their children's education.

THE IDEOLOGUES

The Ideologues explain that they are home schooling for two reasons: They object to what they believe is being taught in public and private

---

[1] The complete study may be found in Van Galen, J. (1986). *Schooling in Private: A Study of Home Education*. Unpublished doctoral dissertation, The University of North Carolina, Chapel Hill, NC.

schools and they seek to strengthen their relationships with their children. These parents are Christian fundamentalists (although not all the Christians in the study are Ideologues), and they have specific values, beliefs, and skills that they want their children to learn. Beyond traditional subject matter, the parents want their children to learn fundamentalist religious doctrine and a conservative political and social perspective. Not incidentally, they also want their children to learn (both intellectually and affectively) that the family is the most important institution in society.

This principled commitment to home education often comes after teaching begins, however, for most of the parents described more practical reasons for first deciding to teach their children at home. These parents had actively been seeking educational alternatives for their children before even learning about home education. The children in several families experienced academic difficulties in the public or private schools they attended. In two families, the parents explained that health problems impeded the children's academic progress and also caused their children to be ostracized by their peers. Only one parent described specific conflicts over public school curriculum that prompted her to consider teaching her children herself.

Indeed, the first choice for most of these families was private school, rather than home school, but the parents explained either that they couldn't afford private school tuition or that they had unsuccessfully attempted to open their own private schools. To be sure, the ideology of these Christian fundamentalists pointed these parents away from public schools when they were seeking educational alternatives for their children, but full ideological commitment to home education usually came sometime *after* the initial decision to teach their children at home.

Intensifying Allegiance

While pragmatic concerns did spark the parents' initial interest in home education, the Ideologues' explanations of why they *continue* to teach their own children, even after other alternatives become available, are far more sacrosanct. As parents begin to interact with other parents through support groups and as they read the literature recommended by these groups, they begin to define home education more frequently and more primarily as an exercise in religious faith. Although they often embark upon home education with some trepidation, the Ideologues explained that they had come to believe they were following God's will and fulfilling their responsibilities as Christian parents in teaching their own children.

Discovering God's will. The Ideologues interpreted a variety of circumstances as further confirmation of their decision to home school. One mother, for example, explained during a discussion at a meeting of home-schooling parents that she interpreted a change in her daughter's attitude as evidence of God's intervention:

> We could really see the Lord's direction. We know it's the Lord's will. At first our daughter was very much against leaving school, but by the next morning, she thought it wouldn't be such a bad idea. This confirmed for us that this was really His will, that she would come around that way overnight.

Another mother, however, recounted in an interview how she interpreted the very negative reaction of her mother as evidence that home education was God's will:

> When we were talking about Christian schools, I had a discussion with my mother. She just really got down on me for teaching him Christian things and that really drove me. I was just determined. And that was, I think, the Lord's way of making up my mind.

From family to family, very different and often contradictory circumstances were described as evidence that God approved of their decision to home school.

The Ideologues also explained that they saw God's intervention in their ongoing work with their children. For example, several parents described how God had enabled them to teach difficult subject matter, even though they, themselves, did not feel qualified to do so. This conviction was demonstrated at a meeting at which several parents new to home schooling explained that they were insecure about teaching. The more experienced parents offered spiritual rather than pedagogical advice. As one father explained to the newcomers:

> If God has established us to be educators, then he'll enable us also. If you make a commitment, the Lord will equip you with the knowledge, the time, and working out your schedule.

For these parents, home schooling is inseparable from their Christian faith. Not only do they believe that God requires them to teach their children at home; their belief that God is personally involved in their home schools also provides the support, encouragement, and guidance for managing their work with their children. In these families, home education is not simply a pedagogical preference; it is also a spiritual exercise in obedience to and reliance upon God.

Accepting responsibility. From such specific circumstances interpreted as God's intervention, the parents move to a more general belief that parents *ought* to teach their own children. More experienced parents and leaders of state and local groups explained to newcomers that teaching their own children is not merely God's answer to specific circumstances, but is a biblical mandate, the moral equivalent of other obligations outlined in scripture. They base these beliefs on several Biblical passages that were often quoted or explained at meetings of Christian home schoolers. An example of this teaching is found in an excerpt from field notes that describe a talk given by a father at a meeting of Central Christian Academy parents:

> Eddie opened his Bible and said that he would now look at what scripture said about education: He read first from Deuteronomy 6:6–7: "These commandments that I give you today are to be upon your hearts. Impress them on your children. Talk about them when you sit at home and when you walk along the road, when you lie down and when you get up." After reading this, he said, "This plainly teaches that the parents are to teach their children. This is given in the context of the law. . . . It is an order that God has established, a method for instructing. It doesn't say that they are to be taught from the state or a certified teacher or even a Christian school. . . . This is God's word. It is external, inerrant, and binding.

While other Christians sharing many of the same doctrinal beliefs as the Ideologues do not interpret such passages to mean that parents are obligated to teach academic subjects to their own children, parents who had brought their children home because of unique circumstances or events came to see these portions of scripture as confirmation of their decision.

Interpreting their adversaries. Defining home schooling as an exercise of their Christian faith, the parents also define opposition to home education as infringements upon their religious freedom and family privacy. This opposition is taken seriously among the Ideologues.

In their publications and at formal meetings, parents were frequently exhorted to be vigilant against efforts to regulate home education, and in their discussions with one another about pending legislation or about their own dealings with local education officials, the Ideologues consistently interpreted opposition to home schooling as evidence of the insidious spread of secular humanism and the erosion of traditional values. With other Christian fundamentalists, the Ideologues firmly believed that schools are primary battlegrounds in struggles between Christians and their opponents.

Warnings of the impending threat of secular humanism abound in the materials read by the Ideologues. For example, an editorial appearing in a newsletter for home-schooling parents published by Christian Liberty Academy (a correspondence school through which many of the Ideological parents receive technical support and curricular materials) warned home-schooling parents of the "real" purpose of public schools:

> I think more Christians need to be aware that the educational systems of the world today are "hot houses"—places where a carefully maintained atmosphere of materialism, humanism, evolution, relativism, and sometimes downright atheism is deliberately created for the impressionable student. (Lindstrom, 1985, p. 2)

In these and numerous other publications (cf. Blumenfeld, 1984; Cumbey, 1983; McGraw, 1976; Morris, 1979; Schlafly, 1984) parents were warned of the spiritual dangers awaiting the students of traditional schools.

Home schooling, then, came to be defined among the Ideologues not only as a means of teaching their children but as a political stance against the persecution of persons like themselves. This position was best articulated at a statewide meeting in November 1984 by a guest speaker, a conservative political activist in the state, who defined home schooling as "Judeo-Christian resistance" to the "growing threats of secularism and statism." His speech, which drew a standing ovation, portrayed the assembled parents as "the supreme threat" to "the race of conditioners" now engaged in "an almost cosmic struggle" for domination of public thought. He then elaborated further on the motives of public educators:

> Fifty years ago, John Dewey made clear how all encompassing he understood his humanistic philosophy to be: "Here," wrote Dewey, "are all the elements for a religious faith that shall not be confined to sect, class, or race."
>
> And Dewey, who is commonly referred to as the father of public education, was not content to allow this secular religion to evolve on its own. Rather, Dewey urged, the goal of educators was "To make it explicit and militant."
>
> Onward secular soldiers, marching as to war. And you, dear friends who wish only to fulfill your responsibilities to guide the moral, the religious, and character development of your children, are in the enemy camp. And that is why home schooling is really, in essence, a means of resistance to the radical secularism and moral relativism—not to mention the mediocrity—which have captured educational philosophy, and which motivates, or blinds, so much of the leadership elite in our society.

This speaker concluded his talk with the prediction that home schoolers would certainly be prosecuted and imprisoned if they did not persevere against the "current anti-religious, relativistic trends."

Faced with such pervasive danger and such an interpretation of the functions of public schooling, the Ideologues view their families and their home schools as part of the last bastions against the impending destruction of "traditional" values and beliefs.

Summary and Implications: The Ideologues

The Ideologues come to believe that they are fulfilling God's general plan for Christian parents and His specific plans for their families. This ideology has implications not only for how the parents shape their children's education but also for how the families negotiate their status in a society that has come to take formal schooling for granted. In claiming that they have personally been called by God to teach their children at home, the parents leave little room for negotiations with those who would seek to restrict or regulate home education. Furthermore, the parents believe that their qualifications to teach their children cannot be challenged since God Himself has appointed them as teachers. Finally, opposition to unregulated home schooling is interpreted as evidence of broader efforts to undermine the family and Christianity. Conflicts between home schoolers and their opponents therefore not only demonstrate to the parents the fundamental differences in the beliefs between the families and traditional educators but also reinforces for the parents the urgency of maintaining those differences.

THE PEDAGOGUES

The second broad category of home schoolers in this study includes parents who teach their own children primarily for pedagogical reasons. Their criticisms of the schools are not so much that the schools teach heresy, but that schools teach whatever they teach ineptly. These parents generally come to their decision to home school with a broader interest in learning—they have professional training in education, they have close friends or relatives who are educators, they have read about education or child development, or they are involved with organizations that speak to issues of childrearing. As with the

Ideologues, their beliefs about education are grounded in broader beliefs about the role of the individual in society.

These parents are highly independent and strive to "take responsibility" for their own lives within a society that they define as pathologically beauraucratic and inefficient. They respect their children's intellect and creativity, and they share a perspective on home education that differs markedly from that of the Ideologues.

Independence and Responsibility

One of the most noteworthy and most obvious characteristics of Pedagogical parents is the value they place on personal independence. This independence is manifested in different ways in different families: In some families, the babies are born at home; other families raise much of their own food. Several of the Christian families in this group belonged to small, nondenominational, loosely organized fellowship rather than to established churches. Home schooling in these families is a powerful symbol of their independence from other social institutions.

Several of the Pedagogues came to home education for reasons similar to those of the Ideologues. Children in several families had also experienced severe academic trouble in school. In many of the families, however, the children had never enrolled in school. One family was homesteading in a remote rural area when their children reached school age. Other families had been influenced by organizations such as La Leche League to build child-centered families and had carried these philosophies over to their children's academic learning. Still others of these parents believed that their children learn in unique ways that could not be accommodated by formal schools.

Also like the Idealogues, the Pedagogues speak of "parent responsibility," but while the Idealogues speak of *acccepting* imposed responsibilities, the Pedagogues describe their independence as a means of *claiming* responsibility for their own lives. As one mother explained in an interview:

> As a parent, I had relinquished all responsibility for learning to authorities. You don't heal yourself, you go to a doctor. You don't learn yourself, you go to someone with a degree and the proper qualifications, so I didn't have the sense that what I was doing with my son involved a learning process. Now I have a very different perspective.

These parents are home schooling because they actively question the professionalization and bureaucratization of modern society, and particularly of modern education. Their decision to home school is a public declaration of their deliberately uncredentialed competence to raise their children with minimal institutional support.

Perspectives on Learning

Their beliefs about education carry over to the Pedagogues' belief that their children will learn more naturally and more completely apart from traditional schooling. The Pedagogues often explain their commitment to home education by describing their beliefs about learning:

> I really think that the individual is created in such a way as to want to grow naturally. That to remove blocks [to learning] is the thing, rather than to build something specifically and impose that view on them. They [children] are builders, too.

> The best thing is not to stifle the creativity that children are born with, their wonderful imaginations. I think that's the very main thing. If my son can maintain his creativity and his vivaciousness for learning, it's worth it.

The methods these parents employ for teaching their children reflect their faith in their children's innate curiosity and creativity. In contrast to the Ideologues who structure their teaching almost entirely around textbooks and workbooks, the Pedagogues are more likely to encourage their children to pursue their own projects and to work at their own pace using resources that are available in the home or the surrounding community. Just as their parents' lives are characterized by striving for independence, the learning of these children is frequently individualistic, independent, and self-directed.

Disregarding Adversaries

When the Ideologues frame the issue of home education in arguments over religious freedom and family privacy, the decision to teach their own children becomes an explicitly political act. Pedagogical parents are more likely to view home education as a personal outgrowth of their beliefs about learning and human nature. Consequently, the Pedagogues are less likely to affiliate with local or state home schooling lobbying and support groups. Several Pedagogical parents explained in interviews that they felt little in common with more dogmatic home schoolers:

> I feel like it's great that there's a state organization, but it's still got to remain personal. Sometimes, people can get out of hand with it—everything has to be like a cause, and I'm not like that. I feel that if it's something you decide to do, well, that's great. . . . We'd just as soon never go to a meeting or never meet with other families unless it seemed like our son was feeling like he was really out of the ordinary or something. There are people who are just gung-ho into making it a real movement, and it's just a home thing for us.

> I don't teach home schooling. I don't advise people to do home schooling. I just say that existentially, I've found that this works in this particular situation at this particular time. My approach is quite different from people who are gung-ho home schooling.

The Pedagogical parents are also less troubled by opposition to home education. Ideological parents repeatedly described the inevitable inquiries from school officials about why their children were not in school as harassment and evidence of hostility that public educators feel toward home schoolers. In Pedagogical families, similar challenges from neighbors, strangers, or school officials often became the subject of family jokes. (An example is the laughter of a mother and father during an interview as they recounted how the police had twice brought their son home from a shopping center where they had gone during the day to get supplies for projects.) Pedagogues attributed such encounters to bureaucratic inflexibility and the ignorance of school officials. In contrast, Ideological families often reacted to even casual inquiries about their home schools by keeping their children in the house behind drawn drapes during the school day.

In sum, the Ideologues pattern their home schools closely after traditional schools, but they are highly suspicious of the motives of school officials and vehemently resist any regulation of home education. The Pedagogues strive to provide an educational environment for their children that is distinctively different from school while they dismiss opposition from public educators with an almost patronizing indifference.

CONCLUSIONS

Opponents of home education frequently argue that common schooling is necessary for the common good, that schools should serve public, not merely private purposes.

The parents in this study share with traditional educators a belief that schooling should serve children's individual needs *and* the needs of society, but they disagree that traditional schools do serve society's best interests. Their criticisms of the schools may often be shrill, but home-schooling parents are joined by other critics of formal schools who have provided ample evidence that schools, at best, adequately serve only limited segments of society (Apple, 1979, 1982; Apple & Weis, 1983; Bowles & Gintis, 1976; Cohen, 1986; Collins, 1971; Oakes, 1985; Willis, 1977). The works of such authors have demonstrated that rather than broadening the perspectives of children, the curricula of formal schools often systematically exclude the life experiences of women and of racial, religious, and ethnic minorities and that schools contribute to the reproduction of racial, gender, and class inequalities rather than equalizing opportunity. The parents in this study may lack the analytical sophistication of the academic critics of schooling, but they recognize that formal education is not a panacea for personal or social ills. For those parents whose children found themselves in academic trouble in school, and for those who dissent from the ideology underlying the formal and the informal curricula of schooling, the limitations of institutionalized schooling are clear.

Further, the rhetoric that the parents use to explain their decisions to teach their children at home is also laden with broader criticisms of the social order. The Ideologues are frustrated not only by the exclusion of their religious beliefs from the formal curriculum of public schools, but also by a society that they percieve to be driven by personal ambition rather than by ethical and moral concerns. The Pedagogues are dismayed not only at the bureaucratization of schooling, but also at the loss of personal efficacy and creativity and in a highly regulated world. The home schooling movement raises important questions about the purposes of schooling and serves as a reminder that education policy makers often lose sight of just such concerns as attention focuses on more tangible matters such as standardized text scores.

Opponents of home education rarely take seriously the parents' criticisms of formal schooling and of the society served by those schools. Consequently, home-school policy frequently addresses only the most superficial issues. Beliefs about education and schooling, or about the social and moral order, cannot be legislated, yet it is such beliefs upon which the home-schooling movement is built. Requiring their children to take standardized tests will not resolve the Ideologues' alienation from public schools and the society served by those schools, nor will requiring the Pedagogues' children to follow a standard curriculum restore the parents' confidence in the effectiveness of formal schooling. Efforts to regulate or restrict home education may represent little more than a diversion from the much larger and much more serious discord over the purposes of schooling that are raised by the home schoolers.

REFERENCES

Apple, M. (1982). *Education and power.* London: Routledge, Kegan and Paul, Ltd.

Apple, M. (1979). *Ideology and curriculum.* London: Routledge, Kegan and Paul, Ltd.

Apple, M., & Weis, L. (1983). Ideology and practice in schooling: A political and conceptual introduction. In M. Apple & L. Weis (Eds.), *Ideology and practice in schooling* (pp. 3–33). Philadelphia: Temple University Press.

Bowles, S., & Gintis, H. (1976). *Schooling in Capitalist America: Educational reform and the contradictions of American life.* New York: Basic Books.

Blumenfeld, S. (1984). *NEA: Trojan horse of American Education.* Boise, ID: The Paradigm Company.

Cohen, E. (1986). On the sociology of the classroom. In J. Hannaway & M. Lockhead (Eds.), *The contributions of the social sciences to educational policy and practice: 1965–1985.* Berkeley, CA: McCutchan.

Collins, R. (1971). Functional and conflict theories of educational stratification. *American Sociological Review, 36,* 1002–1019.

Cumbey, C. (1983). *The hidden dangers of the rainbow: The new age movement and the coming age of barbarism.* Shreveport, LA: Huntington House, Inc.

Glaser, B. G., & Strauss, A. L. (1967). *The discovery of grounded theory: Strategies for qualitative research.* New York: Aldine Publishing Company.

Lindstrom, P. (1985, December). The Bible and education. *The Christian Educator,* p. 2.

McGraw, O. (1976). *Secular humanism in the schools: An idea whose time has come.* Washington, DC: The Heritage Foundation.

Morris, B. (1979). *Change agents in the schools.* Upland, CA: The Barbara M. Morris Report.

Oakes, J. (1985). *Keeping track: How schools structure inequality.* New Haven, CT: Yale University Press.

Schlafly, P. (Ed.). (1984). *Child abuse in the classroom.* Alton, IL: Pere Marquette Press.

Tyack D., & Hansot, E. (1981). Conflict and consensus in American public education. *Daedalus, 110,* 1–25.

Willis, P. (1977). *Learning to labor.* Westmead: Saxon House.

Chapter 4
Culture Acquisition in an Intentional American Community: A Single Case*

Mary Anne Pitman
University of Cincinnati

M. Lynne Smith
University of Maryland
Baltimore County

Educational anthropologists have been able to conclude that through-out our evolutionary past, human adaptation has depended upon our ability to learn. Humans can be said to learn within a fairly standard set of biological parameters. These include the ones defined by pri-matologists who indicate that the major forms of primate learning are observation, modeling, social experience, and play (Lancaster, 1975). Deliberate instruction appears to play a very small part in the learn-ing process of primates. Instead, it would appear that the major forces that shape learning in primates, including humans, are the structures and processes of the entire ecological and social life going on around them (Hall, 1959; Herzog, 1974; Kimball, 1982; Dobbert & Cooke, 1987; Pitman, Eisikovits, & Dobbert, 1989). The biological parameters of human learning are being further defined by neuroscientists who indicate that information in the human brain is processed multi-modally and in interaction with the social/ecological environment.

By positing that the biological structuring of human learning is laid

* This research was supported in part by a grant from the University Research Coun-cil, University of Cincinnati, Cincinnati, OH. An earlier version of this chapter was presented at the 87th Annual Meeting of the American Anthropological Association, Phoenix, AZ, 1988.

down, that humans *are* learners, the anthropologist goes on to focus on the interactive system, on the context of learning, on culture, on the ecology of people, place, affect, and ideology. Researchers who study culture acquisition, therefore, take the nonformal learning environments of home, family, and community very seriously.

This study, conducted in the family-based home school environment, rests on the following assumptions: that humans are extraordinarily sensitive to contextual—that is, cultural—information; that they take in information through a variety of modalities from multiple simultaneous sources; that they do this automatically and unconsciously and at all times; and that the mechanisms by which humans acquire and transmit information in context are very, very complex.

THE RESEARCH SETTING

This ongoing study is occurring in a rural area in the north central United States. It focuses on a community that is part of a small but ubiquitous segment of Americans who are living deliberately simple lives. Together, they form a kind of new intentional community network. These are both rural and urban dwellers, characterized by their advocacy of personal and planetary health. This may take the form of sustainable organic agriculture, bioregionalism, alternative medical care, home birth, home schooling, spirituality, responsible parenting, and peace activism, among other things.

The community in which this research is conducted is made up of a core group of approximately 20 separate and independent households. Dwellings cluster in several different locations within an area that ranges 45 miles east to west and 50 miles north to south. There are no inclusionary or exclusionary rules of group membership. Those who come to community events are welcomed. Those who have chosen to stay in the area have had their settling in facilitated in one way or another by those already there. Still, serious conflicts—some long-standing, others more recent—also exist here. Thus, one rarely finds all members of all the households identified as the core group at any one community event or gathering, and at the same time, there are likely to be members of related or satellite households at most gatherings.

Young adults and their children, living in single-family households, constitute much of the community. The most likely age of the adults is 32–38. Two core networks among them met one another 10 to 15 years prior to the time the research began, when they were students in two colleges, a state college at the southern end of the region, and a private one at the northern end. The households are independent but that independence is maintained via a number of interconnections—a network, if you will—involving the exchange of goods and services and other kinds of support.

The one family that is the focus of this chapter lives in the basement of a three-story wood frame house that is partially completed, sits on 10 acres, and is owned by this couple. The family includes two adults in their mid-thirties and three children under the age of 10. They live within walking distance of two (and sometimes three) other families who live comparable lifestyles. There are nine children in these four households, three of them preschool-aged toddlers. The two school-aged children in the family reported on here were both being schooled at home, mostly by their mother, who was also caring for their 9-month-old brother, Lucas.

The family had lived in the area for three years at the time these observations were conducted. Their sole support at the time was a small family business dependent upon the skilled labor of the father, a farrier. Their pattern, however, had been a mosaic of joint responsibility in family-based business ventures that depended alternately on the skills of both adults. That pattern had changed as the family grew to include more children with the mother taking on more parenting, gardening, and household tasks, including schooling, while the father contracted out as a skilled laborer.

The two learners who are the focus of this chapter are 9-year-old Seth and his sister, 4-year-old Sarah. Seth would have been entering the fourth grade had he been attending the local school when this study was conducted. He had moved into this community when he was 6 and his new sister was just 1. Prior to that time, he had lived in the midwest with his parents who had been working as race horse trainers and managers of several stables before purchasing their own horse, trailer, and travel van. They lived together in the van, traveling to and racing in the state fair race track circuit. When Seth first came of school age, therefore, he did not live in any identifiable school district for an extended period of time. Home schooling was a natural, logical choice for his preschool and primary grade years.

His parents are both college-educated. His mother graduated from the private college in the northern end of the community's boundaries, and had briefly done graduate work in political science at Georgetown University. His father, the son of a university art professor, had attended college for approximately two years. But at the time this research was conducted, these parents, like other community members, were downwardly mobile, and were living a simple economic life, growing and preserving much of their own food, and searching for a home-based business to sustain them for the future.

Family history data derived from formal interviews with both parents indicates that Seth has been less than happy with the arrival of his sibling, Sarah, and disappointed again with the birth of baby brother Lucas. His comfort was reading. He had always read or been read to. When the family had been living in the van, their evening relaxation for many nights had been to read all of C.S. Lewis' *The Tales of Narnia* aloud. Seth had since reread each of the tales 3 or 4 times. His parents would occasionally become concerned about balance in his curriculum. When they first began home schooling, they had three structured hours of schooling every morning. Seth got so that he hated that time, so his parents began tracking his schooling by keeping a daily log of his activities. On that basis, they would occasionally request that he write, play Scrabble, or a World Book game, or do some other "educational" activity. Seth would comply, demonstrate the worried-about skill, and then resume non-stop reading. The one to two dozen books brought home each week from the library were mostly selected by his mother, who took her cues from what he said about his previous week's supply. He would typically select two or three books himself, but then become engrossed in reading one of them rather than continuing to find others.

Seth was somewhat reticent among his peers, and preferred rough and tumble physical play to group games or strategy activities at community gatherings. Because he would prefer to stay intensely focused on one interest or activity, he would typically outlast his peers in that regard. His newfound interest in Cub Scouts and his long-term interest in designing and conducting science experiments were facilitating both his social and intellectual activities at the time these observations were conducted.

Four-year-old Sarah had no memory of a traveling life; this 10-acre homestead was her lifetime home. She would have been one year away from entering kindergarten, if she were to become a public school student. This possibility was being considered, because Sarah was a highly engaging child, very active and interactive. She did not construct any mutually satisfying activities with her older brother; rather, their interactions were conflict-driven. However, she did construct activities with the crawling baby, sometimes friendly, other times antagonistic. She engaged her mother in make-believe play, including the baby in her scenarios. She was always trying to find someone to engage in conversation or activity, including the ethnographer. She particularly sought to have her mother's attention diverted to her during times the baby was most demanding, when, for example, he was nursing or in the early stages of napping. Even when she would do schooling kinds of activities, the social interaction was primary. Thus, she did her new dot-to-dot coloring book when she came home from the store as a way to engage her mother in conversation, and later that evening she took it out again in order to join her father at the kitchen table where he was working on his business ledger. These two very different learners, then, were the focus of the systematic observations described below.

THE STUDY

Data Collection

The first stage of this study involved participant observation during community gatherings and meetings of the parent schooling coopera- tive and informal informant interviews conducted over a period of over 12 months. The second stage of the research forms the basis of the findings reported here. It involved systematic observations of children during typical home school days. I lived with six different families for a period of six weeks from late July until mid-September, 1987.[2] I lived in a tent, close enough to the family's dwelling to sense when their day was beginning, and proceeded to spend the entire day shadowing the children and recording learning incidents. I stayed one week with each family, setting up camp on Monday morning and breaking camp the following Friday afternoon. This was not particularly unusual for the children as I was just one of a number of itinerants in the community at that particular time. A steady movement of like-minded people in and out of the area is part of and facilitated by the community net- work. Observations were recorded four days of the week at most hours of the day, using a kind of time sampling.

The context-dependent, biologically based theory of human learning posited above holds that humans unconsciously and continuously ac-

---

[1] The study was designed and ethnographic data were collected by Pitman, the senior author, as a sole researcher, working alone in the tradition of anthropological fieldwork. Smith subsequently joined the project at the stage of data analysis, developing methods for accessing and displaying large amounts of data, and assisting with the written de- scription of findings. Therefore, "I" in this section refers to Pitman, the anthropologist in the field.

[2] As the community members believe that schooling begins at birth and is lifelong, their school year begins on the Fall Equinox and ends one year later on the eve of the Fall Equinox. Therefore, summer months are theoretically "school" months, but it does not necessarily work that way in practice.

Figure 4.1.   Categories for Structuring Observation and Analysis

Basic Setting and Activity
Setting
Institution
Activity

Immediate Human Context
Group Size
Group Composition
Atmosphere

Learner Role and Behavior
Ability
Act

Response Factors
Responding Person
Response
Expressed Values
Implied Values

quire information from the context and process of all that is going on around them. Therefore, a research strategy was devised to discover and describe this context and process, a strategy which is at the same time both holistic and highly specific in the description of the interactive learning system. The systematic observation is the method that was selected to record this slice of life, to note the human affective and ideological environment, the social structural environment, and the physical resource environment and to note how a learner experiences and is experienced by all of these.[3]

The observation is structured by a learning incident defined as a complete episode or bounded minievent. A focal learner is identified for each incident and detailed fieldnotes are recorded describing the basic setting and ongoing activities, the immediate human context, the learner's role and behavior, and the response factors to which the learner is exposed (see Figure 4.1). The exact setting the learner is in is noted first. Then the details of the activities happening in the learner's immediate environment are described, noting not what the learner is doing but what *everybody else* is doing and, therefore, from and about what the learner is gaining information. This often means describing activities in two or three areas within the learner's purview.

---

[3] The systematic observation is explicated in greater detail in Pitman, Eisikovits, and Dobbert (1989), and the following section of this chapter relies particularly on pp. 66–80. See also Whiting and Whiting (1975).

For example, in the family being observed here, the father and an older agemate of the identified male learner were outside the basement combination living room/kitchen hauling block while Seth was inside on the couch reading. He was not seeing the details of the outside activity but he was aware of the nature of the task, the participants, and their roles.

In order to record the immediate human context, I would describe the number of persons a learner could see or hear within the setting, their connection to the various ongoing activities, their sex and age and relationship to the learner. Markers of relational-affectional atmosphere are recorded, including such information as general noise level, voice tone, and other clues to emotions,[4] being careful to note the emotional atmosphere of the setting rather than the emotional state of the learner.

The learner's role and behavior and the subsequent response factors were then recorded as a complete interaction bounded by a selected minievent. In narrative form, the child's acts, interaction with other persons and with objects, words, gestures, expressions, and focus of attention are described. The environmental and human response is similarly described including "no response" when evidenced by the continuation of ongoing activities. The systematic observation is completed by noting any value statements or explanations cited or implied during the incident.

Data Analysis

The descriptions produced by these systematic observations were initially written by hand on a legal pad and catalogued with a four-part observation number that indicated which family was being observed, on what day the notes were taken, the focal child for that observation, and the chronological order of the discrete observations recorded on that particular day. This simple scheme enhanced the accessibility of the data throughout each succeeding stage of management and display.

The second phase of data management utilized a microcomputer and word processing program and had two distinct stages; first, the field notes for each observation were reduced to brief, capsuled descriptions for each of the 12 categories depicted in Figure 4.1. Then those descriptions were coded, using an ethnographically derived taxonomy of ap-

---

[4] Clues are understood emicly, that is, from the insider's perspective. That is why the validity of this systematic observation depends on a previous/ simultaneous process of standard ethnographic research.

Figure 4.2. Sample Data Reduction Sheet With Codes

Culture	Mountain (M)
Learner	Female, age 4 (F4)
Observation #	2-3-2-1-(3)
Setting	kitchen/livrm: Home (H)
Institution	None: (X)
Group Size	Four: Small (s)
Group Composition	Parent/family group, opposite sex, mother, older brother, baby brother: (P) (o)
Activities	Mother lying on bed, nursing baby to sleep; brother on couch under blanket reading a book: Care giving and deliberate information exchange of reading/studying (Cf) (E/St)
Atmosphere	Quiet, tired (mother and teething baby have been up most of night): Lethargic (B)
Act of Learner	Learner turns to new page/new letter in phonics workbook while mother leaves the table to lay down with the baby; learner has been genuinely excited by what she was able to do and to demonstrate to her mother; alone, she works at copying letter but does not sustain interest and leaves table to get dressed: Deliberate information exchange of practicing, demonstrating skills (E/Dm)
Abilities of Learner	Works at own task and plays alone: Does something different than others (O)
Responding Person	Mother: Parent, same sex, respected person (P) (s) (r)
Response	No response: (N)
Value Expressed	None: (X)
Value Implied	None: (X)

parent options (Pitman, Eisikovits, & Dobbert, 1989).[5] This phase of data management accomplished three important tasks simultaneously: (a) a large amount of handwritten descriptive data was made more accessible; (b) the ethnographer, in the process of reducing the field notes to relatively brief descriptions, relived in chronological order each of the 59 recorded observations, a process that enhanced recognition of both details and patterns; and (c) during the process of writing concise descriptions and then coding those descriptions, the taxonomy was revised and expanded to include categories that emerged from the data but had not been a part of the available codes. At the conclusion of this second phase of data management, a week of handwritten fieldnotes had been reduced to 59 pages of concise, coded descriptions. Figure 4.2 is an example of the reduced, coded data for a single observation.

---

[5] The taxonomy describing specific social, cultural, and ecological options within the interactive system of culture acquisition as well as the codes for each option are presented in detail in Chapters Five and Eight in Pitman, Eisikovits, and Dobbert (1989).

The third phase of data management enhanced data display. Fifty-nine pages of coded descriptions were further reduced to strings of letters that had been affixed to the data during the second phase. Using a Macintosh microcomputer and Microsoft Works software, a database was created to display and manipulate all the categories of coded data. The 59 pages of descriptions became a single page showing all the codes for all the systematic observations conducted in the family that is the subject of this chapter. Figure 4.3 shows the complete database for this family. The database can be sorted and printed in a variety of ways, to assist in the search for patterns in the data. For instance, the learner column can be sorted so that all observations for each learner are shown together, in the order they occurred. Similarly, the data can be regrouped to cluster all observations involving the same categories of responding persons, learner acts, implied values, and so on.

This kind of manipulation provided useful information and concise display of a great deal of data, but was limited in its usefulness for data analysis, because the software was not designed to show relationships between and among categories. Because of this limitation, the remainder of the data from the five other families observed will be recorded with Double Helix, or some other kind of relational database that allows manipulation of the data to search for relationships between and among coding categories.

ONE FAMILY DESCRIBED

What follows is a summary of what the systematic observations revealed regarding learning, during this one week of home schooling in this family.

Basic Setting and Activities

The most likely location of both school-aged children's activities was the family home, especially the combination kitchen/living room area in the walk-out basement level, a space in which all five family members are living while remodeling and construction of additional rooms upstairs continues. Fifty-six of fifty-nine observation records indicate this family living space—an L-shaped basement—as the setting for learning incidents.

A deliberate sampling choice in collecting systematic observations was to avoid institutional settings and rituals, such as the community

Figure 4.3. All Records Family 2

Num	Lr	OBSERVATI	SET	INST	GRP SI	GRP CO	ACTIV	ATM	ACT	ABI	RESP PER	RESPONS	VALUE EX	VALUE IM
1	M9	2-2-1-1-(1)	(H)	(X)	(S)	(MC)	(Cf)	(T)	(E/L)	(O)	(P)(o)(r)	(P+&-)	(H/G. 8.0)	(C/M. 6.0)
2	M9	2-2-1-1-(2)	(H)	(X)	(S)	(MC)	(Cf)	(R)	(So/D)	(I)	(P)(o)(j)	(L-)	(X)	(S/M. 6.5)
3	M9	2-2-1-1-(3)	(H)	(X)	(S)	(MC)	(PC)	(T)	(E/L)	(O)	(P)(s)(r)	(A)	(X)	(M/M. 1.5)
4	M9	2-2-1-2-(1)	(H)	(X)	(S)	(MC)	(E/RK)(PC)	(T)	So/J	(I)	(P)(o)(r)	(M)(L++)	(X)	(C/G. 3.0)
5	M9	2-2-1-2-(2)	(H)	(X)	(S)	(MC)	(SO/VW)(CF)	(J)	(SC)	(U)	(P)(s)(r)	(I-)	(X)	(S/M. 6.5)
6	M9	2-2-1-2-(3)	(H)	(X)	(S)	(MC)	(SO/F)	(H)	(So/f)	(J)	(N)(s)(X-)	(A)	(X)	(S/M. 5.0)
7	M9	2-2-1-2-(4)	(H)	(X)	(S)	(MC)	(Cf)	(T)	(PI)	(I)	(P)(o)(r)	(I-)	(X)	(C/G. 3.0)
8	M9	2-2-1-3-(1)	(OR)	(R/c)	(M)	(MF)	(E/Sr & Bq)	(R)	(E/Md & Cn)	(J)	(N)(s)(X=)	(L-)	(X)	(X)
9	M9	2-2-1-3-(2)	(OR)	(R/c)	(M)	(Soe)	(E/Sr & Rk)	(R)	(E/Sr)	(F)	(P)(o)(r)	(P+)	(X)	(A/M. 4.5)
10	M9	2-2-1-3-(3)	(OR)	(R/c)	(M)	(MF)(o)	(E/Sr & Rk)	(R)	(E/Md)	(F)	(1.2.1.4 T)	(L++)	(U)	(X)
11	F4	2-2-1-4-(1)	(H)	(X)	(S)	(MC)(o)	(I)	(R)	(I)	(F)	(P)(s)(r)	(N)	(X)	(X)
12	F4	2-2-2-1-(1)	(H)	(X)	(S)	(MC)	(Cf)	(T)	(E/Md)	(U)	(P)(s)(r)	(A+)	(X)	(S/G. 5.0)
13	F4	2-2-2-1-(2)	(H)	(X)	(S)	(MC)	(Cf)	(T)	(So/VW)	(I)	(P)(s)(r)	(A)	(X)	(S/G. 5.0)
14	F4	2-2-2-1-(3)	(H)	(X)	(S)	(MC)	(Cf)(I)	(R)	(E/Md)	(J)	(P)(s)(r)	(P+)	(X)	(C/M. 6.0)
15	F4	2-2-2-1-(4)	(H)	(X)	(S)	(MC)	(Cf)	(R)	(I)	(J)	(P)(s)(r)	(L++)	(X)	(X)
16	F4	2-2-2-1-(5)	(H)	(X)	(S)	(MC)	(Cf)	(H)	(PI)	(W)	(P)(s)(r)	(A)	(C/G. 3.0)	(X)
17	F4	2-2-2-2-(1)	(H)	(X)	(S)	(P)	(E/Bq)	(T)	(I)	(O)	(P)(s)(r)	(N)	(X)	(M/M. 1.5)
18	F4	2-2-2-2-(2)	(H)	(X)	(S)	(MC)(o)	(Cf)	(T)	(Cf)	(J)	(P)(s)(r)	(A)	(X)	(H/M. 8.0)
19	F4	2-2-2-3-(1)	(H)	(X)	(S)	(MC)(o)	(I)	(R)	(I)	(F)	(P)(o)(r)	(N)	(X)	(X)
20	M9	2-3-1-1-(1)	(H)	(X)	(S)	(MC)(s)	(PC)	(R)	(I)	(N)	(P)(s & o)	(N)	(X)	(T/M. 8.5)
21	F4	2-3-1-1-(2)	(H)	(X)	(S)	(MC)(o)	(PC)	(R)	(I)	(N)	(P)(s & o)	(N)	(X)	(X)

22	M9	2-3-1-2-(1)	(H)	(X)	(S)	(P)	(A)(Cf)	(R)	(I)	(O)	(P)(o)(r)	(A)	(X)	(A/M.4.5)
23	M9	2-3-1-3-(1)	(H)	(X)	(S)	(P)	(SC)	(H)	(I)	(O)	(P)(o)(r)	(N)	(X)	(X)
24	M9	2-3-1-3-(2)	(H)	(X)	(S)	(P)	(PI)	(H)	(I)	(O)	(P)(o)(I)	(N)	(X)	(X)
25	M9	2-3-1-4-(1)	(H)	(X)	(S)	(P)	(Cf)	(R)	(E/Md)	(O)	(T)	(N)	(X)	(X)
26	M9	2-3-1-4-(2)	(H)	(X)	(S)	(P)	(SO/VW)	(R)	(E/Bq & RK)	(U)	(P)(o)(r)	(P+)	(X)	(X)
27	M9	2-3-1-4-(3)	(H)	(X)	(S)	(P)	(A)	(R)	(A)	(J)	(P)(o)(r)	(A)	(X)	(X)
28	M9	2-3-1-5-(1)	(H)	(X)	(S)	(P)	(Cf)	(T)	(E/Bq)	(O)	(P)(o)(r)	(L++)	(X)	(A/M.4.5)
29	M9	2-3-1-5-(2)	(H)	(X)	(S)	(P)	(Cf)	(T)	(E/RK & Bq)	(O)	(P)(o)(r)	(P+)	(X)	(A/M.4.5)
30	M9	2-3-1-6-(1)	(H)	(X)	(S)	(P)	(Cf)(Sc)	(T)	(E/Bq)	(I)	(P)(o)(r)	(P-)	(X)	(A/M.4.5)
31	M9	2-3-1-6-(2)	(H)	(X)	(S)	(P)	(Cf)	(T)	(E/Md)	(O)	(N)(o)(f)	(D++)	(X)	(X)
32	F4	2-3-2-1-(1)	(H)	(X)	(S)	(P)(o)	(CF)	(T)	(PI)	(PI)	(P)(o)(I)	(L++)	(X)	(A/M.4.0)
33	F4	2-3-2-1-(2)	(H)	(X)	(S)	(P)(o)	(Cf)	(B)	(So)	(I)	(P)(s)(r)	(A)	(X)	(X)
34	F4	2-3-2-1-(3)	(H)	(X)	(S)	(P)(o)	(Cf)	(B)	(E/Dm)	(O)	(P)(s)(r)	(N)	(X)	(X)
35	F4	2-3-2-1-(4)	(H)	(X)	(S)	(P)(o)	(Cf)	(L)	(E/Dm)	(O)	(P)(s)(r)	(I+)	(X)	(S/M.6.0)
36	F4	2-3-2-1-(5)	(H)	(X)	(S)	(P)(o)	(Cf)	(T)	(Cn)	(I)	(P)(s)(r)	(A)	(X)	(H/M.8.0)
37	F4	2-3-2-2-(2)	(H)	(X)	(S)	(P)	(A)(So)	(R)	(A)(So)	(J)	(P)(s)(r)	(A)	(X)	(H/M.8.0)
38	F4	2-3-2-3-(1)	(H)	(X)	(S)	(P)	(SC)	(T)	(Cf)	(O)	(P)(o)(I)	(I-)	(X)	(X)
39	F4	2-3-2-3-(2)	(H)	(X)	(S)	(P)	(SC)	(T)	(PI)	(O)	(P)(s)(r)	(A)	(X)	(S/G.5.0)
40	F4	2-3-2-3-(3)	(H)	(X)	(S)	(P)	(PC)(Cf)	(H)	(Cf)	(J)	(P)(s)(r)	(A)	(X)	(S/G.5.0)
41	F4	2-3-2-4-(1)	(H)	(X)	(S)	(P)	(E/Md)(Cf)	(R)	(Cn)	(I)	(P)(o)(X=)	(I-)	(X)	(E/M.0.5)
42	F4	2-3-2-4-(2)	(H)	(X)	(S)	(P)	(Cf)(E/Md)	(R)	(Cn)	(W-)	(P)(s)(r)	(D-)	(S/M.6.5)	(X)
43	F4	2-3-2-4-(3)	(H)	(X)	(S)	(P)	(Cf)	(T)	(A)	(PI)	(P)(s)(r)	(A)	(X)	(X)
44	F4	2-3-2-4-(4)	(H)	(X)	(S)	(P)	(E/Md)(Cf)	(T)	(Cn)	(I)	(P)(o)(X=)	(I-)	(X)	(E/M.2.5)

(Continued)

87

Figure 4.3. Continued

Num	Lr	OBSERVATI	SET	INST	GRP SI	GRP CO	ACTIV	ATM	ACT	ABI	RESP PER	RESPONS	VALUE EX	VALUE IM
45	M9	2-4-1-1-(1)	(H)	(X)	(S)	(P)	(Pc)	(T)	(Cn)	(N)	(P)(o)(I)	(I-)	(X)	(X)
46	M9	2-4-1-1-(2)	(H)	(X)	(S)	(P)	(Pc)	(T)	(Cn)	(N)	(P)(o)(r)	(I-)	(X)	(S/G.5.0)
47	F4	2-4-1-1-(3)	(H)	(X)	(S)	(P)	(Pc)	(T)	(Cn)	(N)	(P)(s)(r)	(I-)	(X)	(S/G.5.0)
48	F4	2-4-1-1-(4)	(H)	(X)	(S)	(P)	(Cf)(Pc)	(T)	(Cn)	(I)	(P)(s)(r)	(D-)	(X)	(S/G.5.0)
49	M9	2-4-1-1-(5)	(H)	(X)	(S)	(P)	(Cf)(Pc)	(T)	(R)	(J)	(P)(o)(r)	(A)	(X)	(S/G.5.0)
50	M9	2-4-1-1-(6)	(H)	(X)	(S)	(P)	(Pc)	(T)	(Sc)	(O)	(P)(o)(r)	(N)	(X)	(L/M.7.5)
51	M9	2-4-1-1-(7)	(H)	(X)	(S)	(P)	(Pc)	(T)	(Pl)	(O)	(P)(o)(I)	(L-)	(X)	(X)
52	F4	2-4-1-1-(8)	(H)	(X)	(S)	(P)	(Pc)	(T)	(Cn)	(Pl)	(P)(o)(r)	(N)	(X)	(X)
53	M9	2-4-1-2-(1)	(H)	(X)	(S)	(P)	(Sc)	(T)	(E/Sl)	(O)	(S)	(L++)	(A/M.4.5)	(A/M.4.5)
54	M9	2-4-1-2-(2)	(H)	(X)	(S)	(P)	(Sc)	(T)	(Pc)	(F)	(X)	(X)	(X)	(X)
55	F4	2-4-2-1-(1)	(H)	(X)	(S)	(P)	(Cf)(Pc)	(T)	(H)	(J)	(P)(s)(r)	(P)	(X)	(A/M.4.0)
56	F4	2-4-2-1-(2)	(H)	(X)	(S)	(P)	(Cf)(Pc)	(T)	(H)	(J)	(P)(o)(=)	(I-)	(X)	(L/M.7.5)
57	F4	2-4-2-1-(3)	(H)	(X)	(S)	(P)	(Cf)(Pc)	(T)	(H)	(O)	(P)(s)(r)	(P+)	(X)	(A/M.4.0)
58	F4	2-4-2-2-(1)	(H)	(X)	(S)	(P)	(Sc)	(T)	(I)	(O)	(X)	(X)	(X)	(X)
59	F4	2-4-2-2-(2)	(H)	(X)	(S)	(P)	(Sc)	(T)	(Ph)	(J)	(S)	(M)	(X)	(C/M.6.0)

gatherings, potlucks, school meetings, and so on that had been the locus of more than 12 months of participant observation research. Instead, the focus was on the normal, ordinary, and mundane activities of these learners' lives. Still, it is important to note that the normal community pattern, even for this particularly sedentary family group, is to engage in at least one major outing a week. During this week of observations, the major outing was to the local public library, an institution regularly visited throughout the year by this family. Their library trips usually include stops at local stores; the observed outing was typical, in that while systematic observations occurred in the library, some family members were visiting the Salvation Army store and an open-air market. These multiple-purpose outings are a regular part of this family's home-schooling agenda.

The category of activity most likely to be occurring in the main home school setting for this family was one we have called the giving and receiving of care (31 of 59 observations). The actual activities included: changing diapers, nursing the baby, providing direction for children's activities including schooling activities, arranging family outings, grooming, doing kitchen cleanup, and feeding children. (Figure 4.2 is a typical scenario.) These caregiving activities were often accompanied by other kinds of activities or were themselves ongoing during another kind of dominant activity. This occurred nearly half of the time (13 of the 31 instances).

Primary conversion activities—those related to the acquisition of food, clothing, and shelter—was the next most frequent activity going on in this learning environment (16 of 59 instances). Other activities which occurred regularly but less frequently included deliberate exchange of information (8) such as writing, planning, and budgeting, secondary conversion activities (8) such as laundry and cooking; general-purpose socializing (4) such as family conversations regarding grandparents' visits; entertainment (3) such as listening to music[6]; individual, private acts (2) such as quiet reading; and finally, play (1). These data also indicate that a parent's activities in the home school environment often involved performing two, three, or more activities simultaneously. While there is very little evidence that these activities included deliberate instruction, there is ample data on management and guidance of children's self-initiated schooling tasks (see below). Still, what was going on around the focal children most of the time in the setting of their own living room and kitchen was standard child care and household maintenance.

For example, one midmorning the children's father was in the un-

---

[6] This family did not own a television, and it was never a topic of conversation.

finished upstairs of their basement home working on one of dozens of house projects. Their mother, with baby Lucas on her back, had just finished helping him gather items that would be picked up for sale at a local auction house. She returned to the kitchen/living room area, hooked up a home pasturizer for the goats' milk purchased yesterday from another family in the community, and went to lie down on the bed to nurse Lucas and encourage him to nap. Young Sarah had been with her mother, querying her about the objects being gathered for auction. At her mother's request from the bed, Sarah began looking in the antique wooden medicine closet whose four shelves were filled with homeopathic remedies in brown bottles. She picked them up one at a time, looking at the labels for two words that started with the letters R and S. All this time, Seth was sitting at the kitchen table reading *Understanding Weather* and writing information on a chart he had constructed with seven categories. He had not been directed to do this, and continued, for over two hours, without comment to or from anyone. Thus, during this learning incident, as in so many others, "schooling" activities occur in the midst of other family activities, including child care, nursing, and tending to illness, as well as constructing a dwelling and earning income by the sale of household objects.

Immediate Human Context

Group size and composition. The size of the group in the most commonly occurring setting, that is, the family home, was small, usually no more than six people. The composition of the group included people of varied ages, genders, and statuses, similar to the primate communities and human foraging societies that anthropologists have traditionally studied. The immediate family included the baby, two children and parents, though the father was present only one-half the time, and he bore little responsibility for child care and schooling activities when he was there. Thirty-nine of fifty-nine learning incidents occurred with some constellation of family members only. Another 17 learning incidents were recorded in a group which included, in addition to immediate family, an older agemate of 9-year-old Seth.

Atmosphere. The atmosphere in the learning environment of this family was most commonly characterized by moderate expressions of affect rather than either intensity or its opposite, lethargy and boredom. In 33 of 59 observations, the atmosphere was task-oriented with most attention directed toward the activities described above such as infant care, cooking, planning, and so on. For example, Observations 43 and 44 (Table 4.3) describe an afternoon during which Seth is rewriting a story at the kitchen table, using the ethnographer's portable computer, and Sarah is cutting figures like paper dolls out of a mail order catalog while humming and singing made-up songs. Their mother is engaging in afternoon household activities and childcare, including making coffee, baking bread, making phone calls related to scheduling their father's farrier appointments, answering Seth's questions on spelling, finding scissors for Sarah, and getting vegetables from the garden for the teeting baby to chew on. The atmosphere in this learning environment is steady, even, and focused on the tasks of household management.

In another 17 incidents the atmosphere was even more low-key, but relaxed and comfortable rather than depressing or lethargic. An openly happy atmosphere was next most common and it fell between task orientation and relaxation in physical expression. Two incidents during which the atmosphere was decidedly quiet, one loving and one judgmental, indicate occasional variety along both the energy and affect continuums. Still, these learners were unlikely to be in an environment that was intense, either celebrative or angry. Instead, with only three exceptions, the atmosphere was positive, pleasant, and attractive without being particularly exciting. Those few times when it was negative, it was simply boring (1 of 59 incidents) or moderately judgmental (1 of 59) when sharp remarks were directed toward a learner out of line.

Learner Role and Behavior

The learners' acts, what they were actually doing, exhibited great variety. This is in marked contrast with the repetitiveness of ongoing adult activities, the sameness of setting, and the evenness of the atmosphere. Children's activities do not replicate adult activities, nor are the two children in this home school setting similar to each other, either in how they choose to interact with others or in what they choose to do.

Nine-year-old Seth's activities are quite focused and usually independent. Three-fourths (21 of 28) of the systematic observations in which he was the focal learner show him engaged in information getting activities including reading (4), asking questions (4), using the computer (4), writing (2), studying (2), and getting instruction (2). A variety of other activities characterize the remainder of his time. They include socializing, playing, and fighting with other children (8) as well as doing assigned and unassigned tasks such as folding his laundry (assigned) and pasteurizing a fresh supply of goat's milk (unassigned). One instance of ritual activity occurred when both he and his sister were required to take a "time out" by sitting at kitchen chairs for several minutes.

The choices Seth made regarding how to relate to the dominant, ongoing, or adult activities which were occurring around him did range from full, active participation to no participation. However, Seth's activities, more often than not, are unrelated to the ongoing adult or household activity. He does something else altogether, usually one of the information activities noted above (12) or does not participate at all (3).

For example, one sunny fall morning both Sarah and Seth were sleeping late (past 9 a.m.). Their mother had been up much of the night with a teething baby and the whole family was tired. In the kitchen, Joseph, a 12-year-old houseguest, was at the stove making pancakes, while both adults were eating them and simultaneously making coffee and feeding oatmeal to the baby. Seth, in the adjoining sleeping area, rolled off the top bunk on to his parents' bed. Then he got up, went directly to the couch in the living room, sat with his back to the kitchen, covered himself with a blanket, and began to read a library book. He stayed there without comment for some time.

While this loner behavior and voracious reading were his major modus operandi, his interactions, like the behavior itself, did show variety. He exhibits reluctant or unskillful participation (2) in family planning, junior participation (4) in computer use, oral reading, and mealtime socializing, and full skillful participation in library activities and milk pasteurizing (3). Finally, in 4 of 28 observations he was seen interfering with his mother's caregiving activities. This occurred when they focused not on the baby but on his 4-year-old sister's activities. Except for that kind of interference, Seth generally appears to ignore all ongoing activities—mother's, father's, friend's, and sister's—doing something else altogether.

The role that 4-year-old Sarah was fashioning for herself was a much more interactive one. In 19 of 31 observations she is seen as participatory. Her choices regarding how to relate to adult or ongoing activities are diverse and were coded as junior participation (8), watching (2), full participation (2), participating unskillfully (1), and interfering (6).

An example of this diversity in her choices can be seen in several consecutive incidents that occurred one midmorning. While her brother is on the couch doing a World Book social studies game, Sarah sits at the kitchen table with her mother who is nursing baby Lucas and, at the same time, explaining to Sarah how to do the dot-to-dot activities in her newly purchased coloring book. While making a running string of comments to her mother about the dot connecting, Sarah interrupts the nursing by making little chirping sounds to the baby to distract him from nursing, which works. Here she is, in effect, interfering with the ongoing adult activity of caregiving. When her mother moves to the bed to lay down and finish nursing, Sarah retrieves the World Book Game which her brother has completed and returned, at the same time selecting a game sheet she perceives to be at her level— naming letters by upper case and lower case. Alternately watching her mother and the ethnographer, Sarah attempts to complete the reading sheet, but fairly quickly and without commenting in response to her mother's query: "Are you finished with the World Book, Sarah?" she returns the entire contraption to its shelf in the furnace room. Later checking showed her "work" to be incorrect. Here she is participating unskillfully in an ongoing schooling activity. At that moment, her mother gets up from the bed where Lucas has fallen asleep and offers to help Sarah with her morning washing and dressing. Again without comment, either from Sarah or from her mother, who is selecting a radio station that is played when Lucas is sleeping, Sarah chooses clothing from the drawer under the couch/bed where I am sitting and goes upstairs with her mother, exhibiting full skillful participation in the activities of her milieu. She plays (3) or does something else altogether only half as often (7) as her brother. She is a nonparticipant only twice, and one of those times was when she was sleeping late.

Like her choices regarding interaction, Sarah's activities are similarly different from her brother's. They are less focused and reflect the variety of choices she made about interaction. She was as likely to be playing, socializing, and doing art activities (7) as to be engaged in conflict with her brother (7) or to be tending to individual activities like resting, toileting, and dressing, or to be engaged in caregiving and health-related activities, usually in interaction with her mother (6). She also did information-seeking activities (4). But these were her least likely choice, often involved imitating her brother, and may have been an artifact of the researcher's presence, as Sarah knew I was there to "study children and how they learn to live in the country." Thus, this 4-year-old engages in a variety of activities. She tries to do schooling activities, both unskillfully by imitating her brother and therefore doing something well beyond her ability and skillfully by doing a dot-to-dot book. She also socializes by chattering to mother; she goes to the bathroom after eliciting her mother's assistance, and she settles into joyful hopping play. How these activities relate to the ongoing or primary activity also shows considerable variety from interference to watching to junior participation to unskillful participation.

Response factors. Frequencies in kinds of response and persons responding to the two learners in this family indicate that certain structures and processes predominate here. In 39 of 59 observations, the responding person was a parent, usually the mother. Only four instances show the father as the responder, three of those a response to Seth, and the other an accepting nonresponse to Sarah on the evening she sat at the kitchen table doing her dot-to-dot book while her father sat across from her working on his business ledger. The mother's presence and her responses were the primary sounding board in these children's daily lives. The other 20 responses came from a variety of sources. The most likely respondant after parents was a sibling: one response came from baby Lucas to Sarah; three from Seth to Sarah, and five from Sarah to Seth. Again, it is the highly engaging Sarah who elicits a response from the baby and from the focused, solitary Seth and who responds to him. Twice responses came from the visiting friend and from the ethnographer. Twice Sarah monitored and responded to her own behavior and twice the computer program responded to Seth's choices. Finally, in two observations there was no person or thing around to respond; the learner was alone.

The most common response (16) these learners received to their behaviors and choices was a simple accepting, noninstructional response. For example, one quiet afternoon when baby Lucas was asleep and the public radio station was playing classical music, mother was sitting at the kitchen table coloring with Sarah. Seth, the focal learner, was reading on the couch with his back to the kitchen table. He completed a Hardy Boys book, reached to the foot of the couch where he had placed his new stash of library books, looked at a feudal history, put it down and selected a wilderness story. He resumed reading, twisting the new Cub Scout hat his mother had purchased for him earlier that day, a reward for turning in his reading log at the library in time to win a summer Reading Club award. While his mother was surely aware of his book selection behavior on the couch, she did not interrupt, comment, or intrude in any way. This was coded as an accepting noninstructional response. The second most common response (11) was none at all. In such instances, the learner's behaviors go completely unnoticed, as in the day that Seth, alone in the house reading on the couch, noticed that the pasturizer was ready for the next stage. He proceeded to the kitchen and completed the mechanical tasks necessary to finish the job, then resumed reading without commenting to anyone. Implicitly instructional responses, such as praise and reprimands or smiles and scowls, were more often negative (9) than positive (1), the latter occurring only when Sarah expressed pleasure at having made a word in her newly purchased phonics workbook. Sarah, the more active of the two learners, was also the recipient of more negative instructional responses, occurring five of the seven times she had become engaged in conflict, 1 time when she tried to do childcare, and once when she attempted to help with health care. Seth's implicitly instructional negative responses (4) also occurred during conflict, during play that was deemed too rough, and for inadequate performance of a laundry task. Half of the negative responses came not from parents but from siblings or friends, indicating what I observed to be parents' general tolerance (higher than mine) for conflict and for "mistakes." The other two patterns of response were purposefully but indirectly instructional responses such as questioning and responses instigated by the learner's initiative. The purposeful responses were directed more often to Seth (5) than to Sarah (3), were consistently concerned with their studying/reading/writing activities, and came exclusively from their mother. Responses instigated by the learner's initiatives, while no less frequent (8), came only twice from mother, were directed only twice to Sarah, and came from a variety of sources including siblings, friend, self, and the computer. What this analysis reveals is that these learners are not ignored. While codes indicate that an accepting, noninstructional response is most likely, adults and siblings do respond to learners, and the mother offers deliberate purposeful responses.

Values. Statements based on values or world views simply were not made in this family. In only 4 of 59 incidents have I indicated hearing a statement of values. Each of the four is a different value or world view. In slightly over half the incidents, values were implied rather than stated. The most common implication (12) focused on fairness, social balance, the way *we* do things. Parents, for example, were often observed behaving in ways that indicated that they believe they have an equal obligation to tend to all the children. One morning Seth was doing an educational activity in response to his mother's concern that he demonstrate some schooling behaviors. She made no comment to him as he worked on the couch, but she was visually attentive to him. At the same time, sitting at the kitchen table, she was nursing the baby and simultaneously responding verbally to the engaging Sarah's stream of verbal interactions which included questions about her dot-to-dot book, and comments on the baby's nursing behavior. Here, what children were being exposed to and therefore could potentially be learning was that social balance is valued in this family. Another common theme (9) seemed to be achievement of personal growth and related personal skills. All other value implications were only occasional. They included the necessity of obedience and providing direction for children (6), being helpful and maintaining harmony (4), respect (2), frugality (2), aggressiveness (2)—between children only, and the value of knowledge for its own sake (1).

World views that were *not* heard are perhaps as telling. There was no recourse to the sacred, ordained, or spiritual, no cosmic retribution or divine order, and no pessimism, doom and gloom or harshness. Gender and role differences are somewhat evident. Value implications of the mother's actions focused consistently on social balance or fairness and on control in terms of conforming to family expectations. The father's behavior appeared to imply that his place in assuring material survival superceded any agendas in the household, at the moment, including schooling and child care. The current categorization system for values is still being developed and revised as it is used in a variety of studies.

CONCLUSION

The assumptions on which this study rested are neither confirmed nor jeopardized by this one case. But the findings presented above lend support to the salience of those assumptions, and encourage further investigation of human learning along these lines. It does seem correct to assert that these learners were sensitive to contextual, that is cultural, information. While her mother nursed a fussing, teething baby and her brother sat at the kitchen table making a weather chart, Sarah learned about the storing of homeopathic remedies, had a spelling lesson, saw that mothers nurse babies, learned that her brother is paying attention to what she is doing even while he works on something else, and learned something about family values regarding healing, all as part of one small incident. While this incident was ostensibly a spelling lesson ("Find a bottle with two words on it; one starting with 'a' and one with 's'."), Sarah was taking in information from multiple sources including people, objects, affect, and a particular world view, and through a variety of modalities including at least listening, talking, watching, reading. This importing of information was unconscious as culture is unconscious. Rather than Sarah's learning being deliberate, planned, and scheduled, it appears rather to be automatic, unconscious, and constant. We can posit, therefore, that the mechanisms by which human learners receive and transmit information in the context of real life are more likely to occur within a complex interactive system than along a linear continuum.

While these data are inconclusive, they do reveal that in this particular family, children were active and making a variety of choices regarding interactions, even though the activities going on around them were repetitive. Regardless of the tentativeness of this first slice through a large data set, we continue to posit that humans are learners and that they cannot be prevented from learning, even in their own homes.

REFERENCES

Dobbert, M. L., & Cooke, B. (1987). Primate biology and behavior: A stimulus to educational thought and policy. In G.D. Spindler (Ed.), *Education and cultural process* (pp. 97–116). Prospect Heights, IL: Waveland Press.

Hall, E.T. (1959). *The silent Language.* New York: Doubleday.

Herzog, J. D. (1974). The socialization of juveniles in primate and foraging societies: Implications for contemporary education. *Council on Anthropology and Education Quarterly, 5,* 12–17.

Kimball, S. (1982). Community and hominoid emergence. *Anthropology and Education Quarterly, 13,* 124–132.

Lancaster, J. B. (1975). *Primate behavior and the emergence of human culture.* New York: Holt, Rinehart, & Winston.

Pitman, M. A., Eisikovits, R. A., & Dobbert, M. L. (1989). *Culture acquisition: A holistic approach to human learning.* New York: Praeger.

Whiting, B.B., and Whiting, J.W.M. (1975). *Children of six cultures.* Cambridge, MA: Harvard University Press.

Part II
The Implications of the Home Schooling Movement

Chapter 5
State Regulation of Home Schooling: A Policy Analysis

James G. Cibulka
University of Wisconsin-Milwaukee

The educational reform movement of the 1980s has witnessed two counterveiling trends. At one side, in the name of higher educational standards, state regulation has increased dramatically in many states, and such regulation has imposed uniform personnel, program, and testing requirements on local school districts. At the other side, in response to public demand, states have increased choices available to families for selecting a school.

Home schooling represents the second of these policy developments. Its reputed widespread growth in recent years (see Chapter 1) poses a political problem for state policy makers. Given the increasing state regulatory activity of recent years, how should state policy regulate home schools, if at all? What is the balancing point between regulation for quality (what many regard as a legitimate state interest) and the state's desire to preserve and even foster freedom of choice for families (also a compelling, if less universally accepted, state objective)?

This chapter is an analysis of the politics of state regulation of home schools. First, I ask what degree of success "home schoolers" have had in fashioning state laws and regulations which, from their point of view, are fair. Second, the chapter offers an analysis of these developments in various states, attempting to account both for the overall national trend and for differences in particular states; in other words, what factors account for the policy settlement in various states?

THEORETICAL FRAMEWORK

A debate has existed in the politics of education literature about how closed, that is, autonomous, public school decision making is. The classic positions advanced on this question were by Zeigler, Jennings, and Peak (1974) on the one side, who documented that interest group activity in public education is not large, and on the other side Boyd (1976), who challenged their interpretations on several fronts. In his review of the politics of education literature, Peterson (1974) concluded that while interest group activity in education is not high, education may be no more autonomous than other domestic policy areas.

Indeed, research indicates that the mobilization of interests and the structure of governance in some other domestic policy areas favor producer interests rather than interests of consumers. Health and mental health policy frequently are cited as examples (Alford, 1975; Marmor & Morone, 1980). Zeigler, Kehoe, and Reisman (1985), on the other hand, documented greater professional dominance in school government than in reformed municipal government. The principal feature favoring producer dominance of policy making has been the ability of school professionals to structure the policy process so that group mobilization is difficult.

This debate never has been resolved. Wirt and Kirst (1989) pointed out that recently the autonomy of school administrators has been reduced by new consumer and professional constituencies for federal education programs, by court decisions, as well as by other factors. Also, the educational reform initiatives largely led by state-elected officials have reduced the authority of the educational "establishment" such as school boards, superintendents, and even state boards of education.

These arguments over how open or closed educational decision making is—and ought to be—are rooted in pluralist interest group theory. The central tenet of this theory is that policy outcomes reflect the mobilization of interests through groups in the political arena, that competing interests are bargained and compromised, and that no one set of elites dominates policy outcomes because of shifting coalitions, differences in mobilization by these interests from issue to issue, and other factors. Pluralism, in other words, justifies limited popular participation, because groups can mobilize effectively in spite of these limitations. Critics of pluralism, for example, Lowi (1969), have called attention to the many limitations in the way pluralism works.

Thus, a considerable body of research exists on the various kinds of interest groups, why people join them, and their influence over policy outcomes. For example, the debate in the politics of education field over professional dominance addresses the latter issue. While pluralists assert that no one set of elites dominates all policies, various strat-ification interpretations conclude the opposite, namely, that one set of economic, social, or professional elites is in control.

This study of the home schooling movement is framed within these research traditions. The emergence of a home schooling movement, its mobilization into the political arena as an interest group, and the suc-cess of its efforts all provide opportunities to address major themes in the politics of education literature. Moreover, I shall ask what these processes and outcomes suggest about the politics of American educa-tion in the 1980s. Such questions have not been posed in previous re-search on home schooling.[1]

METHODS

Initially, a documentary analysis of legal challenges and statutes in all 50 states was conducted. Preliminary classifications of these stat-utes were done, taking into account such factors as whether the home school is defined as a private school, how the home schools are regu-lated and who is responsible for regulation, and what aspects of the home school are regulated by the state. Phone interviews then were conducted with officials at the Home School Legal Defense Associa-tion, home school leaders, state education agency officials, state legis-lators, and their aides. Based on these data sources, seven states were selected. This "purposive sample" reflects variability in the legal framework confronting home schoolers (e.g., high regulation at one end and almost no regulation at the other) and the degree and kind of political opposition they faced (from state education agency officials, state attorney generals, local boards of education, teachers unions, and others). Phone interviews then were conducted in these seven states. The states are: Colorado, Michigan, Missouri, Nebraska, Pennsylva-nia, Washington, and Wisconsin. While the sample is not intended to be representative from a statistical point of view, the findings reported here are consistent with the perceptions on national trends provided by key informants who operate in a national context. These key differ-ences among states that influenced the selection of the sample were: the state regulatory framework; the degree of political mobilization this framework triggers among home schoolers; tactics of state regula-tors; organizational skills of home schoolers and their opponents; and the perceived quality of the public schools. All these factors will be explained more fully under the "Findings" reported below.

---

[1] See, for example, the special issue of *Education and Urban Society* (November, 1988, Volume 21, No. 1) devoted to home schooling.

FINDINGS

A principal fact which must animate any analysis of states' home school regulations is that, with only some exceptions, home schoolers have been remarkably successful in reshaping state laws and regulations so that these are favorable or at least neutral toward their interests. According to data compiled by the Home School Legal Defense Association (Klicka, 1988), 32 states have adopted home school statutes or regulations since 1956, and 90 percent have been since 1982. While not every new law or regulation has favored home schoolers entirely, in the vast majority of cases, new legislation has resulted from legal challenges or legislative lobbying and direct action taken by home schoolers. For example, higher courts in Georgia, Wisconsin, Minnesota, Missouri, and Iowa ruled in recent years that states' compulsory attendance laws were unconstitutionally vague. State laws which require that instruction in home schools be "equivalent" have been struck down by courts in Iowa and Minnesota, although such laws still exist in seven states. Between 1982 and 1988, 28 states passed laws or regulations which improved the status of home schoolers through reduced state regulation of school approval, staffing, curriculum, or other aspects of school operations. Of the 31 states with explicit home school laws, home schoolers now are generally content with the laws in 27 of these states, according to officials at the Home School Legal Defense Association. For example, only three states any longer require that all home schools, without exception, have a certified teacher involved in instruction at home, and among these, Iowa has placed a moratorium on enforcement.

This is not to say that home schoolers in many states regard state regulation as ideal. Some home schoolers would prefer no regulation at all and argue from a philosophical position of anarchy or religious freedom. Yet most home schoolers, while preferring the least possible regulation, recognize the legitimacy, or at least political reality, of some state regulation. For many home schoolers, Wisconsin's law, which simply requires the home school to be registered, is a model of this minimal regulatory approach. Yet in most states, some greater degree of regulation exists, such as reporting procedures, review of curricula, or inspections.

Home schoolers generally oppose any statute which requires them to be approved by a local school district, an approach operative in 18 states and the District of Columbia. According to many home schoolers, state regulation has the advantage of being more uniform than local regulation and is also generally more enlightened. Despite these reservations about local-approval statutes, such laws do appear to have resulted in surprisingly little conflict in most states, and home schoolers are not actually opposing them.

What reinforces the perception of home schoolers' success in the legal arena is the fact that their movement has grown rapidly and that these statutes have been changed in a period of less than a decade. Considering the typical pace of change in our federal system, a decade is something like moving at the speed of light.

The record of home schoolers can be roughly compared with two other recent social movements: the civil rights movement and the consumer movement. All three movements have waged battles both through aggressive legal challenges/defenses and through direct efforts to change laws. Yet home schoolers have achieved their results without resorting to large-scale, sustained direct action tactics such as marches and boycotts, although occasionally they have sponsored large rallies. While the civil rights movement has largely achieved one of its early goals, the undoing of racially discriminatory laws, those efforts consumed a decade of tumultuous activity at all levels of our federal system. Furthermore, the civil rights movement has had to confront ever more subtle, indirect forms of discrimination, particularly in the face of renewed backlash against civil rights goals in recent years.

The consumer movement, while it has won passage of many specific pieces of legislation at various governmental levels, has had difficulty passing consumer protection legislation which would fully institutionalize consideration of the consumer's interests in governmental decision making, whether before regulatory agencies, before various executive branch agencies, before legislatures, or before the judiciary.

Any comparison of home schooling, civil rights, and consumerism requires careful examination of the goals of these movements, which reflect the range of "wrongs" each has confronted. The differences between the three movements help to highlight the reasons for home schoolers' high percentage of hard-fought, relatively rapid successes. Drawing on interest-group analysis, which is a central framework in the study of educational politics, the next section will identify the conditions necessary for successful political mobilization by interest groups in the three movements.

EXPLANATIONS FOR THE OVERALL PATTERN

The first explanation for home schoolers' success is that they seek *less* state intrusion, not greater state protection through laws and regulations. Unlike civil rights or consumer protection, this social movement argues that its interests are served best by minimal governmental intervention. This position has placed state governments in the defensive position of arguing that there is a compelling state interest attached to their proposed regulation of such schools. From a legal perspective, the precise issues and standards of proof associated with particular laws and regulations can become quite technical.[2] From an overall political perspective, which is influential in legislative debates and does serve as a context for the courts as well, the government is in an awkward position when it attempts to invoke the mantle of state protection of children's interests. Evidence that home schoolers neglect or abuse their children is very scant, while evidence that their educational results are at least equal, and in many cases superior, to that produced by public schools is quite abundant.[3] Here, then, is a difficult case for zealous state intervention.

Home schoolers have had a simpler legal and regulatory environment to counter than that which confronted the early civil rights and consumer movements. First, home schoolers are concerned only with educational policy, not with a range of domestic policy domains such as health, environment, or employment. Second, while they sometimes have been harassed by local school districts, the statutory or regulatory authority they confront always is at the state level. Relief may be sought through various means, of course—changing state regulations (the framework in five states), changing state statutes, or seeking relief through state or federal courts. Yet in each case, the action must be remedied primarily at the state level, since local school districts act principally under state authority. This is to be contrasted with the maze of laws and regulations civil rights and consumer advocates must address at virtually all government levels and in diverse policy arenas.

Further, the effect of raising a largely libertarian claim to be left alone, freed of the reach of state schools and state entanglement, is fiscally appealing to taxpayers and legislators. By contrast, the protection of racial or language minority rights and consumer interests has required government enforcement of those interests. The costs of expanding this governmental machinery has proven offensive to many

[2] See Chapter 8, for an analysis of standards of proof for establishing a compelling state interest.

[3] Such evidence frequently is cited by home schoolers at state board or state legislative hearings. From an educational research perspective, there is no conclusive evidence that the "value added" through home schooling exceeds that in conventional public or private schools. Citing superior educational results alone is not conclusive, of course, since this would require proper controls for "student inputs," which are costly in research designs and, therefore, infrequently done. Even when such designs have been attempted, they are fraught with controversy (e.g., Haertel, James, & Levin, 1988). For further discussion, see Chapter 2.

and is a controversy that home schoolers have been able to avoid. The home schoolers' agenda, if anything, will reduce the tax price of schooling.

In addition, the small size of the home-school population, which is only a minuscule fraction of the total school-age population, gives even greater validity to their appeal to be left alone. Their small size complicates the task of their opponents, who favor either outlawing home schools or creating a high degree of regulation. Under the circumstances, the latter must show some overriding threat to the interests of public schools. This appeal is awkward and raises the countercriticism that public school teachers and administrators are only trying to protect their jobs or that they are putting their finger in a dike attempting to contain a flood of public dissatisfaction with public schools. Also, home schoolers in some states have shown that they drain students from private schools as well as public ones, thereby diluting the assertion that public schools will be harmed by declining rolls. Finally, it has been difficult for public school advocates opposing home schoolers to show harm by documenting the growth of the home-school movement. The problem with this argument is that it focuses legislators' attention on a dangerous issue: Why are the public schools increasingly unattractive to a growing proportion of the population?

In short, the mobilization of home schoolers as a successful interest group (or closely allied groups) in each state has been facilitated by their relatively simpler political task (compared with other reformers), their ideology, including its fiscal appeal, and their small size.

EXPLANATIONS FOR THE VARIABLE SUCCESS OF HOME SCHOOL EFFORTS

Granted that overall, home schoolers have experienced remarkable success, it is nonetheless useful to ask what circumstances have contributed to greater success in some states than in others. I believe that there are five principal reasons for the variation one finds in the degree of success that home school efforts have had in various states. Two of these—the legacy of state regulation and the tactics employed by state regulators which mobilize public opinion against them—trigger the initial conversion of home schoolers from an educational movement alone to a political movement. As long as their aims are narrowly educational, they may well organize, but largely to advance the immediate task of carrying out their responsibilities as parent educators. Once they enter the political arena in court, in legislatures, or before regulatory bodies, their aim is broadly redistributive—to achieve for themselves as a class of persons with common interests their civil rights and to oppose any authoritative claims of state government which interfere with those civil rights.

After home schoolers become politically mobilized, several other factors account for the success of the policy settlement they achieve— their organizational skills, those of their opponents, and the reputation of the public schools in the current period of public school reform. These factors are summarized in Figure 5.1 below.

Figure 5.1   Factors Affecting Varying Policy Successess of Home Schoolers

Factors Affecting Political Mobilization	Factors Affecting Policy Settlement
state regulatory tradition	organizational skills of home schoolers
regulatory tactics which mobilize public opinion	organizational skills of opponents
	reputation of public schools

FACTORS AFFECTING POLITICAL MOBILIZATION OF HOME SCHOOLERS

The State Regulatory Tradition

The inclination of home schoolers to mobilize politically is affected by the legal and regulatory framework that was in place when the home schooling movement arose, or which emerged as the number of home schools multiplied. A good example of a state whose laws triggered political action by home schoolers is Colorado. Home schoolers found uneven local enforcement of state law intolerable. Home schoolers were required to apply to the local district for approval, but school districts were interpreting state regulations pertaining to private schools very differently. Some required curriculum approval, interviews with children, inspection, and other policies perceived by home schoolers as intrusive. If families were in violation of any one requirement, approval might be revoked. Other districts gave blanket denial to any application, while still others approved any request. Home schoolers went to the state legislature to seek relief. Initially they were successful, partly because the several home-schooling organizations disagreed on various points and could not form a united front in representing their interests to legislators. During the following session, parents formed "Concerned Parents of Colorado," and were able to speak with one voice and to keep everyone informed through a computer phone line. It is doubtful, according to home school spokespersons in Colorado, that the new 1988 law could have been achieved without this mobilization. Again, it was the state's uneven interpretation of a vague regulatory framework in place which triggered this political mobilization of home schoolers.

State laws and regulations pertaining to private schools also have an important influence on the political activity and strength of the home-school movement. In states where home schoolers have been treated as a private school, or where proposed onerous legislation affecting home schoolers would increase regulation of private schools (a tactical error made by proponents of regulation in Missouri and Wisconsin), home schoolers have been more likely to win the active support of private schools than in states where the regulatory framework treats them separately from private schools. According to the Home School Legal Defense Association, home schools may now operate as private or church schools in at least 11 states (other options may be applicable as well). In five other states, some home schoolers may qualify as private or church schools.

To be sure, the presence of private schools in the political coalition can prove to be a complicating factor, at least initially because it makes it more difficult to gain consensus among an already diverse set of interests. This occurred in Washington, although eventually the alliance with private schools did prove beneficial to home schoolers.

Regulatory Tactics which Mobilize Public Opinion

Some states blundered politically in their attempt to go on to the offensive by prosecuting home schoolers. Their actions not only had the effect of mobilizing home schoolers, but more importantly, they swung public opinion against the state's regulatory efforts.

One example of offensive enforcement of state laws, from the perspective of home schoolers, is exemplified by Missouri. Prior to 1986, state law had required home instruction to be substantially equivalent to that available in the public schools. State social service officials, accustomed to dealing with child neglect cases, prosecuted home schoolers vigorously for educational neglect. This situation triggered the organization of Families for Home Education, a statewide organization instrumental in assisting prosecuted families in court. This organization filed a federal class action suit against the state, obtained a judgment that the law was unconstitutionally vague, and eventually won passage of a new compromise law. Much news and media coverage throughout this process helped create public awareness of this issue and galvanized public opinion to the point that state officials acknowledged that some change was needed.

Iowa and Nebraska had much national publicity focusing on the state enforcement tactics against home schoolers in their states. Prior to the passage of new corrective legislation in 1985, Nebraska had required private schools to have certified teachers. The state attorney general sent sheriffs to padlock the doors of a Baptist church school operating without certified teachers. Officials at the school objected to state certification on religious grounds and refused to close the school. The state arrested, fined, and jailed several fathers of children attending this school. National media coverage put greater pressure on the governor and state legislature to change the law. The governor asked the attorney general to develop an alternative and submitted a new bill to the legislature permitting any private, denominational, or parochial school (including by implication a home school) to elect not to meet state accreditation or approval requirements. Nonaccredited private schools annually submit to the commissioner of education information on safety, attendance, and the program of instruction. Further, teachers must submit evidence of their qualifications or take a minimum competency test.

A similar scenario of overly zealous enforcement occurred in Iowa, leading to the jailing of a pastor. As a result of the negative publicity, the governor appointed a Task Force on Education, which issued a report in 1985 recommending legislative action that would remove the requirement of certification from all private and home schools. In 1988, the Iowa legislature placed a moratorium on enforcement of certification requirements. In both Iowa and Nebraska, then, home schoolers have benefited from an enforcement posture on the part of the state which raised civil rights claims and engendered wide sympathy for both private schools and home schoolers, making the state look petty and extremist. The same struggle is being repeated in North Dakota in 1989. In each of these states, state enforcement excesses played into home schoolers' hands, swaying public opinion and putting home schoolers on the moral high ground.

Nascent interest groups waging a social struggle for recognition typically benefit from "third-party" mobilization of this kind. Indeed, the battle for public opinion is one important element which distinguishes pluralist from ideological bargaining; ideological bargaining is public rather than private, emphasizing contested values of race, class, and status (Peterson, 1976). In the 1960s, the nonviolent protest tactics of the civil rights movement succeeded in mobilizing public opinion—specifically the middle-class—against authorities when southern law enforcement officials used hoses and dogs against civil rights protestors. Just as the state regulatory tradition triggers mobilization of home schoolers themselves, the enforcement tactics of state regulators can mobilize allies that are critical to the success of home schooling efforts.

FACTORS AFFECTING THE POLICY SETTLEMENT

I have reviewed the factors which shaped the political mobilization of home schoolers. The greater their political mobilization, all other things equal, the greater has been their success in changing laws affecting them. Now, still building on the categories contained in Figure 5.1, I turn to another related factor which influences the actual policy settlement.

Organizational Skills of Home Schoolers

Home schoolers are quite well organized and sophisticated in legal challenges and lobbying. Many who were interviewed by the researcher pointed out, however, that this sophistication was learned from early mistakes. Home schoolers had to learn such things as how to influence the legislative process and how to organize themselves into a unified, effective lobbying force.

Home schoolers have reason to organize themselves for self-help purposes, since organizing a home school is not an easy task. Elaborate networks of regional support groups share educational information. In many states, when it become necessary to mobilize for political goals, an infrastructure was there to build upon.

Home schoolers' efforts have been almost entirely dependent on volunteers. While some home schoolers have ties to the political right and particularly the religious right, they do not share with other conservative causes the financial support from electronic and direct mail fund raising or from philanthropy. Financing of political activity proves a challenge and explains why the organizations seldom have paid staff. While the families are largely middle-class, and in many cases have professional salaries, most have only one member in the labor force while the other member is at home educating. If much of their legal work was not done pro bono by friends or by home schoolers who are themselves attorneys, they could not mount the number of legal challenges and defenses they have.

The personal skills of home schoolers go a long way toward explaining their success. Home schoolers have learned to portray themselves as moderate people, largely to counter critics (sometimes teachers unions) who accuse them of being child abusers, neglecters, and fanatics. They hold coffees for legislators, identify themselves as politically diverse, and eschew portraying themselves as a religious lobby. They distribute moderate printed material to counter their opponents. They seek powerful, respected allies within the legislature or even within the state department of education. At the same time, they employ skillful direct action techniques like capitol rallies and legislative lobbying.

Perhaps the biggest challenge to further legislative inroads by home schoolers is the diversity within their ranks and the resistance to compromise by some elements within the movement when issues of principle are perceived to be at stake. As in many social movements, factions emerge, and this bickering has limited their success in mobilizing national advocacy organizations, with the exception of the Home School Legal Defense Association. Home schoolers include "back-to-the land" freethinkers alongside evangelical Christians, Catholics, Jews, Bahai's and many others. The cultural chasm between these groups is potentially large. They have learned from legislative losses, however, that when divided, their chances of victory are lessened. If the state's laws and regulations are seen as intolerably pernicious by all those factions, it has been easier for everyone to pull together. In other states, particularly those with private school statutes requiring minimum regulation, many parents prefer the status quo, and the problems of mounting a unified organizational base multiply.

However, even where there is agreement on the need for new legislation, different advocacies sometimes emerge. In the State of Washington, for instance, home school bills failed due to the unwillingness of one group of private Christian schools then sponsoring the bills to accept any regulation, even though many less well-organized home schoolers were willing to tolerate some degree of regulation. For a number of legislative sessions, multiple bills were introduced by different home schoolers who solicited different legislative backers. This both reflected and aggravated the problem of in-fighting among home schoolers. Even after a statewide organization was formed, much work was needed before those involved agreed that some level of regulation by the state would be preferable to harassment by truant officers. A skillful survey by one of the organization's leaders, documenting the preferences of home schoolers throughout the state, eventually provided an information base upon which a consensus could be forged that was acceptable to all but some fundamental Christians.[4]

Despite these problems of factionalism, disagreements generally have been subordinated to the broader goals of legislative success. The

---

[4] For a more detailed discussion of Washington State developments, see Chapter 2.

political failures that home schoolers have experienced are not principally due to any tensions which may exist within the ranks. Rather, failures that have occurred can be attributed to the strength of the opposition. It is to this factor that I turn next.

Organizational Skills of Home School Opponents

Not surprisingly, state officials frequently can find powerful friends to support their case for strong regulation of home schoolers. School producer groups in some states have perceived home schooling as a consumer movement which is antithetical to the interests of public schools, including the role interests of public school employees, even though many home schoolers assiduously avoid attacks on public schools. Teachers unions such as National Association (NEA) have opposed home schoolers actively in a number of states, raising concerns about the quality of instruction in such schools, the number of child abusers supposedly among home schoolers, and the threat to public school funding and quality if the number of home schools grows.[5] Home schoolers typically interpret the motives of unions less charitably, citing the probability that many public school teachers would lose jobs if the number of home schools grew. When unions endorse legislation that requires a significant degree of regulation of home schools, home schoolers interpret this as an attempt to put them out of business.

Administrators' associations in some states, such as the elementary principals association or the superintendents association, also may join teachers in opposing home schoolers. State school board associations have taken no consistent position; depending on the state, they may support home schoolers, oppose them, or remain neutral. The National School Boards Association has recommended model legislation which is quite moderate and acceptable to many home schoolers.

The success of NEA state affiliates in countering home schoolers appears to depend on several things: the strength of their Democratic Party support in the state legislature, since they are large and powerful campaign contributors; their resolve to mobilize actively; and their ability to advance a credible attack on home schoolers. Regarding the second of these points, until recently the NEA has been inclined to underestimate the strength of home schoolers. For example, the Wisconsin Education Association Council (WEAC) reportedly boasted that it would "bury" home schoolers during a legislative foray in 1983. In

---

[5] The information in this section is based on interviews with home school advocates, state education agency officials, and state legislators or their aides.

fact, however, WEAC failed to effectively consolidate its considerable Democratic legislative support (and support within the state department of public instruction) to oppose a bill that home schoolers now tout as the nation's model legislative victory. Home schoolers were well organized and obtained active help from some key legislators. Thus, in this instance the organizational skills of home schoolers proved superior to those of their opponents.

In recent years the NEA has awakened to the skill of its opposition. In contrast to the Wisconsin outcome, home schoolers have been delivered bitter defeats by NEA affiliates in Alabama and Michigan.

For example, in Michigan the NEA has fought successfully to prevent home schoolers from changing the existing regulatory framework applied to home schools. Home schoolers have been operating under compliance procedures adopted by the state board of education in 1986, because the laws are silent on home schooling. All teachers of school-age children must be certified in Michigan. Moreover, compulsory public school attendance laws apply to all schools, except state-approved nonpublic schools. Home schools have been deemed to fall under the definition of church schools. The state department of education has tried to close the inevitable loopholes resulting from such a confusing regulatory framework. While it and home schoolers generally have been at odds, they did reach an accommodation on the teacher certification issue, permitting home school teachers to have a four-year college degree in lieu of certification. Home schoolers have argued for an entire overhaul of the laws and regulations, rather than patchwork changes, but they have not been able to get a bill out of committee in the state legislature for two consecutive legislative sessions due to strong opposition by the politically powerful Michigan Education Association.

Several factors may explain the relative success of the opponents of home education in Michigan. Apart from Michigan's reputation as a strong union state, the loss of enrollments experienced by public schools as a result of the home school movement perhaps has been more dramatic in that state than elsewhere. One school district lost 200 pupils in two years to home schooling and was forced to close one building and lay off staff. The difficulties experienced by home schoolers in Michigan do not reflect on their own organizational skills—for instance, home schoolers mounted two large rallies, one with 15,000 people at the state capitol. Instead, the legislative history demonstrates the strength of their opposition.

Another extenuating factor which may explain the Michigan legislature's unwillingness to pass legislation is the State Supreme Court's upholding of the state's teacher certification provision in a challenge launched by two church schools. In many other states where opponents of home schooling also mounted strong campaigns, state legislators were under pressure from court orders to remedy statutes the court declared unconstitutional. The court mandate to act in these other states reduced the strength of home school opponents. Not able to defend the status quo any longer, teachers unions, and other opponents introduced their own hostile legislation. In Michigan, by contrast, the state legislature was under no such court mandate, and home schooling opponents had the somewhat politically simpler task (compared to home schooling opponents in other states where home schoolers eventually prevailed) of defending the status quo. Thus, while Michigan home schoolers do regard the present regulatory arrangement in that state as quite oppressive, they have been unable to change the status quo.

In other states, an important limitation on the success of union opposition to home schoolers has been the union's tendency to adopt a shrill tone and to be inflexible about compromise. When unions have waged arguments about alleged child abuse and poor instructional quality, home schoolers have answered them quite convincingly and dispassionately.

In short, while home schoolers have faced countermobilization by producer groups who support state regulation (sometimes being more adamant about appropriate regulation than state officials themselves), the coalition of home school opponents has wavered in many states, where they have been unable to count on consistent support of all administrator groups or school board associations. Where a powerful anti-home school coalition has emerged, home schoolers have portrayed themselves effectively as underdogs—Davids who must take on Goliaths. Add to this the rather weak empirical case for strong state regulation, and the result has been an interest-group struggle in which consumers triumph over producers. With some exceptions such as those cited above, the efforts of opponents have proven remarkably weak.

Perceived Need for Public School Reform

Again referring back to Figure 5.1, which summarized the factors explaining the high degree of political success home schoolers have had, we turn now to one additional factor which has influenced the kind of policy settlement arrived at in some states. The home-school movement has been helped greatly by its ability to cite shortcomings in public schools. In only one instance were opponents able to turn the reform movement to their advantage rather than the home schoolers', by arguing that the state's public schools perform well on comparative test measures; ergo, accommodations to home schoolers would harm the state's public school system. Generally, the argument has run the opposite way: that performance problems in the public schools legitimate the rights of home schoolers. As stated earlier, home schoolers repeatedly have been able to produce test results that demonstrate excellent academic performance compared to the average achievement in public schools. Thus, the coincidence of legislative efforts to improve public schools with those designed to regulate home schools has been politically beneficial for home schoolers.

To summarize, then, once home schoolers are politically mobilized, several factors affect the policy settlement in each state, and their consequent political success. These factors are the organizational skills of home schoolers, the organizational skills of their opponents, and the perceived need for public school reform in a particular state (a factor which usually, but not always, favors home schoolers).

CONCLUSION

The politicization of the home-schooling movement is a nearly perfect instance of political pluralism at work. The movement has been transformed from an educational to a political movement by a strongly felt perception that participants must organize effectively in the political arena to protect their interests. Having done so, this new interest group garnered diverse allies, depending on the state and local circumstances in which it found itself and depending also on the organizational skills that it developed. While home schooling has been opposed by some producer interests such as teachers unions, this has not been consistently the case. Events have unfolded differently across states and taken on different configurations over time within particular states as issues and alliances evolved in different directions. State regulators and their allies have enjoyed political victories in some states, while home schoolers have triumphed almost totally in other states. Rarely have producers triumphed totally or for very long. Indeed, the balance of power favors home schoolers in most states.

In this analysis I have sought to explain these findings—both the overall pattern and the variations within it—in terms of the goals of home schooling, the character of the specific state's legal and regulatory environment, the small size of the home school movement, its tactics and mobilization skills, as well as those of opponents, and the reputation of the public schools.

At least two of these explanatory factors would make one cautious about interpreting home school developments as an indication of the erosion of public support for public school education generally: The small size of the home-school movement and its libertarian claims probably are atypical of other consumer interest groups in education.

Yet in some respects these findings signal how different the politics of American education had become in the 1980s. If during the heyday of progressive reforms, local school boards and superintendents were able to dominate school policy making,[6] clearly they have been much less able to do so in the 1980s. School professionals lost a great deal of autonomy in the 1960s due to the civil rights and students' rights movements. In the 1970s, criticism of their financial management of enrollment decline, both by citizen groups and by business reformers, contributed to further erosions of public confidence. While the reforms of the 1980s have not been led by grass-roots, populist reformers, but instead by elected officials (particularly governors), foundations, and corporate heads, the reforms still have been imposed on the public school establishment from outside. The home school movement is a specific example of this general development, except that it illustrates an additional point: In the present climate of public concern, citizen activism also can be the source of outside reform pressure on the public schools.

It would appear, therefore, that the success of the home schooling movement is but another instance of a wider trend toward more public influence over educational policies, in contrast to the wide autonomy professionals once enjoyed. While these findings hardly resolve the disputes in the politics of education literature over lay vs. professional dominance, or over class biases in policy outcomes, the case of home school consumer mobilization certainly suggests that pluralist bargaining is, at the very least, useful in explaining *some* policies affecting *some* groups.

Further, there is another theme which emerges from these findings. While home schoolers might be dismissed as unrepresentative of the public at large, their success could well symbolize the depth of public concern over our public schools, such that new schooling arrangements, including alternatives outside the public schools, are no longer viewed as unwarranted or dangerous to the public interest. This level of public concern about public school quality has not led yet to widespread support for the further privatization of schooling in the United States. Yet public opinion polls supporting parental choice, even if confined at the present to market arrangements within the public sector,

---

[6] See Chapter 7 for further evidence on this point.

could be read to indicate that the broad public now accepts the need for more dramatic restructuring policies. Further privatization may be entertained seriously in the future should the public school reform movement continue to demonstrate little success.

Ironically, the possible growth of school choice arrangements which include private schools could cut either way for home schoolers. It could reduce their size and political strength in the face of new competition. Conversely, it could legitimate still greater privatization of education, thereby favoring home school growth and triggering new political coalitions set upon challenging the public schools.

From another angle, it is quite possible to read the home school movement as one which is likely to be short-lived, like so many voluntary movements of reformers whose enthusiasm and support wanes because of the extraordinary commitment and skill such efforts require and because professionals have the organizational capacity to reassert their influence readily through new laws and regulations. With the aid of professional producer groups, state officials may find new ways to legitimate their argument for further regulation. The process of pluralist bargaining, in other words, could retip the scales toward professionals.

Yet even if only the first chapter of this story has been written and told, it seems unlikely that the plot will take any dramatic twists. An incremental model is likely to explain events in most states. The number of home schooling families may be expected to grow, but this growth may be limited by the demands it makes on parents. Some states can be counted upon to seek greater control of home schooling, but most probably will not, since they will find accommodation preferable to confrontation (as bureaucracies almost always do), and since the governmental appetite for regulation may be pursued more productively through public schools.

Since on these matters the prognostications of social scientists are no better than those of fortune tellers (and a good deal less interesting), we shall have to watch patiently for future events to unfold.

REFERENCES

Alford, R. E. (1975). *Health care politics: Ideological and interest group barriers to reform.* Chicago: University of Chicago Press.

Boyd, W. L. (1976). The public, the professionals, and education policy making: Who governs? *Teachers College Record, 77,* 539–77.

Haertel, E. H., James, H. T., Jr., & Levin, H. (Eds.). (1988). *Comparing public and private schools, Volume 2: School achievement.* New York: Falmer.

Klicka, C. J. (1988). *Home schooling in the United States: A statutory analysis.* Great Falls, VA: Home School Legal Defense Association.

Lowi, T. (1969). *The end of liberalism.* New York: Norton.

Marmor, T. R., & Morone, J. A. (1980). Representing consumer interests: Imbalanced markets, health planning, and the HSAs. *Milbank Memorial Fund Quarterly/Health and Society, 58* (1), 125–165.

Peterson, P. E. (1974). The politics of American education. In F. N. Kerlinger & J. B. Carroll (Eds.), *Review of research in education: 2* pp. 348–389. Itasca, IL: F. E. Peacock.

Peterson, P. E. (1976). *School politics, Chicago-style.* Chicago: University of Chicago Press.

Wirt, F. M, & Kirst, M. W. (1989). *Schools in conflict.* Berkeley, CA: McCutchan.

Zeigler, L. H., Kehoe, E, & Reisman, J. (1985). *City managers and school superintendents.* New York: Praeger.

Zeigler, L. H., Jennings, M. K., & Peak, G. W. (1974). *Governing American schools: Political interaction in local school districts.* North Scituate, MA: Duxbury.

Chapter 6

The Best and Wisest Parent: A Critique of John Holt's Philosophy of Education*

Susan Douglas Franzosa
University of New Hampshire

In *The School and Society,* John Dewey (1956, p. 7) attempted to establish the premises for an advocacy of school reform by asserting the following:

> What the best and wisest parent wants for his own child, that must the community want for all its children. Any other ideal for our schools is narrow and unlovely; acted upon it destroys our democracy.

Dewey was addressing an audience of parents involved in the newly founded Elementary School at the University of Chicago at the turn of the century. His remarks were intended to enlist their support not only for their own school but for general public school reform. Their school, he maintained, was to serve as a model for American education. Their responsibility as members of a community, he implied, was to work toward extending the educational advantages enjoyed by their children to all children. What Dewey was proposing was a social ethic for educational reform that demanded that the individual act to assure the educational good of all. "Only by being true to the full growth of

* The author wishes to acknowledge the helpful comments of Ann Diller, Jane R. Martin, Barbara Houston, and Jennifer Radden on earlier drafts of this article.

all the individuals who make it up," he asserted, "can a society by any chance be true to itself" (1956, p. 7).

Dewey's social ethic has characterized much of what has been understood as liberal educational reform in the United States. His proposals derived from what he saw as the interdependence of social and individual welfare and the potentially reconstructive role of the public institution. His work helped to provide an emerging compulsory school system with a rationale for an institutionalized form of social control deemed appropriate for a democratic social order. By universalizing the intentions of an ideal parent and making the school a generalized version of the ideal home, he maintained that public education in the United States could equalize educational opportunity, minimize social conflict, and transmit the knowledge and skill necessary to social continuity and individual growth. That is, Dewey's reform strategy suggested that the school itself could become society's best and wisest parent, and his social ethic suggested that exemplary individuals should act to realize that ideal.

During the last decade Dewey's assumptions about the nature of democratic institutions, social participation, and the promise of public schooling have come under critical scrutiny (Feinberg, 1975). As educational critics began to find in the 1960s and 1970s, the public school has not proven to be the best and wisest parent for all children in our society nor has it always fostered individual growth and development, mediated social conflicts, or provided equality of educational opportunity. Until quite recently, most Americans seemed willing to retain a belief in the potential, if not actual, efficacy of public schooling, but an increasing number of parents are now choosing not to participate in any public arrangements for education and are attempting to educate their children at home (Lines, 1982).

The popular educational commentator John Holt (1982), once an ardent proponent of school reform, now urges such non-participation and advocates home schooling for all parents who love and trust their children. In his recent book, *Teach Your Own: A Hopeful Path for Education,* he chronicles a familiar disillusionment with the educational reform movement of the 1960s and 1970s, offers a critique of compulsory education, and attempts to argue that the parent and home, rather than the teacher and school, are the child's best and wisest educators.

Teach Your Own is a direct assault on the Deweyian tradition. Its very title constitutes a denial of the cogency of Dewey's social ethic and a rejection of democratic reform strategies in education. The "hopeful" path Holt anticipates and intends to foster in education is the withering away of the public school and the reemergence of what he understands as a lost American ideal: self-sufficiency.

Holt, unlike Dewey and his intellectual descendents, does not believe it makes sense to speak of a community's children, or to seek to foster social goals through what he sees as inevitably corrupt educational institutions. In fact, Holt's (1982) contention is that the full growth of the individual is incompatible with any form of institutional control built on community consensus. Unlike the democratic social thesis in Dewey's prescriptions for educational reform, Holt's conservative libertarianism defines a society in which the individual's welfare is not the legitimate concern of the state, one's children can be thought of strictly as one's own, and the individual need feel no responsibility for the good of all. The best and wisest parent within this ideological context chooses to reject social participation in favor of personal independence and autonomy.

This chapter will examine the origins and evaluate the soundness of the arguments Holt offers for home schooling. I believe Holt's philosophy as presented in these arguments demands critical attention, not because it is likely to inaugurate a major home schooling movement, but because it represents and serves to popularize an emerging conservatism that, I will argue, has grave educational implications. I have no doubt that our current ways of educating children need serious re-evaluation and that education at home may prove to be one of a number of appropriate responses to school incompetence and injustice. However, Holt's advocacy of a single solution to the multiplicity of problems we now face in education is naive and misleading. Further, the social thesis he uses to support that solution signifies a retreat from any collective consideration of educational ideals and a dismissal of the idea that communities have any educational responsibilities to their members. Thus, I believe Holt's conservatism ultimately sanctions the educational neglect of the vast majority of children and leads to a tacit acceptance of their plight.

Holt's stance in *Teach Your Own* is a radical departure from his earlier support of school reform, but it is also an extension of the social and philosophical assumptions that have informed his writing from the beginning of his career. That is, Holt has consistently, if not always explicitly, portrayed the child as a kind of noble savage representing authentic human nature, associated social life as unnatural and corrupting, and laissez faire individualism as the terrible but true state of nature. Holt's analyses of education have thus tended to be meditations on what he understands as an irreconcilable conflict between the natural individual and the oppressive and corrupting effects of organized social life.

Holt's first proposals for educational reform are important indications of the concept of human nature and theory of society he has continued to develop and defend. In his early writing he located what he understood as a natural conflict between the individual and society in the pedagogical relationship that he found in schools. "Nobody starts off stupid," wrote Holt in *How Children Fail* (1964, p. 207). Yet it seemed to him that the teacher's unquestioned authority to direct and coerce students according to conventionally understood social goals actually made schools into places "where children learn to be stupid" (1964, p. 196). "Children," Holt has consistently maintained, (1982, p. 1) "are by nature and from birth very curious about the world around them, and very energetic, resourceful, and competent in exploring it." He further contends (1982, p. 196) that "children are by nature not only loving and kind but serious and purposeful." From the beginning of his career as an educational commentator, this romantic view of the child has committed Holt to what Kathryn Morgan (1976, p. 26) has called a "horticultural model" of education in which

> the child is viewed as a subject whose development unfolds from within and who is intrapersonally self-sufficient [and] the child is viewed from within the liberal tradition as highly individualistic and directed toward complete autonomy as the highest form of social and moral development.

Hoping that the schools could provide a context in which children could freely develop their "natural" qualities, Holt (1964, p. 216) first proposed a nondirective pedagogy that he believed could transform the schools into "places where children learn what they most want to know, instead of what we think they ought to know." This strategy, he maintained (1964, p. 206, 220), would result in the production of "the intelligent person" or the "kind of person we need in our society." Holt's major prescription was that the individual child be allowed to proceed individually. By simply "letting him know roughly what is available and where he can look for it" (1964, p. 221) the teacher could provide a natural educative context in the classroom.

For many of Holt's readers this strategy offered an appealing corrective to the authoritarian methods of the past and the beginnings of a critique of existing arrangements for social control. Yet Holt's early work also suggested certain assumptions about the nature of social association that were less obvious. Foundational to his description of the ideal classroom was the implication that social association was not necessary and may even be harmful to human development and learning. Collective activity, group interaction, and a sense of community were not featured in his early models for the classroom.[1] Learning was

---

[1] *How Children Fail* (Holt, 1964), *How Children Learn* (Holt, 1969), and *What Do I Do Monday* (Holt, 1970) illustrate Holt's early nondirective approach to pedagogy.

seen as an autonomous activity, and the goal of education, self-actualization, was mistakenly understood as a product of personal independence from the influence of others.

This was not a critique that looked forward to the possibility of a just and nurturant social organization within the classroom. Rather it was a rejection of that possibility. For, children, as much as possible, were to be protected from social initiation within a community of others. Holt's stress on the need to provide a context for personal autonomy prevented him from recognizing the value of social interaction or that the development of autonomy derives from the mediations a child experiences in group association and requires sociability. Thus, although Holt's early work was compellingly sensitive to the child as an individual, one was left to wonder, as one now wonders about his proposals for home schooling, how emphasis on personal autonomy and independence could allow children to eventually come to value social participation and function responsibly in associated social life; or why they would even want to be defined in Holt's terms as "the kind of person we need in our society."

Holt's early model for the classroom revealed a preference for a social system in which the individual was not subject to general law or social constraint but could freely act without taking account of anyone or anything except his or her own self-interest. This model is compatible with the classical political theory of laissez-faire individualism in which group association is necessarily based on competition and the state's responsibility is simply to maintain a context in which the individual's freedom to compete is assured.

Holt, of course, had no wish to foster competition among children. In fact, it clearly repulsed him. Yet, as he began to extend his critique and look more closely at the societal relations that surround and influence the classroom, it became clear that he was finding it difficult to imagine any public social context in which competition would not be a primary mode of behavior. As his later work illustrates, a competitive and corrupting social organization increasingly assumes the status of a state of nature that cannot be avoided in public life. Thus, the ideal political order that Holt increasingly articulated was based on non-interference and the protection of personal liberty rather than collectivism and strategies designed to foster group solidarity.

In *Teach Your Own* Holt (1982) recalls his optimism in the late 1960s about the possibility of school reform. He writes that he then believed that once individual parents and teachers understood how schooling denied children their personal freedom they would act to change it. However, he became increasingly discouraged by his encounters with what he called "the silent majority" or "the general public" (1982, p. 3). After a decade of arguing unsuccessfully for changes in education, his optimism about the possibility of school reform that would provide a libertarian context for individual learning gave way to disillusionment with public institutions, skepticism about the effects of collective social advocacy, and outright cynicism about the ordinary individual's power, or even desire, to influence the course of public school policy. "I was seeing more and more evidence," he writes (1982, p. 4), "that most adults actively distrust and dislike most children, even their own, and quite often especially their own." Holt soon came to the conclusion that the schools could not be reformed because "they are doing what most people want them to do, and doing it very well" (1976, p. 157). The coercion that he had originally seen in the classroom was now understood as an incidental feature of a thoroughly oppressive educational system sanctioned and maintained by the members of the "general public."

By 1971, a year after the publication of Ivan Illich's *Deschooling Society* (1970), Holt began to shift his attention from pedagogical reform to a more general critique of social institutions and an advocacy of children's rights.[2] In his writing he began to seriously question whether schools or any formalized pedagogy was necessary or desirable. At first Holt's change in strategy was very similar to Illich's. What he now calls "unschooling," as presented in *Instead of Education* (1976), included establishing community resource centers as educational alternatives as well as proposals designed to change the traditionally conceived compulsory "S-chools" into "s-chools"—noncompulsory "doing places for children" (1976, pp. 27–57, 190–199). Yet even as he made these proposals it was clear that he saw little hope for their success. "Those who want humane schools for their children," he wrote, "can hardly add up to 5 percent of the population" (1976, p. 207). And he added, "Even if S-chools become s-chools, it will take many years to rid them of the many teachers who don't like or trust children" (1976, p. 157).

Holt (1976, p. 157) now suggested that the school's "true social tasks" were to shut the young out of society while ranking and sorting them according to discriminatory standards and socializing them into docile future citizens and employees. Because he assumed that this was what most people wanted them to do, he also believed that these purposes, however tacitly, would necessarily govern alternative schools as well (1976). Thus, he suggested that good and loving parents should find ways of helping their children escape from schooling alto-

---

[2] Holt's *Freedom and Beyond* (1972) and *Escape from Childhood* (1974) reflect his concerns during this period.

gether. "Education—compulsory schooling, compulsory learning," he wrote, "is a tyranny and a crime against the human mind and spirit. Let all those escape it who can, any way they can" (1976, p. 222).

At this point, Holt was ready to reject collectively organized efforts to reform the nature of schooling because he had begun to formalize a social thesis. Public life and group association, as Holt saw it, inevitably led either to a totalitarian consensus or social conflict and disintegration. This principle of group behavior appears to be drawn from his analysis of the historical ascendency of the evil nation state. In a variation of laissez faire economics, he argued (1976, pp. 115–116):

> As among people in any given society, so among human societies, the bad is most likely to rise to the top. If two societies live side by side, one modest, peaceful, kindly and happy, the other a greedy and violent tyranny, the bad society must always swallow up the good. . . . Thinking of ourselves as history's glorious final product, we like to say that it illustrates what we call the law of the survival of the fittest. It would be truer to speak instead of the survival of the morally least fit.

In *Teach Your Own* the ascendency of the "morally least fit" appears to infect all human social association except that of the family. Perhaps the clearest indication of this is that Holt now explicitly argues that an escape to a parallel structure of free or independent schools is untenable. According to Holt (1982, p. 168), "such schools have little power to multiply, while home schooling does." Further, he contends (1982, p. 168) that "even in supposedly 'free' or 'alternative' schools, too many people still do what conventional schools have always done." That is, if some parents have ideas about what must be learned, they will try to enforce an arbitrary curriculum that denies the individual child's right to self-direction (1982, pp. 187–188).

However, it is not simply adult association in which the morally unfit hold sway. In *Teach Your Own* Holt also argues against collective educational arrangements because he sees the society of children as potentially corrupt as well. He quotes with agreement the report of a parent who has written to him contending that sadistic behavior among children only occurs "when there is a group" (1982, p. 47–48). He points out that peer groups have "powerful and harmful effects" (1982, p. 49) and maintains that it is common to find that even among first graders "the social life of the children is mean-spirited, exclusive, status seeking, snobbish" (1982, p. 45).

At the time he wrote *Teach Your Own,* then, Holt was thoroughly committed to the assumption that the full spectrum of group association outside the family, from the relations between "mean-spirited" first graders to the relations between nation states, was inevitably characterized by a collective will to oppress the individual and deny his or her freedom. That is, for Holt, there was no longer the possibility of a good society capable of nurturing its members. Given the inevitability of the corruption of individual human nature in group association, the only plausible educational course for Holt was the private alternative of home schooling.

In Holt's view (1982, pp. 346–347) the home is the only social arrangement that can escape totalitarian tendencies because

> it is a natural, organic, central, fundamental human institution, one might easily and rightly say the foundation of all other institutions. . . . [W]e cannot even imagine a society without homes, even if these should be no more than tents, or mud huts, or holes in the ground.

The home, according to Holt, is the only human institution that can be genuinely concerned with the individual's welfare. And although he doesn't state it, it seems clear that the home he wants to defend as a natural center for individual growth is not a dwelling, but the private family that has somehow remained insulated from the corrupting effect of any larger social or political context. He fails to adequately explain, however, how the home can maintain this independence or why the family within it can resist the influence of the morally least fit.

He offers no refutation to the charge, for example, that in some cases the family can serve as a context in which the individual may be subject to the oppressive will of others. Although Holt himself has recognized this possibility in *Escape from Childhood* (1974, pp. 24–31), here he simply observes that parents who dislike their own children will rarely try to educate them at home. If they do, he maintains (1982, p. 57), "such families are likely to find home schooling so unpleasant that they will be glad to give it up." These families, he implies, simply do not love and trust their children enough to sustain the effort to educate them at home. Like the rest of the general public, they will ultimately prefer to sanction the morally least fit's governance of their children's education. The ideal home schooling family, however, will contain parents who have willingly undertaken "the heavy responsibility of having and bringing up children because they deeply want to spend a part of their life living with them" (1982, p. 22).

Holt's descriptions of the home schooling parent and, even more importantly, his critique of the parent who chooses to keep his or her child in school, reveals the nature of his social thesis and the weaknesses in his analysis of the process of social change. His directive to "teach your own" operates as a moral imperative to parents who claim to love their children. Those who choose home schooling exemplify the highest ideals of parenthood. Members of this elite and their children, Holt believes, will become models of natural authority. Through example they will eventually convince others that self-sufficiency and personal autonomy should be one's highest educational goals. At first, however, not many parents will choose this course.

> The number of people who, even if it were easy to do so, would want to take their children out of school and teach them at home, is small. Not many people enjoy the company of their children that much, or would want to give that much attention to their interests and concerns, or take that much of the responsibility for their growth. (1982, pp. 316–317)

Membership in the moral elite is thus understood by Holt as a matter of individual choice. The only relevant criteria to a decision to school at home appear to be the strength of parental affection and a willingness to take responsibility. This is illustrated by his refusal to acknowledge the legitimacy of any condition that might affect a loving parent's determination to educate his or her own child. For example, in response to letters he has received from parents considering home schooling, he makes the following assertions:

> Working-class parents as well as middle-class parents can find the appropriate resources for their child's education. Single parents concerned with having to work, provide day care, and find time to teach their children can leave their children alone during the day and teach them in the evening. Parents of exceptional children can adequately meet their children's therapeutic and educational needs by themselves. (1982, pp. 74–76, 81–82, 144–146)

Holt even maintains that illiterate parents have the appropriate competencies to educate their own children if they *want* to (1982, p. 58). He thus dismisses class, lifestyle, the child's special needs, and the parent's competencies as irrelevant considerations in a decision to home-school one's children.

Although the strength of affection appears to be primary, there are nevertheless other characteristic beliefs that describe Holt's best and wisest parents. Home-schooling parents are likely to be independent thinkers. According to Holt (1982, p. 68) they will "go their own way without caring, or even looking to see whether anyone is following them." The home schooler then, like the child in Holt's early model classroom, will not be dependent on, or responsible to, a community of others. He or she can willingly reject the conventions of social association and remain self-sufficient.

Home-schooling parents may thus appear to have no uniform political or social beliefs. Holt notes, for example, that people of all religious and political affiliations can and should educate their own children. At first this appears to be no more than an acknowledgement of the intergenerational process implied in his assertion (1982, p. 41) that "people have the right not only to believe what they want but to try to pass their beliefs along to their children." But Holt goes further. He records what he takes to be a particularly definitive and "eloquent" statement from one of his correspondents. The letter he chooses to quote (1982, p. 23) stresses what he understands as "the central convictions" of the home-schooling parent.

> The fact that my children exist and that I am their father confers upon me, (and likewise upon every man so situated,) by natural law, an eminent domain, and with that the inescapable original obligation, and, with that, the sole natural right (and authority) to rear and to train them accordingly to the dictates of my own conscience before God; therefore, by what law of justice (if any) can I be required or compelled to allow that obligation to be fulfilled by (or that right to be exercised by) another?

Thus, home-schooling parents assert ownership and eminent domain over their children and claim sole responsibility for their education. This represents a political stance in regard to the rights of children that Holt has failed to examine. For the freedom to educate one's children as one sees fit clearly might include restricting the child's liberty to choose what and how he or she will learn. By assigning exclusive rights to the parent and denying that the community has any right to approve or disapprove educational practices in the home, the child is left unprotected.

At this point in his argument, Holt's theory of society and his belief in the evil nature of social association have become more powerful than his wish to preserve the natural instincts and personal autonomy of the child. If this were not the case, Holt would continue to assert, as he did in *Escape From Childhood* (1974, pp. 156–157, 186–198), that children should be allowed to pursue their education in any manner they please even when this means rejecting their parent's expectations and leaving home. In *Teach Your Own*, however, the parent's claim to his or her child's education is prior to the child's freedom of self-direction and, indeed, to the child's right to his or her own education.

Holt's mistake is to assume that within the romantically conceived private family the belief that one has a right to educate his or her children will necessarily be accompanied by a love and trust that can be easily translated into an open and nondirective pedagogical relationship (1982, p. 57). This faith is unfounded, and Holt offers no real explanation of how parental love and trust are necessarily compatible with a belief in ownership. He (1982, p. 22) merely observes:

> Having chosen to have children, [home schoolers] feel very strongly that it is their responsibility to help these children grow into good, smart, capable, loving, trustworthy, and responsible human beings. They do not think it right to turn that responsibility over to institutions, state or private, schools or otherwise.

One must ask Holt to explain why a majority of parents do continue to think it right to send their children to "institutions, state or private, schools or otherwise," or why he regards this choice as a surrender of all parental responsibility for the child's education. Presumably for Holt, those parents who "turn over" their responsibilities are willing to conform to the collective will of the morally least fit and, like "most people" within the general public, "distrust and dislike" children. But how does this disaffection develop and why do parents make this choice?

Holt's explanation is drawn from an analysis of his encounters with individual members of the general public. In *Teach Your Own* (1982, p. 4) a representative working-class adult, Holt's cab driver, serves as his chief informant. Holt introduces their discussion by asserting:

> People whose lives are hard, boring, painful, meaningless—people who suffer—tend to resent those who seem to suffer less than they do, and will make them suffer if they can. People who feel themselves in chains, with no hope of ever getting them off, want to put chains on everyone else.

What Holt is arguing is that disadvantaged adults are more likely to sanction the perpetuation of even the most intolerable social order and grant public institutions the authority to control the socialization of their own as well as others' children. Thus sufferers are more likely to collaborate in their own and their children's oppression. Although at first this may seem to indicate a critique of the social conditions that give rise to what some writers have addressed as the problem of false consciousness, Holt, in his contention that the sufferers "want to put chains on everyone else," persists in seeing it as a matter of personal moral choice.

In the case cited, Holt's driver, not unlike Holt himself, sees no hope of successful collective action and is convinced that as an individual he is powerless to change the way schooling or society operate. Because he believes that his own children have succeeded as adults because they have done well in an authoritarian school, he can only propose that the schools become even more authoritarian in order to achieve success with other children. Thus, although it may be argued that the driver's defense of the "way it is" does ultimately serve to perpetuate an oppressive educational system, it does not testify to a lack of affection for children or a willingness to see them in chains. Rather, it appears that the driver's desire is to make children accede to school authority so they can achieve whatever later success is possible for them.

Holt's analysis does nothing to counteract the convictions that render powerless this working-class representative of the general public. Rather, his arguments only serve to reinforce the belief that one cannot succeed in changing public arrangements for education either as an individual or through collective action. The only practical choice Holt poses is between supporting the schools or rejecting them. The moral course for Holt is an individual rejection of all educational institutions. Because sufferers are less likely to follow this course, socioeconomic status certainly does seem to be a relevant characteristic of Holt's best and wisest parent, despite his (1982, p. 7, p. 76) protests to the contrary. This, however, remains hidden by Holt's insistence that all parents can find ways of educating their own children if they want to. Thus, the general public—which is primarily composed of sufferers—is dismissed by Holt as morally imperfect. Further, and perhaps more damning to his argument as a whole, his celebration of personal autonomy and laissez-faire principles and his rejection of collective social responsibility commit him to an acceptance of the "choices" of those parents he disparages regardless of the educational consequences for their children.

The argument Holt advances in *Teach Your Own* has grave educational implications. It offers no protection to children from parents who may see themselves among the elite and choose to exercise their "right" of educational "eminent domain" unjustly. It also legitimates the educational neglect of those children who must remain in school. For Holt believes that as more people defect from the public schools, it will become increasingly difficult to find compelling reasons to support education with public funds.[3] But somehow, perhaps because these are the children of the morally imperfect, this doesn't seem to bother Holt very much. To the charge that an acceptance of home schooling will mean that middle-class parents will increasingly flee from the public schools leaving only the children of the poor and powerless, he (1982,

---

[3] Holt points out that the decline of the birth rate, the voucher system, and "today's antischool climate" will also be contributing factors (1982, p. 227, 229, 237).

p. 326) contemptuously responds, "well what's so bad about that? You [public school proponents] will then at last be able to give these poor children your undivided attention." Clearly this is an inadequate response to the very real threat of the institutionally defined underclass of children Holt's proposals imply. It is perfectly consistent, however, with Holt's social thesis and strategy for social change.

Holt (1982, pp. 66–67) mistakenly believes that home schooling will accomplish a gradual change in which the morally imperfect (that is, the schools) will either wither away or be transformed. What he foresees is that children educated at home will begin to serve as models of goodness, intelligence, and authority. They will be happy, self-reliant, and personally successful. Their success will operate as a powerful incentive to other parents who will then begin to choose home schooling. Schools will be forced to radically alter their goals and practices in order to compete for clients or they will disappear. Eventually, as the increased number of individuals who have been educated at home become adults, society itself will become more humane, intelligent, and open. Holt believes this process is likely to take a long time, however. He (1982, p. 67) estimates the number of people who will choose home schooling as currently "no more than one percent of the population, if that."[4] And he notes (1982, p. 66), "important and lasting social changes always come slowly, and only when people change their lives, not just their political beliefs or parties or forms of government."

Holt's "hopeful path" for education and society is untenable. To assume that the family can or should isolate itself from the political and social relations in which it is situated is naive and misleading. People cannot "change their lives" without changing the context within which they live—a context that extends beyond the home. Further, an increase in the number of those who are home schooled in what he explicitly sees as a multiplicity of conflicting family traditions is much more likely to lead to intensified social conflict than social harmony. Holt, however, has given up on any hope for a positive utilization of the community and, as a result, can only present us with a series of false alternatives derived from what he sees as the necessary opposition of self and society.

In Holt's system, the individual self, not social relationships, has become the object of reform. The choice Holt mistakenly presents is between personal autonomy, self actualization . . . . and private

---

[4] The reader should note that Holt's estimate of the number of parents wanting a humane alternative for their children has decreased since he wrote *Instead of Education* from "5 percent of the population" to "no more than one percent."

responsibility for one's own, as opposed to a slavish conformity to the collective will of others. This positioning of alternatives rests firmly on the philosophic tradition of romantic individualism with which Holt's work began. It is not unprecedented nor is it eccentric. Today disillusionment with public institutions is widespread. The refusal to participate in society's arrangements for social welfare is increasingly seen as a healthy exercise of personal power and self sufficiency within an inflexible and corrupt social order. Holt's ideal for the best and wisest parent speaks to that disillusionment, in the same way his call for a nondirective pedagogy spoke to the classroom concerns of the 1960s and early 1970s.

Christopher Lasch (1981, p. 23) has recently observed of popular social scientists:

> by redirecting their attention from public policy to consumer tastes . . . they unavoidably help to sustain the illusion that people can initiate sweeping changes without resort to politics, merely by exercising their right to make individual decisions as consumers of goods, services, and ideologies.

Holt's cottage industry approach to education fosters this illusion. Further, his romantic descriptions of the home-schooling parent serve to conceal the political implications of his proposals for educational change. In *Teach Your Own* he quotes extensively from the letters of enthusiastic home schoolers to establish that educating one's own children is a workable, personally satisfying, and even courageous alternative to the dehumanizing experience of schooling. The letters he chooses to quote are often compelling, and his proposals appear to derive, not from any special interest or rigid political position, but, from the unimpeachable integrity of personal experience. The decision to educate one's child is presented as an individual's reasonable exercise of personal choice and not a proposed social program.

Yet Holt is proposing home schooling as a general social program. His imperative to "teach your own" must be understood as the endorsement of a social thesis that can only lead to what Dewey called the "narrow and unlovely." The best and wisest parents in our society may share Holt's critique of the schools and his diappointment with school reform but they need not agree that his latest educational strategy is a "hopeful path for education." Rather, good parents, if they are also wise, will recognize that their own child's good is dependent on the good of others and that taking adequate responsibility for one's own requires continued participation in the crucial debate about what constitutes the best education for all our children.

REFERENCES

Dewey, J. (1956). *The school and society.* Chicago: University of Chicago Press.

Feinberg, W. (1975). *Reason and rhetoric: The intellectual foundations of 20th century liberal education.* New York: John Wiley.

Holt, J. (1982). *Teach your own: A hopeful path for education.* New York: Delacorte Press.

Holt, J. (1976). *Instead of education.* New York: Dell.

Holt, J. (1974). *Escape from childhood.* New York: Elsevier North-Holland.

Holt, J. (1972). *Freedom and beyond.* New York: Elsevier North-Holland.

Holt, J. (1970). *What do I do Monday.* New York: Elsevier North-Holland.

Holt, J. (1969). *How children learn.* New York: Pitman.

Holt, J. (1964). *How children fail.* New York: Pitman.

Illich, I. (1970). *Deschooling society.* New York: Harper & Row.

Lasch, C. (1981, December 3). Happy endings: A review of Daniel Yankelvocich's new rules: Searching for self-fulfillment in a world turned upside down. *New York Review of Books, 28*(19), 23–26.

Lines, P. M. (1982). *Private educational alternatives and state regulations.* Denver, CO: Education Commission of the States.

Morgan, K. (1976, April). Children, bonsai trees and open education. *Journal of Educational Thought, 10,* 22–23.

Chapter 7

The Shifting Roles of Family and School as Educator: A Historical Perspective*

Joseph Kirschner
Youngstown State University

Public schools! No one loves them. Few defend them. People of whatever political persuasion—right, left, or center—complain about the schools, and a growing number outright reject them by turning to private or to home schooling. The purpose of this chapter is to suggest a historical explanation of this phenomenon. This is done by exploring the shifting roles of family and school as educator. The explanation of these social changes, as framed by modernization theory, (Berger, Berger, & Kellner, 1973) suggests that they have been driven by the evolution of the idea of a quasireligious national mission for public schools.

One conclusion that emerges is that the American love affair with public schools and their civic mission has ended. A civic faith flowered in a 19th-century America that was both optimistic and chronically uneasy about the stability of the social order. What emerged in the 1830s was an ideology for common schools that would serve almost as an established church. Schooling came to be regarded by increasing numbers of people as the messianic hope of an American millenialist

* My thanks to Youngstown State University for its support, both temporal and material. I am especially grateful for a Faculty Improvement Leave for 1988–89 which provided me with the time to pursue this study. I also appreciate the financial support of the University Research Council to purchase needed software.

mission (Tuveson, 1968, pp. ix-x). But over the past century-and-a-half a widely shared religious faith in the mission of public schools to assure civic virtue has vanished (Church & Sedlak, 1976, p. 471).

Signs of this loss of a widely shared faith in a messianic civic mission for public schooling is quite evident in recent reports (see, for example, National Commission on Excellence in Education, 1983; Task Force on Teaching as a Profession, 1986; and Bennett, 1988). They offer no vision, no mission; rather, they focus on what's wrong, why schools aren't working. One reads about declining SAT scores and teacher accountability. Urban schools are criticized for being little more than custodial institutions plagued with discipline problems and inadequate security. One is offered statistics on the number and kinds of high school graduates who can neither read nor write, much less demonstrate literacy in mathematics, science, geography, or history. A recent "best seller" suggests a lost legacy with its dictionary of cultural literacy, a book of "basic facts" that all Americans should know (Hirsch, 1987).

Besides this formal public criticism, there are those who "vote with their feet." Since the 1960s, a growing number of parents have taken their children out of public schools and sent them to various private schools. For a period, some turned to those alternative schools known as "free schools." Others sought out fundamentalist Christian schools and academies. And now one sees the "pedagogues" and "ideologues," as Van Galen (1988, p. 54) describes them, reject all schools and turn to what is paradoxically labelled "home schooling."

This chapter charts the development and demise of the quasireligious ideology informing a civic mission for American public schools and their interplay with family and community educational needs and desires. The conceptual framework provided by Berger's modernization theory (Berger et al., 1973 p. viii) indicates that the public school story can be seen both as defense of modernization and a protest against modernity, depending on the historical period. This framework reveals not only the genesis of an essentially religious faith in common schools (as public schools were called in the 19th century), but its transformation and ultimate demise.

This history of public schooling, then, traces the source and transformation of beliefs in the mission of public schools. Over the span of a century-and-a-half, we can witness a kind of dialogue betweeen defenders of modernizing tendencies and challengers, or "discontents," as Berger (1973, pp. 181–184) calls them.

This chapter begins with an examination of the uncertain years of the early 19th century when religious and political leaders worried about the excesses of individualism and thus turned to the idea of universal education in state-run school systems. As less and less hope was placed in churches and families to assure the kind of America congenial to economic progress and social order, these political figures and their educational and clerical allies turned to the schools. Education, it was hoped, would offset a trend toward a radical individualism with little regard for the larger welfare. The faith in public schooling as an "engine of democracy" grew so strong that schools became a veritable secular "established church."

The period between the 1840s and 1880s witnessed the successes of reformers with the consolidation of district schools, the rise of state commissioners and superintendents of education, and standardization of text books. The continuing transformation of the public school mission in the new century is examined in the context of the Progressive critics of these now bureaucratic public schools. These critics wanted to turn schools into little "families" and communities.

The period of the 1920s to the 1960s is characterized by an increasingly frantic search for educational panaceas to address particular social ills and national crises. By the end of the 1960s the idea of a national mission for public schooling had disappeared. The 1970s proved to be a time of a crisis of faith, both civic and religious. Distrust of social institutions of all kinds were never deeper. Out of this era of deep disillusionment with government, schools, and even organized religion, many turned inward to self-nurturance, family, and neighborhood. This was the cultural setting for the home-school movement.

A COMMON SCHOOL IDEOLOGY EMERGES

Our story begins with the origins of a reassuring civic/religious faith in a common schooling whereby a common morality would be achieved by all. The eventual loss of this faith along with nostalgic recollections of a sort of moral golden age have recently convinced some to abandon public schools and turn to home schooling. An understanding of where this faith in public schooling came from as well as the strength of its appeal may help to explain the intense disillusionment that fueled the passion and commitment of home schoolers.

Political, economic, social, and religious factors all contributed to the common school movement of the 1830s and 1840s. The faith in public schooling has, among other factors, been closely tied to national identity. This was true not only in the U.S., but elsewhere in the West. With the emergence of the nation-state came the triumph of an ideology of faith in the state as the source of ultimate social value, with national values transcending those of family, community, and even religion.

The American Revolution itself was, in an important sense, both an expression of and a challenge to a nationalism, reinforced by an established church, that had been evolving in the West since the 16th century. The growing diversity of sects, even in New England, precluded any viable role for established churches in the new states. With the Revolution came an optimistic new democratic religious and social vision growing out of a fundamental challenge to dogmatic authority, whether religious or secular.

But there is a gloomier side to the early American story. Along with the optimism there was a chronic uneasiness over the cohesiveness of the nation.[1] In 1796 Benjamin Rush, a physician and signer of the Declaration of Independence, worried about excessive individualism. He believed that "we had yet to effect a revolution in our principles, opinions, and manners" (cited in Knight & Hall, 1951, p. 306). Like many others he turned to education. To support the Republic he argued that "each youth must be taught that he does not belong to himself but that he is public property and a warrior in the cause of liberty" (Knight & Hall, 1951, p. 306). The state would take precedence over family or church as educator of the young.

The schooling ideology that emerged in the 1840s offered the prospect of a centripetal force that would offset centrifugal tendencies of modernization in the early Republic, such as the proliferation of religious sects, industrialization, and the spread of social unrest. Ironically, the schooling that originated as a counterpoise to the isolating and fragmenting aspects of modernization developed into an institution that exacerbated the impact. As universal public schooling developed, it contributed to the diminished control parents felt they had over the education of their young.

The birth of the Republic witnessed the beginnings of a factory system that contributed to radical transformations in the economy and social relations. These included the institutionalization of education as well as transforming the family and the roles of women and men within it.

---

[1] Many studies have dealt with the ferment and unrest of the early years, especially during the Jacksonian period. Two will be mentioned here. One monograph that confines its story to Vermont is John J. Duffy's and H. Nicholas Muller, III's *An Anxious Democracy: Aspects of the 1830s* (1982). A considerably older but still valuable study that relates education to this period of ferment, concentrating on New England and New York, is Sidney Louis Jackson's *America's Struggle for Free Schools: Social Tension and Education in New England and New York, 1827–42* (1941).

The idea of publicly supporting schools was not new to this era. What was new were enhanced expectations for them and their growing dominance in the lives of children. One can detect the growing presence of school in a child's life by looking at attendance figures. While they are notoriously sketchy prior to the 1830s, we can get some idea by looking at New York figures. Albert Fishlow estimates that in 1800 there were about 14 school days per year provided for each child with about 60 percent of the 5–19-year-olds enrolled. By 1840 enrollment was about 70 percent, with a 20-day school year. These figures are undoubtedly on the high side, even for New York, and certainly for the United States as a whole. Fishlow estimates that by 1860 the national enrollment was at 60%, up from 40 percent in 1840 (Church & Sedlak, 1976, p. 57).

Even by midcentury, while schools still did not dominate the lives of children as they did later, interest was nevertheless strong. As early as 1787, the Northwest Ordinance reflected an accompanying interest in the necessity of and mission for schools in the new territories. "Religion, morality, and knowledge being necessary to good government and the happiness of mankind, schools and the means of education shall forever be encouraged" (Mattingly & Stevens, 1987, pp. 1, 45). Religion, morality, and knowledge had long been viewed together. The joining of these via schools to national aims was what was unique.

The family itself underwent basic changes between the 17th and 19th centuries (Aries, 1962). Prior to the 19th century, families in rural/agrarian societies were productive as well as procreative units, often closely tied to extensive kinship networks in the community. These ties provided a resource system for economic survival and valuable support for parents in the rearing and socialization of the young. In America, they were strongest in more settled regions and considerably weaker on the frontier.

By the early decades of the 19th century, the family had become more isolated from the larger community. As production tasks shifted more and more to commerce, business, factories, and mines, men increasingly worked away from the home. Childhood emerged as a stage in life needing special protection and nurture (Aries, 1962), and women became the prime source of child nurture. This is evident in childrearing manuals which, between the 17th and 19th centuries, changed from mainly addressing fathers to speaking almost exclusively to mothers (Degler, 1980, p. 73). The resulting stress on the childrearer provided one impetus for turning to public schooling for help.

It is no coincidence that the 19th century, known as the "century of the child," was also the age of the "cult of domesticity" with the woman viewed as the home guardian of social morality. The moral education of the young was now the woman's unique "calling."

In 18th century rural/agrarian society, especially in Protestant New England, literacy education occurred at home and included some rudiments of writing and arithmetic and enough reading so one could read Scripture. This carried over into the early 19th century. What little schooling people had by then was at most a supplement to this diet. The educational expectations of most parents was for little more than their children being able to read the Bible, do some writing, and reckon well enough to get by on the farm.

Before children of both sexes were eight or nine years old, the mother was "the prime inculcator of values, and perhaps their sole formal educator as well. "Keeping school" appeared in letters and diaries of women. This was a common as well as an important responsibility of mothers, and not only for those of the urban middle class who might have had children" (Degler, 1980, p. 74).

The key role of the mother as moral educator is exemplified in the childhood of Harriet Worden, later a central figure in the Oneida Community in upstate New York. Harriet, born in 1840, recalled spending much time with her mother. While her mother sewed, Harriet would leaf through the family Bible and ask her mother to identify the fancy gothic-like letters that began each chapter. Bit by bit, with the help of her mother, she learned her letters, how to sound them out, and recognize words. Harriet remembered standing up on the sofa and reading Bible passages.

As for school, she didn't attend one until she was eight, and then only after her mother had died and she and her father moved to Oneida (Worden, 1869). By way of comparison, it was common for most children in those days to attend school for three months out of the year, for three to four years.

In some households maternal teaching was more directed and intentional than that experienced by Harriet Worden. In the tradition of the dame schools, women sometimes took in neighbor children as well. Thus, any Scriptural literacy was learned from the mother, with father's role, if he had any, being evening Bible readings.

The changes in family and women's role within it did not happen all at once. But with these changes we can chart the move of education from home and community to the school.

By the 1830s political and religious leaders keenly felt the lack of a common civic morality. Society by then had become quite diverse denominationally, ethnically, politically, and even linguistically. The only ultimate and shared faith that seemed possible in a pluralistic society "fraught with crime, disorder, and radicalism" was a civic morality that had to be instilled in everyone. Marty (1987) has referred to this morality as a civic religion that served to hold the American pluralist society together (Marty, 1987, pp. 79–80). During the early and mid-19th century, this "religion" amounted to a generic "non-sectarian" Protestantism informing a Christian America. (Noll, Hatch, & Marsden, 1983, p. 114)

The common faith that began to join republic, religion, and school was well-articulated in 1820 by Lyman Beecher. He invoked the necessity of a common morality in order to get social unity. "The integrity of the Union demands special exertions to produce in the nation a more homogeneous character and bind us together with firmer bonds. . . ." Schools will "produce a sameness of views, and feelings, and interests" and will "lay the foundation of our empire upon a rock. Religion is the central attraction which must supply the deficiency of political affinity and interest" (quoted in Marty, 1987, pp. 231–232)

Hatch's (1988) description of the rapid increase of Methodists and Baptists in the late 18th and early 19th centuries is further evidence of the new social morality. He sees the religious movements growing out of the great revivals as a kind of religious populism that empowered ordinary people to take their deepest impulses at face value, which in turn inspired them to want to spread the word, to prepare the way for God's influence in human affairs (Hatch, 1988, pp. 13–14)

Evangelical Christianity was very much a part of a drive for a state-supported school system grounded in a common Christian morality. In the early 19th-century Evangelicals, along with Unitarians and others, advocated a grounding in morality and piety for the upcoming generation in order to assure a strong, prosperous America. Handy (1967) makes clear the Evangelical role in *The Protestant Quest for a Christian America: 1830–1930*. It "was from among the ardent evangelicals that the liberal pioneers came" (Handy, 1967, p. 13). Findley (1986) identifies the centrality of the evangelical role by noting the awareness of historians "of the intimate linkages between nineteenth-century evangelical Protestantism and education" (Findlay, 1986, p. 125).

Methodism, (more strictly, the Methodist Episcopal Church) and Unitarianism both played key roles in the early years of the school movement.[2] The Methodists provided considerable inspiration and effort in setting up state-supported common schools in the old Northwest, such as in Ohio where they dominated state and school politics. Unitarians, by the 1830s, had come not only to dominate Massachusetts politics, but also common school advocacy and later its control. Moreover, the annual reports of Horace Mann (Unitarian and Massa-

---

[2] For a fuller discussion, see Kirschner, 1988.

chusetts' first commissioner of education) were widely read by common school reformers throughout the country.

Evangelical Methodists as well as mainline Unitarians took for granted that beyond the divisive specifics of particular sects, all Americans shared a common Christianity—a "Publick Religion," as Benjamin Franklin called it. Both were worried about increased diversity in American society. This worry was reinforced by a fierce anti-Catholicism. While such sentiments came with the first Puritan settlers, anti-Catholicism in the 1840s was enflamed by Protestant uneasiness over the large numbers of Irish Catholic immigrants.

This was by no means an insignificant factor in the arguments for social stability and common schools. An annonymous letter in the *Princeton Review* in 1841 makes a case for a general Protestant religion being taught to everyone. "Unless the protestant religion is taught in the public Schools, Protestantism will drift into irreligion, and the Roman Catholics will gain the predominance over our governmental institutions. The spirit of Protestantism is the spirit of liberty, and the Protestant religion must therefore be taught in the schools" (Culver, 1929, p. 154).

The leading educators of the first generation of common school advocates, regardless of denominational affiliation, all agreed that schools were to be the moral educator of the new republic. The Unitarian minister, Henry Ware, JR., was typical in his explicitly joining religious instruction to the mission of common schooling. He spoke of the intimate connection between religion and universal education. Indeed, he suggested in 1838, " universal education is a religious idea." People should not rest until everyone could read for themselves the law by which they are to be judged. "Hence the necessity that every man should be educated—that he might know those Holy Scriptures which make wise unto salvation" (Ware, 1838, p. 506). Without such a faith, Ware wondered if the very idea of universal education would have occurred to anyone.

And another Unitarian minister addressed the intimate relation of religion, government, and schooling. "If the voice of the people is *not* the voice of God, we must endeavour, since we are to be governed by it, to *make* it the voice of God by educating intellectually, morally, and religiously those who utter it. . . . The masses MUST be educated. This is the great business of the patriot and philanthropist. . . . By this transforming process, the child of the rudest emigrant [sic] shall be prepared in a few years, to enjoy and perpetuate our noble institutions. The school-house and the church, these are the hope of the Republic" (Burnap, 1844, pp. 17, 21).

The evangelicals saw a similar connection. Methodist minister

Fitch Reed linked the Methodist evangelic faith to school and nation. When addressing what it is that will give consistency of moral character to the rising generation, he offered the following answer in 1831. "Constant and familiar precepts and examples in the domestic circle; facilities for popular education in all ranks of society; and a frequent interchange of correct feelings and sentiments—these alone will give that consistency of moral character to the rising generation, necessary to the happiness of domestic life and the well being of civil government"[3] (Reed, 1831, pp. 184, 187). School and family are to be partners in the education of the young.

To avoid the divisiveness that resulted from a morality too closely tied to a particular religious sect, school reformers, such as Horace Mann of Massachusetts, Calvin Stowe of Ohio, and Henry Barnard of Connecticut (to name but three) sought to articulate a common nonsectarian morality, or a veritable secular "established church."

At its core, the ideology that came to dominate by the 1850s amounted to "God's providential Protestant express promoting commerce, westward expansion, schools, and churches . . . a native Protestant ideology" (Kaestle, 1983, p. 95). The ideology that emerged stressed self-discipline for insiders and cultural conversion for outsiders which helped explain its varying popularity among different groups in different antebellum Northern states. The need for common schooling was a central tenet of native Protestantism.

For the next period (the 1850s to 1880s), morality and literacy were the twin goals of education. Yet in the process of working for universal, state-supported schools, the moral ideology of schooling came to be less frequently articulated. In its stead school rhetoric increasingly was about means, the organizing and running schools. With this rhetorical shift something basic happened to the mission of the public schools. Instead of schools being viewed as a bulwark against the worst excesses of modernism, they became its very agency. The home/school gap, consequently, widened as more and more education moved from home to bureaucratic school.

FROM HOME EDUCATION TO SCHOOL EDUCATION

Clearly articulated by midcentury was a widely shared but by no means universal public school ideology, one shared mainly by northern white Protestants, though not without support in more urban parts

---

[3] This and other published Methodist sermons I have consulted are located in the Garrett-Evangelical Theological Seminary library. My thanks to Dave Himrod, research librarian, for his valuable help.

of the South. Along with this ideological development came moves to realize it in statewide school systems. It is now possible to chart the move of certain educational practices out of the home. Such movement is the reverse of what took place a century later with home schooling. The dominance of schooling in childhood in the late 19th century is all the more striking when one remembers, as discussed above, that only a half-century earlier most of childhood was spent at home.

Nevertheless, by midcentury, the teaching of basic literacy for many European Americans outside the South was shifting to schools. One factor in this move was that Americans grew less and less interested in religious matters, and thus in maintaining religious practices in the home much less attending church. Yet, despite the sectarian decline, parents maintained a concern for the moral education of their young. The only basis for such morality, people believed, was the Bible. When this education was not provided at home, it was urged on the schools by parents and others. Not only was this wanted for one's own children, but was proclaimed from pulpits to be essential for the development of good morals and law-abiding citizenship.

The burden women felt in their home tasks contributed to pressures for increased schooling. Besides virtually having the entire job of educating the young, women had to take care of the household. This involved all the husband's and other members' personal needs, including food and clothing. It was an exhausting full-time job. As Degler (1980) points out, before the 19th century "the rearing of children and the maintenance of the home had never been a full-time job" (Degler, 1980, p. 81). But it was so now.

One woman, Charlena Anderson, found the daily round of household chores overwhelming and difficult to organize, especially given her desire to spend more time with her children. She writes to her husband in 1887 that her answer to her problems would be living in a boarding house. If the family lived there, she could "get rid of that 'what shall we eat and drink' and have only the 'wherewithall shall we be clothed' to contend with" (Degler, 1980, p. 65).

The burden of rearing a child at home was intensified as young males had to be better prepared so they could succeed in an industrializing America. Many middle-class parents felt a growing anxiousness that they might not be able to assure the success of their sons. So, getting ahead became another motive for schooling.

These middle- and upper-class parents, however, were not without uneasiness in the move of moral education from home to school. As parents moved away from the older network of social controls, they worried about how children would be affected by the resulting compromises with older values. "Choosing schooling for their children as an antidote to their own compromises allowed parents to appear greatly concerned about their own backsliding without having to alter their own behavior in any way" (Church & Sedlak, 1976, p. 80). Mixed motives have often inspired school reform.

While the Whig Party was another source of support for common schools, it exacerbated parent/school conflict. This Party was made up of many old-line Protestants of the commercial classes uneasy over the influx of Catholic immigrants into their communities. They wanted schools to teach their values to their children. Yet, these Whigs "expected the schools to make immigrant children more like native Americans than like their parents, to make the poor economically ambitious and socially virtous, to make Catholic children Protestant" (Church & Sedlak, 1976, p. 84). Schools for these children would modify rather than reinforce habits learned at home.

What the Whigs sought was an institutional form of social control to substitute for the personal network of the small town. This, they believed, would assure that people would perform their responsibilities and work to promote the general welfare. Especially for the urban population, schooling would efficiently internalize a sense of social control and social duty (Church & Sedlak, 1976, p. 73).

There were many tensions between parents and teachers over socializing children. Self-reliance was a decided virtue. Yet, parents also wanted deferent and obedient children. The more they came to worry about their own lack of control over their children, the more they supported the school aim of character formation. It was this anxiety over not feeling able to shape the young at home that contributed to what Tyack (1974) sees as the shift of educational responsibility from home to school (Tyack, 1974, p. 69).

In general parents wanted schools to take custody of their children and train them in basic skills and attitudes. The price was loss of authority and control over the child's education, creating what Tyack regards as a tradeoff for letting the state have the right to discipline all children in values deemed desirable. In return, schools would confer opportunity and status. The exchange was not realized, however, without reluctance and some resistance (Tyack, 1974, pp. 160–161). As we will later see for home schoolers, when public schooling no longer seemed to instill the values desired by some parents for their children, resistance became rebellion.

FROM LOCAL CONTROL TO PROFESSIONAL CONTROL

Over the last half of the 19th-century schools changed dramatically in terms of complexity and locus of control. Not only did age-graded schools replace most one-room schools, for example, but control over curriculum and texts shifted from parents and the local community to the professional staff, mainly administrators at the district and state levels.

With these changes came a transformation of mission, as more and more parents saw the public school as a vehicle of opportunity and mobility for their children. Thus we witness a radical change from a desire for a common set of values to be taught to all, to an interest in different things being taught to differing groups of children. Confidence in public schooling was strengthened or weakened depending on how each group of parents saw schools serving their aspirations for their children. By century's end, the civic and moral school mission had become "Americanization" for some and getting ahead for others. With this development was to come a serious test of citizen commitment to public schooling.

To understand what was happening to schools in post-Civil War America one must notice, as always, what was happening at large in the United States. Rapid population growth, along with technological and social changes, fueled what Berger et al. (1973) would call modernizing influences. These were shaping all walks of life, including schools. The watchwords became sequence, order, steps, specialization, and compartmentalization with everything in its place and a place for everything.

There is ample evidence of this tendency in public schools. The local district school system was yielding to increased state-wide regulation. As populations built up in urban settings, one-room generalized schools were being replaced by age-graded specialized schools. The highly decentralized tradition of each child bringing their own textbooks from home came to be supplanted by systemwide textbook adoption (Kaestle, 1983 ch. 6).

There were other modernizing signs. One was the professionalization of school administration, as schools became far more centralized and hierarchically controlled by the 1880s than they ever were in the 1840s. Educational literature came to be dominated by pedagogy and teaching methods. The expansion of normal schools and the institution of certification laws affected teacher training and licensing, removing even more control over schools from the local community. The concern for organizing, running, and maintaining schools began to dominate the rhetoric of school administrators and reformers alike.

The rapid growth of population in many towns and cities only served to augment bureaucratizing tendencies of many public schools. Numbers came not only from migration from country to city, but from a general westward movement and immigration from abroad, swelling new towns and villages. Chicago grew from a muddy village in 1830 to a metropolis of over 100,000 by 1860. Boston in a single year, 1847, added 37,000 Irish immigrants to its population of 114,000 (Tyack, 1974, pp. 30–31).

All the population growth between 1830 and 1890 compounded the educational burden on school districts. Added to this was the fact that a growing *percentage* of children and youth of what we now call "school-age" were attending school instead of working (Tyack, 1974, pp. 66–70). The very expression "school-age" indicates a bureaucratizing trend. A certain age group in the population is catalogued, slotted. In just 28 years from 1870 to 1898 the number of pupils in schools grew from less than 7,000,000 to 15,000,000, outstripping the overall population growth (Tyack, 1974, p. 66).

Population and financial pressures were such that despite the presence of compulsory attendance laws, they were rarely enforced. There were not nearly enough spaces for those who wanted to enroll. Tyack observes that in 1886 in Chicago if "all the children who were legally obliged to attend school had come to classrooms," only one third would have found seats (Tyack, 1974, p. 71).

Even with reform fervor energizing calls for more money for schools, support lagged far behind need. Thus one sees a strong impetus for cost efficiency in building and running schools. With this drive came diminished parental and community control.

The efficiency argument was evident in discussions about age-grading. In the district school system that dominated in the early 19th century, children of all ages were taught in one room by one teacher. School reformers wanted to end this practice.

Henry Barnard declared as early as 1838 that the one-room school was not only inefficient but inhumane. One of the "conditions of success" for a system of public schools was a "classification of scholars" that brought "a large number of similar age and attainments, at all times, and in every state of their advancement" together under the exclusive charge of the same teacher (Tyack, 1974, p. 44; Katz, 1975, p. 35).

In the early 1860s Frederick A. Packard, too, addressed the age grading of schools. Speaking of Ohio, Packard observed that the "practice of grading the schools—that is, the very natural arrangement of them into departments, as primary, secondary, grammar, principal, &c.—has been introduced to some extent in the larger towns, and is regarded with favour by the school authorities of Ohio, but this only *facilitates* the work of instruction; it does not *perform* it" (Packard, 1866, p.59; emphasis in original).

The move to consolidate textbook acquisition in the hands of school authorities offers an instance of how a move for efficiency contributed to the decline in parental prerogatives. In the early 19th-century schoolbooks were provided by the pupil's family. In many schools it was not unusual for there to be as many textbooks as there were children in attendance. Often children brought to school old tattered family textbooks their parents had once used.

Not surprisingly as reform pressures for common texts grew in the 1840s rural parents often resisted. Not only did they resent school intrusion into textbook selection, but they felt such an action was too costly and so voted down school taxes. For educational reformers, however, more school uniformity would insure better quality. For the overworked teachers, often having several different texts for the same subject, teaching was made even more difficult. For them the very diversity of textbooks undermined efficiency and professional expertise (Kaestle, 1983, p. 134).

Let us now recap the transformation of school mission. At first the stress was on the need for education for all in the new Republic. By the 1840s concerns over disorder and social unrest reoriented thinking toward schooling for character development as a way of preserving the social order. While this was a change, it was still a common aim, and the tone was still basically optimistic. A faith in human agency to assure a more perfect society predominated.

By the post-Civil War period, common schools were publicly funded, centrally regulated, and professionally managed. Yet Americans retained their faith in the cosmopolitan ideal of inclusive public schools. Though inequities abounded, Americans "widely shared a belief in fairness and cohesion through common schools" (Tyack, 1974, p. 222).

The growing numbers of the poor in cities by century's end contributed to growing doubts in a faith in commonality. Many educational theorists recommended replacing common education with special education. This meant schooling had to be designed to recognize the differing roles some children would play in American society compared to those that others would play (Church & Sedlak, 1976, p. 192). Domestic science and manual training, for instance, would provide the "hand training" lower-class children needed.

The effect of changes in the public schools and their mission was to turn schools from being a protection against the worst of modernizing tendencies to its facilitator. This resulted in the earlier enthusiasm and vigor for reform being drained out by the late 1880s. Not until the early 20th century with the progressive critics did any real reform energy return.

PROGRESSIVE DISSENT

Progressive education is often thought of as being a countervailing force to modernizing tendencies. Yet progressivism, in its political and economic as well as educational dimensions, is a somewhat paradoxical movement when viewed on the screen of modernism. One thinks of moves to humanize industrial society, curb its excessive tendencies toward greed and materialism, and to balance a move toward bigness with attention to restoring a stake in society at the level of family and local community.

The paradoxical side of progressivism is that it also carried within itself the very spirit of modernism. Progressives shared a widespread interest in the methods of science. For many this was accompanied by a belief in social efficiency which meant a trust in governance by "scientific" experts. Applied to schools it contributed to a moving away from locally elected school boards and towards the superintendancy and its office of expert specialists.

The wing of progressivism that Church calls the "liberal progressives" is the one we know best. It provided the vision and language of reform. But it was the "conservative progressives" who, with their modernist bent, actually transformed what was done in schools through the use of experts trained in the new social science, new measurement techniques, and curriculum design (Church & Sedlak, 1976, pp. 255–257)

Two key words recur in the rhetoric of progressives: "society" and "community." For the conservatives the preferred word was "society." The controlling metaphor was the efficiently running machine. Ideally, society itself was a machine with its many parts (such as schools, families, and religious organizations) meshing smoothly.

For the liberal progressives "community" was the key. The biological metaphor "organism" was central. It encompassed the idea of interaction, interrelatedness. This image shaped the visionary aspect of progressivism in education.

Between 1890 and 1910 the liberals defined the dialogue over school reform, only to be eclipsed in the next decade by conservative progressives with their social efficiency through educational engineering.

As the 19th century neared its close, liberal critics looked at America's schools and saw lockstep teaching, rote memorization, passive students, and an irrelevant curriculum. They believed the schools were separating family and community, parent and child. Among these critics one finds Francis Parker, Jane Addams, Ella Flagg Young, and John Dewey.

The successes and failures of progressive moves for school reform are better understood when one observes the world of the public school teacher. It is all too easy to forget about the teacher and get caught up in the fervor, energy, and commitment of the reformers. Low pay and status, a tightly monitored social life, crowded classrooms with pupils of a variety of ages, often inadequate training, and poor and too few textbooks were the teacher's lot.

One way they coped with large numbers of pupils was to use the recitation method and require much reciting from memory as a check on pupil learning. Even with a desire to teach for understanding, teachers found little time and less support. Coverage, after all, was what interested school examiners when they came into classrooms and listened to student recitations. And the teacher knew her (rarely his) job depended on this visitation.

Both liberals and conservatives were concerned about what they saw as meaningless rote memorization. Both were interested in better teaching and better organization of subject matter so as to reduce the widening gap between societal needs and school and neighborhood. Liberals stressed working with children and their families to foster assimilation into American society while strengthening neighborhood ties and involvement. Conservatives looked to making schools more relevant to the needs of adult society. For the conservative education was social group specific; for the liberal it was for commonality, at least in rhetoric.

John Dewey's work (Dewey, 1915) exemplifies the liberal reformers' common faith. The task of the school is to prepare students for life in a "great community" by encouraging their involvement in a variety of activities in school, always working "along common lines, in a common spirit, and with reference to common aims." Schools are tragically weak, Dewey believed, because they endeavor to prepare "future members of the social order in a medium in which the conditions of the social spirit are eminently wanting" (Dewey, 1915, pp. 14–15).

Educational reform by 1910 came down to either instilling "the spirit of service or the more indidividualistic one of self-direction . . . in building communities that were 'worthy, lovely, and harmonious' " (Church & Sedlak, 1976, p. 269). The aspect of liberal progressivism that educators were inclined to notice was that of self-direction. And even here, when it was tried out, it was more likely to be directed to the young of the well-born and affluent. For the children of the lower-middle and lower classes, the aspect of Progressivism that most influenced the school was that of the conservatives. Thus, as far as practice was concerned, even the liberal side of progressivism led to class-specific educational goals.

Like the liberals the conservative reformers, with their vision of a smoothly functioning social order, eschewed social conflict. They believed that what students learned in school should be relevant to what they were to do in society. Fitting schooling closely to the adult destiny of the child meant a school designed and run by experts. For the conservatives, the task of meshing school and society was clearly too complex for any direct democracy and mass participation. Thus "individuals could not be expected to fulfill their social roles adequately unless they were guided to them and supervised as they performed them" (Church & Sedlak, 1976, p. 256).

Although it was meant as a solution to the alienating aspects of modernization, the progressive legacy contributed to the problem. The family/school gap widened. With this came a weakened faith in public schools. In the 1930s and beyond, reformers turned to public schools to find panaceas for the various crises, social and otherwise, that arose. And when even this mission had clearly failed by the 1970s, many parents turned to alternatives to public schooling, including education at home.

A SEARCH FOR EDUCATIONAL PANACEAS— ACTIONS AND REACTIONS

Dominating the period after 1916, marked by Woodrow Wilson's election for a second term to the White House, were a series of crises relating to booms, busts, and wars. The first crisis, World War I, framed the end of political progressivism. Ten years after the war's end in 1919 the "great depression" commenced, and only ended after America's entry into World War II. Soon after that war, the United States was fighting in Korea as well as deeply engaged in a "cold war" with the Soviet Union. We may also recall hydrogen bomb testing, civil rights, Vietnam, and Watergate.

By the late 1920s progressive educators were speaking of projects, units, class discussions, and field trips. Yet, despite all this, most schools went about their usual business, largely unmoved by all the reform rhetoric.

With the onset of the Second World War little remained of progressive education beyond unit plans, field trips, and increased verbal attention to creative expression in classrooms. Feelings of being left out of decisions involving the education of their children was causing many parents to lose interest and some to seek alternatives.

With parents becoming disillusioned, the field of educational reform was ripe for the group of conservative critics who emerged in the late

1940s and early 1950s. As they saw it, schools had been captured and corrupted by progressive education. In *Crisis in Education*, Iddings Bell, in 1949, accused the school establishment of having not only taken over domestic functions that were properly parental, but having excluded religion, without which education could have no ultimate purpose (Cremin, 1961, p. 339).

Four years later Arthur Bestor, in his *Educational Wastelands,* claimed that American education had been taken over by a powerfully entrenched " 'interlocking directorate' composed of professors of education, the school administrators they trained, and the state departments of education that required their courses for teacher certification" (Cremin, 1961, pp. 344, 345).

With the fears and passions generated by the Cold War, schools were pressured to adopt such curricular reforms as the new math, new biology, new chemistry, and new physics as a part of national policy. The launching of a Soviet satellite in 1953 loosened federal moneys for these projects.

During the period from the mid-1950s until the mid-1960s liberals turned to school desegregation as a vehicle of racial justice. As activity moved from the courts to the streets, numbers of black parents in the South felt for the first time in a century some measure of control over at least the educational destiny of their children. In the process of banding together in civil disobedience they found a new source of meaning growing out of collective action in their quest for educational equity.

By the mid-1970s the realization of this dream was proving ephemeral indeed. So too were the hopes for the various curriculum reform movements, with new math, for example, being virtually abandoned by 1970.

Waves of social hope and disillusionment followed in rapid order, furthered in the 1960s by a series of assassinations of charismatic leaders. By the 1970s the faith in a national destiny that shaped American dreams throughout the 19th century was lost, as was the faith in human agency to solve social problems. Gone was a belief that public schools could shape a virtuous citizenry. Instead, feelings of powerlessness and meaninglessness came to predominate.

One other event will be singled out, the "free school movement" of the late 1960s and early 1970s. One of its leading advocates and practitioners later provided pedagogical leadership for home schoolers (see Holt, 1981). The movement amounted to a radical critique of public schooling.[4] Although it involved only a small fraction of the school population, its impact was felt far beyond its domain.

---

[4] For a fuller discussion see Kirschner, 1981.

It was a movement for a more holistic education. At its best, free schooling meant practicing such ideals as parental control, student and teacher involvement in actually running schools, personal engagement, a reaching out beyond school walls, and a linking of young and old. It was a countercultural challenge to the traditional, hierarchical model of school control that had emerged in the late 19th century and been institutionalized in the 20th by the conservative progressives.

Two events signaled the growth of free schools in the late 1960s: the U.S. publication in 1959 of A.S. Neill's *Summerhill: A Radical Approach to Childrearing* and the Free Speech Movement at Berkeley in 1965. A whole generation of teachers who were educated in the 1960s and early 1970s read *Summerhill*. They noticed his call for freedom, not coercion, in schools and his urging teachers to always be on the side of the child. This meant respect; more strongly, it meant unconditional love and trust.

Out of the Free Speech Movement grew a dialogue about schools and what they were for. What emerged was a desire for empowerment as a challenge to the traditional mission of schools as agencies for molding the young. While the movement began in elite universities, its concerns were soon directed at what was happening in elementary and high schools. Out of these efforts grew the move for alternative schooling. The sense of empowerment parents came to feel as they got involved in running some of these schools helped them find the courage to take the education of their young into their own hands and not trust the "experts."

A notable free-schooler, in this regard, was John Holt. By the beginning of the 1980s he had become a staunch advocate of home schooling. Up until his recent death he edited the home-schooling newsletter, *Growing Without Schooling* (see also Holt, 1981).

The writings of that poet of the free school movement, Peter Marin, show how basic was the questioning of public schools. He might well be speaking for many home schoolers as he describes in essentially religious language the concerns of free schoolers at the opening of the 1970s. Redemption is at the "heart of any decent teaching, healing or loving." Change is needed, not in the methods of the school system, but its aims. "What is troubling the young and forcing upon their teachers an intolerable burden is the idea of childhood itself: the way we think about adolescents, and their place in the culture itself" (Marin, 1969, p. 50).

Today free schools seem like a page from ancient history. Desegregation controversies, school violence, new math, Bible-reading and lawsuits, teachers' unions, textbook complaints, accountability, and school-levy failures—all are signs of the times. Many parents who gave up hope for any changes in public schools settled for safer, more disciplined schools and a reduced dropout rate. Others turned to private schools, both secular and religious. Still others gave up on schooling altogether and turned to education at home.

CONCLUSION

What insights can we gain from this history of American faith in the civic and moral efficacy of public schooling? What can we make out of the apparent loss of faith in public schooling as a vehicle of national cohesion? How may its history inform our present gropings for a better future for our young, one of empowerment, promise, and meaning?

History provides one with perspectives. For home schoolers, it helps explain the source of the profound disillusionment with public education. Within this history, one also finds possibilities in ventures tried and later abandoned, as in the free school movement or in certain of Jane Addams ventures.

The socialization of the young and parents' and schools' role in the process is what this history has been about. The 19th-century story was one of education moving from the home to the school, bringing forth the issues of a schooling mission and locus of control. By the 20th century, the vision of a common schooling had come to be replaced by a specialized one. As these failed to work for most of the poor, and even many not-so-poor, faith in the promise of public schooling waned. As the faith waned, alternatives became thinkable.

In our own times, we find many Americans turning to "family values" and scriptural religion in a search for stability and something to believe in. This is a defensive posture laced with a heavy dose of nostalgia. But it is a search: for personal empowerment, for meaning, for a hope for a worthy future for the next generation. In the home-school movement one finds a hint of optimism in this age of cynicism not seen in quite a while. What remains is to join this to a sense of the larger welfare.

REFERENCES

Aries, P. (1962). *Centuries of childhood: A social history of family life* (Robert Baldick, trans.). New York: Vintage Books. (French original 1960)

Bennett, W.J. (1988). *American education: Making it work.* (A Report to the President of the United States and the American People.) Washington, DC: U.S. Department of Education.

Berger, P., Berger, B., & Kellner, H. (1973). *The homeless mind: Modernization and consciousness.* New York: Vintage Books.

Burnap, G. W. (1844). *Church and state: Or the privileges and duties of an*

American citizen. (A Discourse, Delivered in the First Independent Church, on Thanksgiving Day, December 12, 1844.) Baltimore: John D. Toy.

Church, R. L., & Sedlak, M. W. (1976). *Education in the United States, an interpretive history.* New York: The Free Press.

Cremin, L. (1961). *The transformation of the school: Progressivism in American education, 1876–1957.* New York: Alfred A. Knopf.

Culver, R. B. (1969). *Horace Mann and religion in the Massachusetts public schools.* New York: Arno. (Original work published 1929)

Degler, C. N. (1980). *At odds: Women and the family in America from the revolution to the present.* Oxford: Oxford University.

Dewey, J. (1915). *The school and society.* Chicago: University of Chicago. (Original work published 1899).

Duffy, J. J., & Muller, H. N. (1982). *An anxious democracy: Aspects of the 1830s.* Westport, CT: Greenwood.

Findlay, J. (1986). Nineteenth-century Protestantism and American Education. *History of Education Quarterly, 26,* 125–129.

Handy, R. T. (1967). *The Protestant quest for a Christian America: 1830–1930.* Philadelphia: Fortress.

Hatch, N. (1988, March). *The Democratization of Christianity and the Character of American Politics.* Paper presented at the Religion and American Politics Conference, Wheaton, IL.

Hirsch, E. D. (1987). *Cultural literacy: What every American needs to know.* Boston: Houghton Mifflin.

Holt, J. (1981). *Teach your own: A hopeful path for education.* New York: Delta/Seymour Lawrence.

Jackson, S. L. (1941). *America's struggle for free schools: Social tension and education in New England and New York, 1827–42.* Washington, DC: American Council on Public Affairs.

Kaestle, C. F. (1983). *Pillars of the republic: Common schools and American Society, 1780–1860.* New York: Hill and Wang.

Katz, M. B. (1975). *Class, bureaucracy, and schools: The illusion of educational change in America* (Expanded Ed.). New York: Praeger.

Kirschner, J. (1981). Free Schooling and the "Fourth Great Awakening". *Review Journal of Philosophy and Social Science, 6,* 72–82.

Kirschner, J. (1988, November, 4). *Methodism, Unitarianism, and the Quest for Common Schools.* Paper presented at the Annual Meeting of the History of Education Society, Toronto, Canada.

Knight, E., & Hall, C. (1951). *Readings in American educational history.* New York: Appleton.

Marin, P. (1969). Adolescence and the Apocalypse. *This Magazine Is About Schools, 3,* 40–63.

Marty, M. (1987). *Religion and republic: The American circumstance.* Boston: Beacon.

Mattingly, P. H., & Stevens, E. W., Jr. (1987). *". . . Schools and the means of education shall forever be encouraged": A history of education in the Old Northwest, 1787–1880.* Athens, OH: Ohio University Libraries.

National Commission on Excellence in Education. (1983) *A nation at risk.*
Washington, DC: U.S. Government Printing Office.

Noll, M., Hatch, N., & Marsden, G. M. (1983). *The search for Christian America.* Westchester, IL: Crossway.

Packard, F. A. (1969). *The daily public school in the United States.* New York: Arno. (Original work published 1866).

Reed, F. (1831). Sermon 11, The Influence of Moral Principle, Secured by early Culture, Essential to National Prosperity, by Rev. Fitch Reed. Middletown, Connecticut: July 4, 1831. In E. Ireson (Ed.), *The Methodist preacher: Or monthly sermons from living ministers* (Vol. 2). Boston: Putnam and Damrell.

Task Force on Teaching As a Profession. (1986) *A nation prepared: Teachers for the 21st century.* Washington, DC: Carnegie Forum on Education and the Economy.

Tuveson, E. L. (1968). *Redeemer nation: The idea of America's millennial role.* Chicago: The University of Chicago.

Tyack, D. B. (1974). *The one best system: A history of American urban education.* Cambridge, MA: Harvard University Press.

Van Galen, J. A. (1988). Ideology, curriculum, and pedagogy. *Education and Urban Society, 21,* 52–68.

Ware, H., Jr. (1838). *The duty of promoting Christianity by the circulation of books.* A Discourse Delivered Before the Unitarian Book and Pamphlet Society, at the Annual Meeting, May 31, 1838. Boston: Book and Pamphlet Society

Worden, H. (1869). Unpublished Diary. Rare Books and Special Collections of Syracuse University Library.

Chapter 8

Home Schooling Law

Sharon Nalbone Richardson
School District of Springfield Township Oreland, PA

Perry A. Zirkel
Lehigh University

INTRODUCTION

While education occupies a cherished position in our country, the reputation of its mass institutional form has become tarnished. A growing number of citizens individually are reacting to institutional education by literally taking matters into their own hands and homes. For a variety of reasons, ranging from the pragmatic to the spiritual, these educational vigilantes have removed their children from school and are instructing them at home (Klicka, 1988). While most of these people are sincere, they differ in their ability to provide their children with a valuable education outside of an institutional framework. They all face a legal barrier in the form of state compulsory school attendance laws. These statutes vary. Some, for example, do not allow home instruction or permit it only under certain, sometimes quite restrictive, conditions.

Not surprising, as the "home schooling" movement has gained in momentum and become more widespread, state and local officials have responded with more vigorous enforcement of their compulsory education laws. The inevitable result is more litigation and, in some instances, new regulations. As both parents and school officials evidence increasing intransigence, the statutes play a central role in this legal tug-of-war over the education of the child. A secondary, but no less significant, role is played by the courts which, in resolving the disputes between parents and the schools, must test and interpret the statutes.

CONSTITUTIONAL ISSUES

Historical Overview

Historically, the education of children in the United States was a matter of parental discretion. Decisions to educate or not to educate, and the substance of that education, were made by parents. It was not until after the Civil War that states began to preempt what had traditionally been viewed as a parental prerogative. By 1900 all the northern states had adopted some form of compulsory attendance statute. Southern states were a bit slower to respond, but eventually they, too, followed the trend for mandatory attendance. Today every state has some form of compulsory attendance statute.

State power to compel attendance and regulate the form and content of education was acknowledged by the Supreme Court in the landmark case of *Pierce v. Society of Sisters* (1925). Although the case dealt specifically with the constitutionality of an Oregon statute that required attendance at public school, the Court acknowledged a general right of states to require that a child be educated and to regulate that educational process. The Court stated:

> No question is raised concerning the power of the state reasonable to regulate all schools, to inspect, supervise and examine them, their teachers and pupils; to require that all children of proper age attend some school. (*Pierce,* p. 534)

Interestingly, the Supreme Court did not find it necessary in *Pierce* to explain or justify this shift in power from parents to the state. Accepted without any other comment than "no question is raised," the shift was a legal fait accompli. Until recently, parents challenging compulsory attendance laws usually focused on issues less basic than the very right of the state to compel attendance. Recent home instruction cases have partially shifted the focus back by more frequently challenging, on constitutional grounds, the power of the state to compel attendance and regulate basic educational choices. For the most part these challenges have been unsuccessful.

Constitutional Framework: Four Critical Cases

While the right of the state to require education is well accepted, the extent to which that right may be exercised is not unlimited. In a number of cases, most occurring in the 1920s and including *Pierce*, the Supreme Court defined the boundaries of state power.

The first successful Supreme Court challenge to the state's right to regulate education was *Meyer v. Nebraska* (1923), in which the Court established the principle that the state's right over education was not absolute. In *Meyer*, the Court held unconstitutional a Nebraska statute that prohibited the teaching of a modern language other than English to students who had not completed the eighth grade in any private, parochial, or public school. The authorities charged and convicted the defendant, a private school instructor, for teaching German to a child who had not advanced beyond the eighth grade. Overturning the conviction, the Court struck down this transparently anti-German, jingoistic statute, ruling that it violated the defendant's right to teach, the students' right to learn, and the parents' rights to choose, within bounds, what their children would be taught. Regarding these rights as liberties protected by the due process clause of the Fourteenth Amendment and recognizing "[t]he power of the State to compel attendance at some school and to make reasonable regulations for all schools" (*Meyer*, p. 402), the court found Nebraska's statute to be unreasonable and arbitrary.

Two years later, in *Pierce*, the Court again applied the principle established in *Meyer*. The Court ruled that the Oregon statute compelling attendance at public school, without providing for a private school alternative, "unreasonably interferes with the liberty of parents and guardians to direct the . . . education of children under their control" (*Pierce*, pp. 534–535). Although the plaintiffs were not parents but private school corporations seeking injunctive relief from Oregon's essentially "public school only" compulsory attendance law, the Court acknowledged the right of parents to have some choice in the education of their children. The Court noted:

> As often heretofore pointed out, rights guaranteed by the Constitution may not be abridged by legislation which has no reasonable relation to some purpose within the competency of the State. The fundamental theory of liberty upon which all governments in this Union repose excludes any general power of the State to standardize its children by forcing them to accept instruction from public teachers only. The children is not the mere creature of the State; those who nurture him and direct his destiny have the right, coupled with the high duty, to recognize and prepare him for additional obligations. (*Pierce*, p. 535)

The principle established in *Meyer* and in *Pierce*, limiting the power of the state to control the terms and content of education, was relied upon again by the Supreme Court in 1927. Applying the due process clause of the Fifth Amendment to the Federal Territory of Hawaii, the

Court in *Farrington v. Tokushige* (1927) struck down stringent laws regulating the Island's private schools and thereby set further limits on state power. The express purpose of the Hawaii statute was to assimilate and indoctrinate a large alien population and to promote Americanism. The act, together with the implementing regulations, gave the Territory pervasive power over foreign language (mostly Japanese) schools. After reciting a lengthy listing of the act's provisions and the various regulations, the Court, in rather summary fashion, struck them down, stating:

> The foregoing statement is enough to show that the school Act and the measures adopted thereunder go far beyond mere regulation of private-ly-supported schools where children obtain instruction deemed valuable by their parents and which is not obviously in conflict with any public interest. They give affirmative direction concerning the intimate and essential details of such schools, intrust their control to public officers, and deny both owners and patrons reasonable choice and discretion in respect to teachers, curriculum, and textbooks. (*Farrington,* p. 298)

The *Farrington* Court acknowledged there was a right to regulate private schools, but that right could not be so extensive as to effectively eliminate the alternatives offered by private schools. The Court set forth the principle that the state cannot excessively control the terms and content of nonpublic schools, so as to rob them of their character as alternatives to public schools.

These three Supreme Court decisions established the due process framework for the constitutional limits on the right of the state to require and regulate education. The issue of state power versus parental power remained relatively dormant for almost half a century until the Supreme Court squarely confronted the issue in *Wisconsin v. Yoder* (1972). Whereas in the earlier cases the Court relied upon due process, specifically the freedom to choose educational alternatives, in *Yoder* the Court applied the First Amendment right to the free exercise of religion.

Affirming the Wisconsin Supreme Court's reversal of a conviction of Amish parents for violating the state's compulsory attendance law, the Court set this other constitutional boundary on the states. The Court in *Yoder* ruled:

> [The] State's interest in universal education . . . is not totally free from a balancing process when it impinges on [other] fundamental rights . . . such as those specifically protected by the Free Exercise Clause of the First Amendment, and the traditional interest of parents with respect to the religious upbringing of their children. (*Yoder,* p. 214)

While this ruling might appear to be a rather significant limit on the power of the state versus the power of the parent, the Court was quite careful to narrowly circumscribe its scope. The *Yoder* Court insisted that in order to trigger constitutional protection, the parental interest must be religious in nature rather than philosophical or personal; the religious interest must pose a real, rather than perceived, threat to the religious interests involved; and the disruption to the child's education should not seriously impair the child's future nor should it threaten the public order in any significant way. In order to tip the balance away from the strong state interest in compulsory education, the parents would have to satisfy all of these narrowly defined criteria.

Based on uncontested evidence, the Court in *Yoder* found an interdependence between Amish fundamental religious tenets and the self-sufficient Amish way of life, an interdependence that was clearly threatened by continued attendance in secular schools. There was also no dispute as to the sincerity of the Amish claims, nor that they were religious in nature rather than philosophical or personal values. The Court emphasized it was "not dealing with a way of life and mode of education by a group claiming to have recently discovered some 'progressive' or more enlightened process for rearing children for modern life" (*Yoder,* p. 235). Furthermore, the Amish parents only wanted to remove their children from public schools after the eighth grade. Thereafter, they would continue to be educated in Amish schools "characterized by the undisputed testimony of expert educators as "ideal" vocational education" (*Yoder,* p. 224). The Court concluded the Amish system would not harm the child in any significant way, nor would it threaten the public safety, peace, or order.

The extended applicability of *Yoder,* even for other religious groups, is dubious. The *Yoder* Court was careful to narrowly circumscribe its ruling. For example, the Court commented:

> [The Amish made] a convincing showing, one that probably few other religious groups or sects could make, and weighing the minimal difference between what the State would require and what the Amish already accept, it was incumbent on the State to show with more particularity how its admittedly strong interest in compulsory education would be adversely affected by granting an exemption to the Amish. (*Yoder,* pp. 235–236)

One is hard pressed to give an example, outside the Amish, where the Court's narrowly defined criteria for a successful First Amendment challenge would be met. Chief Justice Burger, writing for the majority warned: "Nothing we hold is intended to undermine the general applicability of the State's compulsory school-attendance statutes or to limit the power of the State to promulgate reasonable standards" (*Yoder*, p. 236).

These four cases, *Meyer, Pierce, Farrington,* and *Yoder* combine to form the legal framework for the power of the state to require and regulate education. While not dealing specifically with the right of home instruction, these cases form the constitutional backdrop against which home instruction cases are viewed.

Constitutional Challenges: Overview Sampling

Increasingly, parents who are prosecuted for instructing their children at home are attacking compulsory school attendance statutes on constitutional grounds. These challenges, if successful, would restructure the state-parent balance set in *Meyer, Pierce, Farrington,* and *Yoder*. This balance, while recognizing restrictions on state power, now tilts in favor of the state. Although no case dealing specifically with home instruction has yet reached the Supreme Court, the increased number of court challenges and the increased activism of the home instruction movement may well produce a Supreme Court ruling in the future. Constitutional challenges have generally been based on the First or Fourteenth Amendment.

Religious claims. In many of the home instruction cases parents have removed their children from school for religious reasons. Prosecuted for violating the compulsory attendance laws, these parents have argued that they have a highly protected First Amendment freedom to educate their children according to their religious percepts and values.

The most recent court decisions provide consistent continued confirmation of the *Yoder* decision. In *Howell v. State* (1986), Texas' intermediate appellate court rejected *Yoder* protection for parents who argued that their religious conviction was to educate their children at home. In *State v. Schmidt* (1987), the Ohio Supreme Court held that the state's explicit-exceptions statute, which requires that home education programs be approved by the local school superintendent, did not violate the free exercise clause. Similarly, in line with parallel private/parochial school decisions such as *Fellowship Baptist Church v. Benton* (1987) and *Sheridan Road Baptist Church v. Michigan* (1986), North Dakota's highest court held in *State v. Patzer* (1986) that the teacher certification requirement in the state's home schooling statute did not violate the free exercise clause. Likewise, the highest court in Maine rejected the parents free exercise claim against that state's prior approval requirement.

In an earlier case, a North Carolina parent wanted to educate his five children at home and refused to send them to public or private schools; in his view, "exposing his children to others who did not share his religious beliefs would corrupt them" (*Duro v. District Attorney,* 1983). Although the father charged that the North Carolina compulsory school attendance law violated his first Amendment right to the free exercise of his religion, the Fourth Circuit denied his *Yoder*-based claim and held that North Carolina had a compelling interest in compulsory education which overrode the father's religious interest. More recently, the Eighth Circuit held that the Arkansas Home Schooling Act did not violate the free exercise clause (*Murphy v. State,* 1988).

Another religious issue has surfaced when parents have challenged the constitutionally of different requirements concerning the qualifications of the home teacher. A few states, namely Iowa, Michigan, and North Dakota, require all teachers in home schools to possess a teaching certificate. This requirement has been controversial enough to cause the Iowa legislature to place a moratorium on the enforcement of certification requirements until the matter could be studied further (Klicka, 1988).

Absent a similar moratorium, Michigan's state law requiring teacher certification of all individuals providing instruction was challenged in 1980 and again in 1986. In *Hanson v. Cushman* (1980) the federal district court found the statute to be reasonable because the parents had not proven that any of their fundamental rights had been violated. In the private school case of *Sheridan Road Baptist v. Department of Education* (1986), other Michigan parents challenged the certification requirement as a burden on the free exercise of religion. Michigan's highest court rejected that argument, regarding certification as a minimal burden that was outweighed by the State's interest in providing proper education.

North Dakota's statute requiring teacher certification has also been under attack several times in this decade. In 1980, the statute was upheld because the court found no evidence that the family's religious convictions would be affected (*State v. Shaver,* 1980). In a subsequent case, North Dakota's highest court conceded that the certification requirement imposed a burden on religion, but concluded that the burden was outweighed by the compelling state interest in sufficient educational quality, as legislatively determined to include certified teachers (*State v. Rivinius,* 1982). More recently this statutory requirement was again challenged and again upheld, with the court ruling that this requirement was the least intrusive means of ensuring the children are taught by competent staff (*State v. Patzer,* 1986). Two very recent North Dakota decisions have continued to maintain this position; in *State v. Melin* (1988) and *State v. Toman* (1989) the court held that the certification requirement did not violate the free exercise clause.

Prior to *Yoder,* the free exercise arguments for home instruction were consistently rejected by the courts. Not surprisingly, given the narrowness of the ruling in *Yoder,* the free exercise argument has met with negligible success in the years since *Yoder.* The reasons have varied. In some instances parents have not presented sufficient evidence to show their interest was religious in nature. In others, even though the interest was religious in nature, it did not rise to the level required by *Yoder* to trigger preponderant constitutional protection.

In contrast, successes, based on a First Amendment, *Yoder*-like religious interest are rare. In two Ohio cases, parents have successfully employed the First Amendment *Yoder* defense in gaining reversals of their convictions by the state's highest court. However, both cases involved instruction in unaccredited, religiously affiliated schools.

The parents in *State v. Whisner* (1976) and *State ex rel. Nagle v. Olin* (1980) were convicted for failing to send their children to state-approved schools, choosing instead to educate them at nonpublic, religiously oriented schools which did not conform to the "minimum standards" promulgated by Ohio's state board of education. The earlier case, *Whisner* (1976) was broader in scope than the later case, *Olin* (1980), but both were Ohio Supreme Court cases that involved similar factual patterns. Furthermore, the First Amendment issue was decided in the same way and for the same reasons; in fact, the *Olin* decision relied extensively on *Whisner.*

The group of parents in *Whisner* were "born again" Christians who maintained that attendance in schools adhering to Ohio's minimum standards was incompatible with their religion. The defendant in *Olin,* although not Amish, sent his daughter to an unaccredited Amish School, fearing that if she were educated according to the "humanistic," un-Christian values mandated by Ohio's minimum standards, he would subject himself, and his daughter, to eternal damnation. In both cases, the Ohio Supreme Court concluded that the claims satisfied the rigid criteria established in *Yoder.* The court accepted that the beliefs were religious in nature, rather than philosophical personal. The beliefs were sincerely and deeply held and there existed a strong interdependence between the educational experience and the inculcation of the parental religious values. The court also found the application of the minimum standards to nonpublic schools, while not a direct regulation as in *Farrington,* indirectly allowed the state to control the content and terms of education in Ohio including the curriculum, the method and hours of instruction, the teachers, the physical plant, and even the educational policies. In both cases, the court concluded the result was the "obliteration" of the distinction between public and non-public schools and the "absolute suffocation" of religious education.

It is difficult to assess the significance these two cases hold for the home instruction movement. Any such assessment raises a number of questions. Are these decisions directly applicable to cases where parents instruct their children at home rather than in an unaccredited, religiously affiliated school? If so, do these decisions add to *Yoder* either by broadening the scope of protected "religious" interests or by tightening the limits on acceptable state regulation of education? Or are they only aberrations, limited in scope to Ohio?

It would appear reasonable to assume the religious rights protected in *Whisner* and *Olin* are not contingent upon where the child is instructed. The court's rulings in both cases were at unreasonable state regulation that infringed upon the free exercise of religion of the parents. It was the content of the minimum standards (unreasonable regulation) and their effect (abridgement of basic religious of basic religious freedoms) that concerned the court, not the source of the alternative religious education. Home instruction on religious grounds would thus appear to come within the *Whisner-Olin* rubric, whatever its strength may be.

An unpublished Michigan decision supports this conclusion and offers some guidance for the answers to the other questions. However, its significance is limited by its fact pattern and its unreported status. In *State v. Nobel* (1980), the court held that the religious interests of the defendants in educating their children at home overrode Michigan's statutory requirement of teacher certification. Because Mrs. Nobel possessed all the qualifications necessary for teacher certification but refused on religious grounds to obtain it, the court found the requirement a mere formality. Relying on *Whisner,* the court reasoned that because of the religious nature of the defendants' claim and because of the superfluous nature of her certification, the requirement was an undue restriction on the defendants' religious freedom. Dismissing the criminal charges against the defendants, the court cryptically concluded: "the Nobels have a documented and sincere religious belief and this court won't and no Court should interfere with the free exercise of a religious belief on the facts of this case" (*Nobel*, p. 12).

More recent decisions support a nonacceptance of the expansive view of *Yoder* in the home schooling contest. These decisions are discussed below under the three basic categories of home instruction statutes.

Nonreligious claims. Aside from void-for-vagueness challenges, which are treated elsewhere in this chapter, the other constitutional attack on compulsory attendance laws is nonreligious, primarily on Fourteenth Amendment due process grounds that parents have the right, that is, the liberty, to educate their children as they see fit. Like the First Amendment free-exercise theory, this argument cuts across statutory categories and has the potential, if successful, to restructure the current state–parent balance. Unlike the First Amendment theory, there is no relatively recent Supreme Court decision, like *Yoder*, that expressly and unequivocally advances this position. Although the theory has popular appeal among those advocating a right of home instruction, modern courts have generally restricted the argument to a position subordinate to a state regulation.

The crux of the Fourteenth Amendment due process argument is that parents have a fundamental liberty to choose how their children are to be educated, and absent a "compelling state interest," this right is superior to the state's right to compel attendance and regulate education. It has long been recognized that parents have some rights relating to their children's education. The issue now raised is the degree of constitutional protection afforded such rights.

The conventional judicial view is that parents have a right to a voice in the education of their children, but this right not rise to a sufficiently protected level to outweigh the state's interest in regulating, or even prohibiting, home instruction. This position has been consistently adopted in the earlier, as well as the more recent, home instruction decisions. For example, in an early Ohio Supreme Court decision, *Parr v. State* (1927), the court addressed the issue of the constitutionality of the state compulsory attendance statute. Affirming the conviction of the parents for educating their children at home in violation of the statute, the court summarily weighed the balance in favor of the state:

> Compulsory education laws have very generally been upheld by the courts. Statutes making the education of children compulsory have become very general in the United States, and their constitutionality is beyond dispute, for the natural rights of a parent to the custody and control of his infant child are subordinate to the power of the state, and may be restricted and regulated by municipal laws. (*Parr,* p. 556)

As a more recent example, a New York appellate court, in *In re Franz* (1977), affirmed the defendant's conviction for violation of the compulsory education law. The court upheld the constitutionality of the law, reasoning that "our . . . [statute] strikes a happy balance . . . There is no rigid robotlike regimentation of children; nor conversely, can each child step to the music that he hears, however measured or far away"

(*In re Franz*, p. 944). The court refused to accept the defendant-parent's argument that her nonreligious claim was entitled to the same level of constitutional protection that was given the parents in *Yoder,* stating "[h]owever we may try to fit the . . . argument, procrustean-like into *Yoder,* therre is no credible analogy between the two" (*Franz*, p. 944).

In more recent federal cases, *Scoma v. Chicago Board of Education* (1974), *Hanson v. Cushman* (1980), *Blackwelder v. Safnauer* (1988), and *Murphy v. State* (1988), the courts specifically and emphatically rejected the contention that the parents had an independent, nonreligious, fundamental right in the education of their children. In *Scoma,* the parents sought an injunction and declaratory judgment to prevent the Chicago Board from interfering with their decision to educate their two school-age children at home. The federal district court in Illinois observed that the plaintiffs were asserting new and wideranging fundamental constitutional rights that included:

> [The] right and duty to educate their children adequately but as they see fit; to rear their children in accordance with their determination of what best serves the family's interest and welfare; to be protected in their family privacy and personal decision-making from governmental intrusion; to distribute and receive information; and to teach and to ensure their children's freedom of thought and inquiry. (*Scoma*, p. 460)

The Scomas were not claiming a religious interest in the home instruction of their children, relying instead on substantive due process, privacy, and equal protection. Rejecting the Scomas' direct assault on the Illinois law, the court distinguished *Pierce* and *Yoder,* stating:

> The courts have held that the state may constitutionally require that all children attend some school, under the authority of its police power. Plaintiffs have established no fundamental right which has been abridged by the compulsory attendance statute. . . . Under the test of *Pierce* and *Yoder* the Illinois statute . . . is reasonable and constitutional. (*Scoma*, p. 460)

The parents in the *Hanson* case, which was decided six years after *Scoma,* also sought a declaratory judgment that Michigan's compulsory school attendance law was unconstitutional. As with *Scoma,* the parents' claim hinged upon the court's recognition that they enjoyed a fundamental nonreligious right to control the education of their children. Refusing to recognize the fundamental status of their claim absent a religious interest, the federal district court in Michigan dismissed the action, stating: "Plaintiffs have cited no cases to the Court that have held that parents have a fundamental constitutional right to educate their children at home, nor has the Court's research uncovered any (Hanson, p. 112). In disposing of the parents' claim the court further stated:

> [The] plaintiffs have established no fundamental right that has been abridged by Michigan's compulsory attendance statute ... Thus the state need not demonstrate a "compelling interest" but only that it acted "reasonably" in requiring children to attend school and that children be taught only certified teachers. (Hanson, pp. 114–115)

In Murphy v. State (1988), parents challenged the constitutionality of the Arkansas Home Schooling Act on both religious and nonreligious grounds. In addition to determining that the Act neither violated the free exercise clause (religious argument) nor the equal protection clause (nonreligious argument), the Eighth Circuit further held that the constitutional right of privacy does not extend to protect parental decisions concerning the direction of their children's education from state interference.

Decisions such as Blackwelder v. Safnauer (1988) and State v. Edgington (1983) have rejected parents equal protection claims under the Fourteenth Amendment. In a recent state decision, Blount v. Department of Educational and Cultural Services (1988), parents lost their nonreligious constitutional claim when the highest court in Maine held that neither the state constitution nor the equal protection and due process clauses of the Federal Constitution afforded parents additional protection beyond that provided by the First Amendment.

Although most courts have refused to recognize that parents have a Fourteenth Amendment fundamental right to control the education of their children or have summarily weighed the balance in favor of the state, there are some exceptions. However, these decisions are limited in their precedential value.

The afforementioned Whisner decision is undoubtedly the most notable exception because of the status of the court and the unequivocal nature of the ruling. While the crux of the Whisner court's decision to reverse the parents' convictions was based primarily on a First Amendment Yoder-like theory and was specifically related to a private unapproved school, the court additionally elaborated on the nature of the parental rights in due process terms, stating:

> [In Farrington, Pierce, and Meyer] the court utilized the "liberty" concept embodied within the due process clause of the Fourteenth Amendment to invalidate legislation that interfered with the right of a parent to direct the education, religious or secular, of his or her children. Thus, it has long been recognized that the right of a parent to guide the educa-

tion, including the religious education, of his or her children is indeed a "fundamental right" guaranteed by the due process clause of the Fourteenth Amendment. (*Whisner*, pp. 213–214)

Other courts had recognized that *Farrington, Pierce,* and *Meyer* placed limits on state action, but none prior to *Whisner* had taken the extra step of recognizing a Fourteenth Amendment fundamental right of parents to control the education of their children. The extra step taken by the *Whisner* court has the effect of restructuring the state-parent balance so as to tip it in favor of the parents, unless the state can show a compelling interest that cannot be satisfied with less restrictive means.

Another exception is *Perchemlides v. Frizzle* (1978), an unreported Massachusetts lower court decision that dealt specifically with home instruction. After local school authorities rejected their home instruction program the parents sought a declaration by the court that the rejection violated their constitutional and statutory right to educate their child at home. The parents had removed their six-year-old son from school because they were dissatisfied with the education he was receiving and were convinced they could give him a superior education at home. Their decision was not religiously motivated. The Massachusetts statute exempted from public school attendance a child "otherwise instructed in a manner approved in advance by the superintendent or the school committee." In 1893, the Massachusetts Supreme Judicial Court, applying a slightly different statute, had construed the language "otherwise instructed" to include home instruction as an exemption, provided it was "given in good faith and sufficient in extent" (*Commonwealth*, p. 403). On the basis of the statute and the earlier case, the *Perchemlides* court concluded that "[w]ithout doubt, then, the Massachusetts' compulsory attendance statute might well be constitutionally infirm if it did not exempt students whose parents prefer alternative forms of education" (*Perchemlides*, p. 9). Without identifying a specific constitutional amendment, the court attributed the potential infirmity to a right of privacy independent of the First Amendment. The court included within the notion of privacy the right of "non-religious as well as religious parents . . . to choose from the full range of educational alternatives for their children" (*Perchemlides*, pp. 8–9). Presumably contained within this right was a constitutionally protected choice of the alternative of home instruction. Ironically, the case was decided on a constitutional issue, but that issue proved to be procedural rather than substantive.

The significance of the *Perchemlides* decision should not be overstated. As mentioned, it is an unreported Massachusetts lower court decision that is subject to widely different interpretations. For all the publicity the case generated, its judicial acceptance has been markedly limited. The somewhat skewed logic of the case, particularly in the area of the substantive rights of parents, has not become more popular among other courts.

In a more recent Massachusetts case, *In re Charles* (1987), the state's highest court recognized that parents do have a constitutional right to direct the education of their children. However, the court upheld state regulations requiring parents to seek approval by submitting their home schooling proposal outlining the curriculum, materials, and qualifications of instructors. This approval process was designed to promote the state's substantial interest in ensuring the education of its citizens and, therefore, did not infringe upon the parents' constitutional rights to direct the education of their children.

In sum, although the power of the state to control educational choices is limited by several key Supreme Court cases, parents do not have an unqualified constitutional right to home instruction. States retain the power to compel attendance at public or private schools and to regulate, at least minimally, the terms of education. The Supreme Court's decision in *Wisconsin v. Yoder* offers some support for a First Amendment claim to home instruction. However, the vast majority of such suits has failed to satisfy the Court's criteria. Other constitutional theories attempting to limit state power to prohibit home instruction have been similarly unsuccessful. The various constitutional cases will be discussed below in relation to the categories of compulsory education statutes.

STATUTORY ANALYSIS

Like several other issues in education law, the law of home instruction is largely dependent upon state statutes. Much of the relevant case law is comprised of state court decisions interpreting compulsory education statutes and the state policies or regulations adopted thereto.

The statutory backdrop for home instruction is a shifting landscape. Of the 32 states that have adopted home school statutes or regulations, 90 percent has been passed between 1982 and 1988 (Klicka, 1988). Although there have been some exceptions, the overall trend in recent years has been in favor of home instruction, making it an explicit to compulsory institutional education under specific circumstances or criteria.

An up-to-date compilation of state statutes and regulations by the Home School Legal Defense Association (Klicka, 1988) reveals that over half of the 32 states require home schools to be "approved" by the local school district; that three states require home-school instruction to be "regular and thorough;" that five states require the home teachers to be "competent," "qualified," or "capable of teaching," and that only three states require home schools to utilize certified teachers. In another category, seven states require instruction ot be "comparable" to public schools.

The definition of home schools has also been an issue of debate. According to the Home School Legal Defense Association (Klicka, 1988), in at least 13 states, statutory language permits home schools to designate themselves and operate as private schools or religious schools. In an additional six states, home schools may qualify as private schools or church schools.

Monitoring student progress and achievement has also been an issue in the passage of home-schooling laws. According to the same source, which is an advocacy group, 25 states require standardized testing, but they do not necessarily require submission of test results. Several other states require district testing. There are six states that provide an alternative to testing.

Relevant case law can best be understood within the framework of three basic types of relevant state statutes. Some compulsory education statutes, hereinafter referred to as the "no-exception" type, require attendance within certain ages at public or private schools only. Other compulsory attendance statutes, hereinafter referred to as the "implied exception" type, provide another alternative with broad language like "equivalent instruction elsewhere." The third type provides an "express exception for home instruction."

Category One Cases: "No-Exception" Statutes

The cases occurring within jurisdictions that requires attendance in public or private schools without any express or implicit exception for home instruction have tended to cluster around two dominant issues. One issue has been the constitutionality of the no-exception compulsory school attendance law. The other frequently encountered issue has been whether, in the no-exception type of statute, home instruction qualifies as a private school.

Constitutional challenges. As discussed above, the argument that there is a constitutional right to instruct one's child at home has been unsuccessfully advanced in a number of cases within the no-exception category. The Supreme Court dictum in *Pierce*, stating "[n]o question is raised concerning the power of the State . . . to require that all children of proper age attend some school" (p. 534), continues to hold sway. Since *Pierce,* courts have either not reached the constitutional question or have rejected the argument that parents have a nonreligious constitutional right to instruct their children at home. Only one case discussed earlier (*Nobel,* 1980) has succeeded on the basis of a First Amendment religious claim. In that instance, a Michigan court, applying the *Yoder* balancing process, concluded the state's interest in uniformity was not sufficiently compelling to justify enforcement of the compulsory school attendance laws against the defendants.

Private school. In the jurisdictions that expressly require attendance at either public or private schools, the primary question has been whether home instruction qualifies as a private school. The courts have split about equally on this issue. One group of decisions has interpreted private school narrowly to not include home instruction. The other group has interpreted private school broadly and liberally to include home instruction. Within this latter group, the courts have required that home instruction must nevertheless be equivalent to the instruction offered in the public schools.

One of the earliest cases to interpret private school narrowly was *State v. Counort* (1912). In *Counort,* the defendant was convicted for refusing to allow his two children to attend a local public school or an approved private school, as required by Washington's compulsory attendance statute. The father appealed, claiming he was experienced as a teacher, capable of teaching all branches required to be taught in the public schools, and that he maintained a private school at home for his daughters. The Washington Supreme Court rejected his appeal, finding the evidence did not show that he maintained a private school at his home. Commenting on the distinction between home instruction and a private school, the court stated:

> Such a requirement means more than home instruction. It means the same character of school as the public school, a regular, organized and existing institution, making a business of instructing children of school age in the required studies and for the full time required by the laws of this state . . . The parent who teaches his children at home, whatever be the reason for desiring to do so, does not maintain such a school. (*Counort,* pp. 911–912)

For home instruction to be acceptable under this interpretation, it would seem to have to become so institutional in character as to lose any intimate, homelike quality.

The rationale for denying home instruction a private school status was sharpened and tightened in the oft-cited *State v. Hoyt* (1929). As in *Counort,* the parents claimed they were maintaining private schools at their homes and therefore were not in violation of the state compulsory school attendance law. Their children were instructed in their homes by private tutors in the courses required to be taught in the public schools to children of their age. Affirming the convictions, the New Hampshire Supreme Court rejected the contention that such instruction qualified as a private school. According to the *Hoyt* court, home instruction could not be comparable to school institutional instruction because it necessarily lacked the socialization a child would acquire in the group learning experience. The rationale that home instruction is inherently inadequate because of the absence of socialization has been used by courts in a number of subsequent cases to rule that home instruction cannot qualify as a private school. The *Hoyt* court also reasoned that home instruction would place an unreasonable administrative burden on the state to supervise the various home learning experiences and therefore could not qualify as a private school. This administrative rationale has been infrequently relied on by courts.

Although a socialization rationale has not been frequently followed in modern decisions, it was at least implicit in the Kansas Supreme Court's decision in *State v. Lowry* (1963). The only question before the *Lowry* court was whether the defendants' home instruction program constituted a private school and therefore exempted them from the compulsory school attendance law. Affirming the convictions, the court concluded the defendants were not operating a private school. The court based its conclusion on the defendants' failure to fulfill all the statutory curriculum requirements and on the absence of an appropriate institutional atmosphere. Reasoning similarly to *Hoyt,* the *Lowry* court stated:

> To determine whether or not the defendants were operating a private school, this court will look to the purpose, intent and character of the endeavor. The defendants' school was located in their home. The only pupils were their children. The only grades offered or taught were the ones in which their children were enrolled, and, of course, the instruction did not meet the statutory requirements . . . When all the facts and circumstances are considered together, the only conclusion that can be reached is that this was not a private school conceived or promoted for the purpose of educating anyone desiring to attend, but is really only scheduled home instruction. (*Lowry,* p. 964)

Given the strong inference, if not outright endorsement of a *Hoyt*-like socialization rationale, it seems unlikely the court's decision would have been different had the defendants satisfied the curriculum requirements. Other courts have similarly construed Category One statutes to preclude instruction at home.

Approximately the same number of courts within the co-exception jurisdictions have interpreted attendance at public or private school broadly to include home instruction provided it was equivalent to that offered in the public schools. In *State v. Peterman* (1904) the court ruled home instruction qualified as a private school under Indiana's public-or-private-school-only compulsory attendance law. Emphasizing the educational rather than the social aspect of "school," the court stated:

> A school, in the ordinary acception of its meaning, is a place where instruction is imparted to the young. If a parent employs and brings into his residence a teacher for the purpose of instructing his child or children, and such instruction is given as the law contemplates, the meaning and spirit of the law have been fully complied with . . . We do not think the number of persons, whether one or many, make a place where instruction is imparted any less or more a school. (*State v. Peterman,* p. 551)

Almost 50 years later, the Illinois Supreme Court applied the *Peterman* reasoning in *People v. Levisen* (1950). This case perhaps best illustrates a broad interpretation of "private school" to include home instruction. Convicted under Illinois public-or-private-school-only compulsory attendance law, the Levisens appealed, claiming the state had failed to prove their child was not attending a "private school" within the intent of the legislation. The Levisens, Seventh Day Adventists, were instructing their seven-year-old daughter at home because they believed instruction with other children produced a competitive, "pugnacious" character, and that the public school atmosphere was not conducive to fostering faith in the Bible. They also believed that for the first eight or ten years of life, the field or garden was the best schoolroom, the mother the best teacher, and nature the best lesson book. Motives aside, the evidence indicated the Levisen's daughter was receiving equivalent or superior instruction at home for five hours a day in all the required courses, and that she showed a proficiency comparable to her third grade peers.

Reversing the convictions, the court agreed with the parents' contentions that school is a place where instruction is imparted; its existence is not dependent on the number of persons being taught. The court also noted "[t]he object is that all children shall be educated, not that they shall be educated in any particular manner or place" (*People v. Levison,* p. 215). According to the majority in *Levisen,* academic training, not the development of social skills, was the *sine qua non* of school. The dissent, referring to the *Conourt* decision, argued that allowing home instruction would thwart the legislature's intent and would "do violence to the letter and the spirit of the law" (*Levisen*, p. 216).

While the *Levisen* court held that home instruction would qualify under the Illinois statute, it emphasized the decision "[did] not imply that parents may, under a pretext of instruction by a private tutor or by the parents themselves, evade their responsibility to educate their children" (p. 215). A sound education was still a prerequisite, with the court noting:

> Those who prefer [home instruction] as a substitute for attendance at the public school have the burden of showing that they in good faith provided an adequate course of instruction . . . commensurate with the standartds prescribed for the public schools. (p. 215)

The court did not clarify what this burden entailed.

Almost 25 years later, the federal district court in *Scoma v. Chicago Board of Education* (1974) reasserted *Levisen's* holding that home instruction could, so long as commensurate with public school standards, qualify as a private school. However, the court balked at going beyond *Levisen*, rejecting the parents contention that home instruction was a fundamental constitutionally protected right.

In the recent unreported state trial court decision of *Leeper v. Arlington Independent School District* (1987), the court interpreted the Texas statute to allow home instruction programs under the option for private schools. Further, the court invalidated the guidelines for private schools contained in a resolution by the state school board of education, finding that the guideline had been arbitrarily, capriciously and unconstitutionally applied to home education programs.

Most recently, a Colorado appellate court held that children who pursued their daily instructional coursework in their home were "enrolled" in an independent or parochial school within the meaning of the state statute (*People in Interest of D.B.*, 1988).

Overall, Category One cases reflect a clear and almost equal split between the *Levisen/Scoma* view and the *Hoyt* position. This issue is replayed in the equivalency context in Category Two cases.

Category Two Cases: "Equivalency" Statutes

Cases dealing with Category Two statutes greatly outnumber the cases occurring under either Categories One or Three. In part, the large number of cases is directly attributable to the inherent ambiguity of Category Two statutes. The larger number of cases may also be explained by the adoption of this type of statute in many of the more populous states. These statutes do not expressly limit instruction to public or private schools, nor do they expressly provide for home instruction. Rather, the statutes provide an exemption from public school attendance with ambiguous terms like "equivalent instruction elsewhere."

Other commonly occurring issues include: (a) What standards are employed to measure equivalence? (b) Who has the burden of proving equivalence, the state or the parent? and (c) Who determines equivalence, the court or school authorities? In addition, constitutional challenges have frequently occurred in Category Two cases.

Constitutional challenges. A number of cases occurring within Category Two jurisdictions have involved constitutional challenges. However none of these challenges has been successful. In several cases involving First Amendment free exercise arguments, the court rejected the parents' contentions. In *Commonwealth v. Renfrew* (1955), the defendant's argument, in part, consisted of a religious claim that, as Buddhists, they had a right to remove their child from school and instruct him at home. The Massachusetts Supreme Judicial Court flatly rejected their argument, stating, "[t]he right to religious freedom is not absolute" (p. 111). In *State v. Moorhead* (1981) the Iowa Supreme Court rejected the defendants' religious claim because they failed to present evidence that their First Amendment religious freedom had been infringed by the compulsory education law. It was the absence of a genuine religious claim, however, and not the validity of the First Amendment argument that produced the court's ruling in *Moorhead*.

Similarly, when a father refused to send his child to school in Arkansas, the court held that the language of the applicable statute was clear enough to put father on adequate notice that his course of home study would not constitute a school within the meaning of the statute and that the statute did not violate the father's First Amendment free exercise right (*Burrow v. State*, 1984).

In contrast to *Moorhead*, an Alabama court, in *Jernigan v. State* (1982), found the parents had presented sufficient evidence to show a religious interest in home instruction. However, the court dismissed their appeal concluding their claim did not satisfy the *Wisconsin v. Yoder* criteria. More specifically, the court found the parents' claim had not "shown that their entire way of life [was] inextricable from their religious beliefs or that public education would substantially interfere with their religious practices" and "that the home education they practice[d] [was] an adequate substitute or replacement" for public school (*Jernigan*, p. 1245).

In the most recent challenge, the North Dakota Supreme Court rejected all constitutional claims (*State v. Anderson*, 1988). Parents convicted of violating the compulsory school attendance law challenged the statute on several fronts. The court held that the state constitution authorized the legislation to regulate nonpublic as well as public schools; their requirement of advanced governmental approval for religious schools as well as their requirement that religious schools employ only certified teachers did not violate the establishment clause of the First Amendment; and finally that a requirement concerning employment of certified teachers did not violate the free exercise clause of the First Amendment.

The defendant-parents' arguments based on other constitutional theories have been similarly unsuccessful in Category Two cases. In *People v. Turner* (1953), for example, a California appellate court rejected the defendants' main contention that the compulsory education law deprived them of their Fourteenth Amendment right to determine how and where their child might be educated. Upholding the constitutionality of the California statute, the court stated:

> There can be no doubt that if the statute, without qualification or exception required parents to place their children in public schools, it would be unconstitutional . . . The statute here, however, . . . does not so provide. It recognizes the right of parents not to place their children in public schools if they elect to have them educated in a private school or through the medium of a private tutor or other person possessing certain specified qualifications. (*Turner*, p. 887)

Other cases, including a subsequent California decision, have similarly upheld the constitutionality of their respective compulsory school attendance statutes (*In re Shinn*, 1961; *Knox*, 1950; *Stephens*, 1937).

While most of the nonreligious constitutional challenges have centered on a Fourteenth Amendment theory that parents have a right, or "liberty," to choose how their children are to be educated, there have been some variations on this argument. For instance, in a New York case, the defendant argued, without specifying the constitutional source, that the education law impinged upon her guarantee of privacy (*In re Franz*, 1977). As the court observed:

> The rationale of this argument is that [the defendant] holds a sincere moral and philosophical belief that the children can best be taught at home under her sole and individual guidance; and that she should therefore be allowed her own way. (*Franz*, p. 948)

The court rejected this, as well as a second, considerably more abstruse, constitutional argument.

A considerably different Fourteenth Amendment argument was successfully advanced in an unreported Massachusetts case. The court, in *Perchemlides v. Frizzle* (1978), held that once a right to home instruction was recognized under state law, parents were constitutionally entitled to a "high level of procedural due process protection from arbitrary, capricious, or even malicious conduct on the part of the authorities who are authorized to evaluate and decide on the equivalence of a given program." The protection ranges from ample notification to a fair and open hearing where certain "factors" are to be considered and others ignored. The *Perchemlides* court found the parents had not been provided the necessary procedural protections and, therefore, ordered a new hearing by the local school authorities that would follow the court's procedural directives.

A number of procedural issues have arisen under constitutional guise, but parents have been unsuccessful in each case. For example, when parents brought action against the state for alleged deprivation of constitutional rights in connection with actions finding them in civil violation of state compulsory attendance laws, the district court held that no claim upon which relief could be granted had been stated (*McDonough v. Ney*, 1984). In a case where the court determined that the language of the applicable statute was clear enough to put the father on notice that his home study course would not constitute a school within the meaning of the statute, the court ruled that the father lacked standing to raise a claim that the statute was unconstitutionally vague (*Burrow*, 1984). Similarly, parents who had never sought an exemption from the state's compulsory school attendance laws could not assert the alleged unconstitutionality of the exemption provision as a defense to the prosecution for violating the attendance law (*State v. Toman*, 1989). In another procedural challenge, parents sought to enjoin the prosecution on the basis that it was being conducted in retaliation for exercising their constitutional rights (*Trower v. Maple*, 1985). The court of appeals held that a federal court could not enjoin a valid state court proceeding instituted in good faith merely because of conduct by a state official involved in the proceeding.

"Equivalent instruction elsewhere." Because of the ambiguity of statutory language like "equivalent instruction elsewhere," courts have sometimes concluded that home instruction is not a permitted exemption in jurisdictions with this type of compulsory attendance statute. Although a majority of courts have held home instruction qualifies under the equivalence exemption, a substantial minority, adopting the socialization rationale of *State v. Hoyt* (1920), have concluded home instruction is not, nor could it be, equivalent to the institutional, group learning experience.

Commonwealth v. Roberts (1983) was probably the earliest case in which the equivalence issue was discussed. Reversing the conviction of the defendant, Frank Roberts, the Massachusetts Supreme Judicial Court interpreted the statutory language "otherwise instructed for a like period of time in the branches of learning required by law" to include equivalent instruction offered in other than a public or approved private school. Although the defendant's daughter was instructed in a private unapproved school, the court, in dicta, recognized the right of parents to instruct their child at home so long as the education was equivalent and offered in good faith. In construing the statutory exemption broadly, the court reasoned the goal of the law was that "all the children shall be educated, not that they shall be educated in any particular way" (*Commonwealth v. Roberts*, p. 402). The *Roberts* academic-only interpretation of this type of statute reflects the majority view, although a substantial minority of courts have followed the *Hoyt* rationale.

The judicial evolution of this issue is clearly reflected in a series of decisions in New Jersey. Interpreting the statutory language, "equivalent instruction elsewhere than at public school," New Jersey courts have come up with completely opposite conclusions. In the two older cases, *Stephens v. Bongart* (1937) and *Knox v. O'Brien* (1950) the language was interpreted to require an equivalence not only in terms of academic input but also in terms of social development. In a more recent case, *State v. Massa* (1967) the court reasoned and interpreted the same language to require only academic equivalence. During the same decade, the New Jersey Supreme Court implied that home instruction could qualify as an exemption from public school attendance (*State v. Vaughn*, 1965).

In *Stephens* the trial court found the parents to be disorderly persons for instructing their two sons at home rather than sending them to school as required by law. While the evidence indicated their home instruction was not academically comparable to that offered in the public school, the judge preferred to rest his decision on the broader basis of the inherent lack of equivalence of home instruction, stating:

> I incline to the opinion that education is no longer concerned merely with the acquisition of facts . . . A primary objective of education today is the development of character and good citizenship. Education must impart

to the child the way to live. This brings me to the belief that . . . it is almost impossible for a child to be adequately taught in his home. I cannot conceive how a child can receive in the home instruction any experiences in group activity and in social outlook in any manner of form comparable to that provided in the public school. (in *Stephens*)

The trial court in *Knox* reiterated and elaborated upon the view expressed in *Stephens* that home instruction could not be equivalent to an institutional group-learning experience. Holding the defendant guilty of being a disorderly person for instructing his two children at home and not sending them to school, the court explained:

The underlying philosophy of modern life is that people, through social intercourse with one another, shall live in amity, and to absorb unto ourselves that which is good in our neighbor, and to shun that which is bad . . . Research discloses that even the siblings of royalty were encouraged under supervision to have contact with the commoner. The entire lack of free association with other children being denied to Mark and Eileen, by design or otherwise, which is afforded them at public school, leads me to the conclusion that they are not receiving education equivalent to that provided in the public schools in the third and fifth grades. (*Knox*, p. 392)

This rhapsodic view of the benefits of public school socialization was apparently not shared by the Massas, who removed their daughter from public school and instructed her at home. Fined $2,490 by a local magistrate for failing to comply with New Jersey's compulsory school attendance law, the Massas appealed and were granted a trial *de novo*. As framed by the court, the central issue in this case was equivalence; specifically, what the word "equivalent" meant in the context of the New Jersey statute. Unequivocally rejecting the earlier interpretation of the statute, the *Massa* court said:

[T]he . . . [O'Brien court] interpreted the word "equivalent" to include not only academic equivalency but also the equivalency of social development. This interpretation appears untenable in the face of the language of our own statute and also the decisions in other jurisdictions. (p. 257)

Interpreting the New Jersey statute as requiring only academic equivalence, the *Massa* court ruled home instruction was permissible. Based on the evidence presented, the court found the defendants' home instruction program was academically equivalent, in large part because the state had failed to prove the reverse, and overturned the municipal court's conviction. The view expressed by the *Massa* court that "equivalent instruction elsewhere," or other such language refers only to academic equivalence has been, by a narrow margin, the favored and more recent view.

Standards of equivalence. Where home instruction has not been excluded per se as an alternative, the issue frequently shifts to what standards or criteria are used to measure equivalence on a case-by-case basis. Generally, courts are guided by their state's statute if it sets out standards for determining equivalence. Those provisions vary from a single requirement, such as teacher competence, to a much more elaborate and detailed set of standards.

One of the standards most frequently at issue in determining the equivalence of home instruction programs has been that of teacher qualifications. Where the statute has not provided a teacher qualification standard, courts have usually implied a requirement of teacher competence but not teacher certification. For instance, in *State v. Massa* (1967) the court refused to require that Mrs. Massa have state certification. In fact, the court was satisfied that Mrs. Massa, who did most of the instruction, was qualified to teach her daughter the basic subjects from grades one to eight even though her formal education did not go beyond high school, and even though she had no prior teaching experience. The judge concluded that Mrs. Massa was a competent teacher based on his observation of her while testifying and during oral argument.

Other courts, applying open-textured statutory provisions like New Jersey's, have similarly implied that teacher competence, and not teacher certification, was all that was required (*Commonwealth v. Roberts*, 1893; *Perchemlides*, 1978). For instance, in New York, where the statue only called for teacher competence, a series of decisions involving the qualifications of the teacher have held the standard did not demand teacher certification (*In re Falk*, 1981; *In re Foster*, 1972; *In re Franz*, 1977; *In re Thomas H.*, 1974; *People v. Turner*, 1950).

When the statute specifies teacher qualifications, however, courts have scrupulously followed the statutory requirement. For example, in *State v. Moorhead* (1981) the defendants contended it was unclear whether the term "certified teacher" meant the teacher must be "certified" by a licensing agency or merely "competent." Summarily dismissing the argument, Iowa's Supreme Court referred the defendants to the certification requirement established by the board of public instruction, and stated, "[t]he term should cause no difficulty for citizens who desire to obey the statute" (p. 64). Conversely, a Minnesota statute requiring that a home instructor's teaching qualifications "be essentially equivalent to the minimum standards for public school teachers" was struck down for vagueness (*State v. Newstrom*, 1985).

In addition to teacher qualifications, a number of other factors have influenced courts in determining the equivalence of a home instruction program. As with teacher qualifications, where there are specific statutory standards, courts have tended to apply them rigorously. For instance, in New York, the statute allows for education elsewhere so long as it is "substantially equivalent" to that offered in the public schools. New York courts have generally been quite strict in applying the statutory standards that, in addition to teacher competence, provide for days of attendance, daily hours of instruction, and the subjects to be covered. Thus, in *In re Franz* (1977) the court was sympathetic to the motives and intentions of Mrs. Franz, but was not swayed by them and concluded her home instruction program was inadequate. Tactfully sidestepping the question of Mrs. Franz's competence to teach, the court found her home instruction not substantially equivalent to that offered in the public schools because she only instructed her two children for one-and-a-half hours per day, as opposed to the five hours of daily instruction in the public schools, and because the subjects she covered were determined by the children's interests rather than New York's education law.

Sincerity and good intentions were also not enough in *In re Thomas H.* (1974). Convicting the defendants of neglect for failing to send three of their children to school, placing the children under court order to attend school, and placing the parents on probation for 18 months, the court applied New York's standards strictly and literally. The sole issue before the court was the academic equivalence of the defendants' home instruction program. Both parents were well educated. The evidence clearly indicated the parents were making a good faith, conscientious effort to train their children in an alternative, if somewhat offbeat, manner; however, the instruction was not systematic. For example, it was admitted that United States and New York history were not given much attention, although numerous field trips were taken to points of historical interest. A psychological evaluation of the three children indicated all three had above average intellectual ability and advanced reading skills. The parents objected to the public schools, maintaining "schools can't touch creativity in our way" (*In re Thomas H.*, p. 388). The New York court, however, refused to accept what some might consider an ideal and idyllic learning experience. Finding that defendants' home instruction did not satisfy New York's standards, the court concluded it was not substantially equivalent.

When confronted with a general statutory provision like "equivalent instruction elsewhere" without specific standards, courts have varied with regard to the specificity and rigor. For example, in *State v. Massa* (1967), the court, while admitting that under a more definite statute with sufficient guidelines the defendants' home instruction might have been found inadequate, adopted its own vague criteria of "sufficient and proper instruction." This criteria included the subject matter covered, the method of teaching, the time devoted to instruction, and the results of achievement tests. The court appeared to be less concerned with teacher qualifications, and declared social development an irrelevant criterion.

Perchemlides v. Frizzle (1978), an anomalous and highly publicized home instruction case, illustrates a much more specific and rigorous approach. The Massachusetts statute applied in *Perchemlides* provides an exemption for children who are "otherwise instructed in a manner approved in advance by the superintendent or the school committee." Although the court acknowledged it was outside its purview to set standards for the local school authorities, it nevertheless instructed the school committee to consider certain factors and completely disregard others in evaluating a proposal for home instruction. Factors to be considered were teacher competence (not necessarily certification), the number of hours and days devoted to instruction, subjects taught, adequacy of educational materials, and availability of periodic tests for measuring academic progress. Factors to ignore were the parents' motives, the lack of an identical curriculum to that provided in the public schools, socialization, and the creation of a precedent for future home instruction proposals if the plan was approved. No court has followed the lead of *Perchemlides* in imposing such a specific set of factors upon local school authorities in the absence of statutory direction.

Whatever standards, criteria, requirements, or factors are specified in the statute or identified by the courts, it is clear they play a critical role in determining the equivalence of a home instruction program. Where the statute elaborates standards, courts have, as mentioned, consistently and scrupulously applied them. For jurisdictions with only a general statutory provision and no specific standards, the issue has remained relatively dormant. However, in at least one reported case, *Matter of Chapman* (1985), the parents' home schooling program was upheld due to a lack of articulated state standards. In *Chapman,* a New York court held that in the absence of sufficient evidence from the commissioner of education of the nature and quality of instruction available at public school for children of like age and attainments, it could not be determined that the home instruction program was not substantially equivalent to the public instructional program. *Chapman* illustrates that as home instruction becomes an increasingly feasible and frequent alternative to public schools, the issue of standards promises to become increasingly important.

Who determines equivalence. Unless a state statute has expressly provided otherwise, courts have generally determined whether a home instruction program was equivalent. For example, in New Jersey and New York, where the statute does not specify who is to evaluate "instruction elsewhere" for equivalence, the courts have automatically assumed the role themselves.

Where instead the statute provides that an administrative agency is to evaluate instruction elsewhere for equivalence, courts in at least three jurisdictions have refused to usurp that statutory authority (e.g., *Commonwealth v. Kollock*, 1936; *Commonwealth v. Renfrew*, 1955; *State v. LaBarge*, 1976). For example, in *Commonwealth v. Renfrew* (1955), the Supreme Judicial Court of Massachusetts affirmed a judgment against the defendants who had not obtained approval for their home instruction program from the local school superintendent or school committee as required by statute. The Renfrews contended they were giving their child equivalent instruction at home and attempted to introduce evidence to that effect. The court refused to even consider the evidence of equivalence, stating "[h]ome education of their child by the defendants without the prior approval of the superintendent or the school committee did not show a compliance with the statute" (p. 111). Whether the court would allow evidence on equivalence following a disapproval by the local authorities was not addressed.

Many statutes incorporate language such as "substantially equivalent" or "equivalent instruction;" numerous cases have challenged this terminology as either being unconstitutionally vague or overbroad. There is wide discrepancy amongst the courts on this issue.

In several cases, equivalency language has not been found to be void for vagueness. For example, one Court of Appeals judge wrote: "The term 'equivalent instruction' may be brief, but brief is not vague. A wordier description would not be clearer" (*Mazanec*, 1986. In a partially related challenge as it pertained to private school education, the judge ruled that the term "equivalent instruction" could be capable of objective measurement and verification (*Bangor*, 1982).

Courts in Alabama (*Jernigan*, 1982), Iowa (*State v. Moorhead*, 1981) and West Virginia (*State v. Riddle*, 1981) have all determined that equivalency language is not constitutionally void for vagueness or overbroad. In contrast, a number of courts have determined that equivalency language is void for vagueness. In Minnesota, the compulsory education statute was found unconstitutionally vague for purposes of imposing criminal liability when a parent failed to comply (*State v. Newstrom*, 1985). In a Missouri case, since neither regulations nor guidelines had been developed to clarify the statutory meaning of "substantially equivalent," a federal district court found the compulsory education statute unconstitutionally vague (*Ellis*, 1985). In a private school case, Iowa's statutory term "equivalent instruction" was struck down as unconstitutionally vague (*Fellowship Baptist Church,* 1987); subsequently new regulations were adopted in Iowa. The same sort of language was struck down in Pennsylvania in the *Jeffrey v. O'Donnell* case (1988) and also resulted in new state regulations being adopted.

The courts are split over the constitutionality of equivalency language. Where they have struck down this type of statue as unconstitutionally vague, more specific legislation and/or regulations typically follow, sometimes resulting in the shift from a Category Two to Category Three jurisdiction.

Technical compliance. A number of cases in Category Two jurisdictions have been decided on whether parents have met their statutory obligations in order to be eligible for home schooling. For example, parents in Alabama were convicted for failure to comply with the state statute requiring home schooling parents to be certified teachers (*Jernigan,* 1982). Typically, parents have urged that as long as their home instruction program was equivalent to public school instruction, the details of compliance were insignificant.

One line of cases has developed around the matter of truancy. For example, in *State v. McDonough* (1983), parents appealed a conviction that they had committed a civil statutory violation for permitting their children to be habitually absent. The Supreme Judicial Court of Maine upheld the conviction. The court found that the statutory requirement of prior approval of home instruction programs is not constitutionally improper, and therefore there was no denial of the parents' asserted right to educate their children at home. Furthermore, the court held that the parents' constitutional privilege against self-incrimination was not violated by a requirement that they apply for and obtain prior approval: "Where the state has provided a reasonable procedure whereby defendants may vindicate their asserted right to educate their children at home, they may not ignore the procedure and then appeal to this court claiming that their right has been denied" (p. 980). This same theme was evident in *Matter of Kilroy* (1983), when a New York court concluded that despite parental constitutional rights to privacy, child rearing, and religion, the parents were still subject to state regulation and control.

In a North Dakota case, *In Interest of C.S.* (1986), children were labeled "unruly" by the Juvenile Court due to habitual truancy. The state Supreme Court held that despite the fact that the Juvenile Court had correctly determined the children had been habitually and without justification truant, the children could only be found "unruly" if they were habitually defiant of parental directives to attend school. The court held that children who were removed from public schools by their parents were not "unruly children;" this court "won't visit the sins of the parents onto the children." However, the court held that intentional noncompliance with the state's compulsory school attendance law was a violation by the parent.

Parents in Iowa sought discretionary review after being convicted of failure to cause their children to attend public schools. The school district had filed their claim on September 30th after the children had failed to report for school. The State Supreme Court found the parents had been convicted on the basis of crimes not yet committed: "no parent . . . could be in compliance with the statute [requiring 120 days] by September 30 of any given year . . . the Truckes still had approximately 220 days left in the year to comply with the statutes" (*State v. Trucke*, 1987). Although the parents won a technicality, this decision is somewhat surprising since the truancy factor had been raised with the presumption that the parents had no intention of sending their children to school in the future.

In two recent New York cases, the issue of parental neglect has been raised. In *In re Andrew TT* (1986), parents refused to cooperate with school district authorities who were seeking to evaluate the parents' home schooling program. The court held that the parents' reluctance to cooperate permitted an inference of neglect. In a subsequent New York case, *Matter of Christa H.* (1987), parents were charged with educational neglect. The court held that proof that a minor child is not attending public or private school constitutes a prima facie case of educational neglect, which the parents must rebut with evidence that the minor is attending school and receiving the required instruction in another place.

In an unusual case where parents presented an affirmative defense, parents of home schooled children brought action for declaratory, injunctive and monetary relief against the superintendent and others in connection with the enforcement of state's compulsory attendance law (*Mazanec*, 1986). The Court of Appeals held that the act of the superintendent in investigating the educational arrangements and providing that information to a prosecutor, resulting in initiation of proceedings under the compulsory attendance law (that ultimately ended in dismissal), was not a valid basis for awarding parents monetary relief against the superintendent. The parents were prosecuted not because their actions were deemed incapable of meeting the requirements of the law, but because they frustrated the attempts at verifying compliance with the law. The court held that the superintendent did not act because of a hostility to the home schooling proposed by the parents or to their religious precepts.

In North Carolina parents sought declarative judgment and injunctive relief which would permit them to educate their children at home in lieu of attendance at public or private school (*Delconte v. State,* 1985). The State Supreme Court held that the parents' home instruction met the statutory requirement for attendance at a nonpublic school. The court held that the statute dealing with compliance with their compulsory school attendance requirement by attending a religious school or qualified non-public school does not prohibit home instruction as a means of complying with the law.

Burden of proof. Another frequently encountered issue is the question of who has the burden of proving equivalence, or the lack thereof, of a given home instruction program. Where the statute specifically allocates the burden of proof, courts have consistently followed the statute's directives. For instance, New York's statute, which places the burden on the parent, has been strictly adhered to in all of the home instruction cases (*In re Falk,* 1981; *In re Meyers,* 1953; *In re Thomas,* 1974).

The burden of proof issue was central in the 1981 case, *In re Falk.* The Falks, high school graduates with some technical training but no previous teaching experience, removed their nine-year-old son from school and were instructing him at home. They were philosophically opposed to the group learning experience, viewed routines and regulations of public school skeptically, and felt public school "overstimulated" their son. Restating the New York position that "the onus of demonstrating that the home instruction is substantially equivalent education falls on the parents" (*In re Falk,* p. 389), the court was satisfied that the parents had sustained their burden. Although doubtful about their ability to provide substantially equivalent education at the secondary level, the court concluded that up through the eighth grade the parents could provide their son with the minimal education required by law. However, in at least one earlier New York case where the evidence appeared to be equally persuasive, the court concluded that the parents had not sustained their burden of proving substantial equivalence (*In re Thomas,* 1975).

In a more recent New York case, *In re Adam D.* (1987), the court partially sidestepped the burden-of-proof issue by pointing to the district superintendent as responsible for determining substantial equivalency. The court reasoned that such an evaluation necessarily involves school officials because they possess the educational expertise needed to make such a judgment. Finding that the parents had been hostile, uncooperative, and guilty of educational neglect, the court ordered that the parents be placed under the supervision of the court social services agency. Should the agency wish to pursue the home schooling option, then the court cited curriculum review, teacher competency, on-site inspection, and standardized testing as permissible prerequisites for the superintendent's determination.

In a recent Michigan case entitled *Waddell v. State* (1987), a Seventh Day Adventist refused to send her child to school and refused to supply school officials with information demonstrating the equivalency of home instruction. Under Michigan state law, the parent has the burden of proving equivalency, but the state has the burden of determining whether a child is being educated. The parent's refusal to provide information rendered the school officials incapable of determining whether the child was receiving any education. Although the parent sought a *Yoder*-type exception, the Michigan State Court held that the parent's religious freedom had not been violated by the state compulsory education law. On appeal to the United States Supreme Court, the case was dismissed for lack of a substantial federal question.

Where the statute is silent or ambiguous on the allocation of the burden of proof, court decisions have varied. Some courts have ruled that the burden rests on the parents to prove, as an affirmative defense, that their home instruction was equivalent to that offered in the public schools (e.g., *State v. Moorhead*, 1981). Other courts have insisted that because of the criminal or quasicriminal nature of the offense, the burden was on the state to prove, beyond a reasonable doubt, that the children were not receiving an equivalent education at home (e.g., *Sheppard v. State*, 1957, *Wright v. State,* 1922). A third line of cases has divided the burden between the parents and the state (e.g., *State v. Vaughn,* 1965).

The allocation of the burden of proof was decisive in the 1981 case of *State v. Moorhead* (1981). Convicted for violating Iowa's compulsory attendance law, the parents appealed, arguing that in a criminal prosection the state had the burden of proving, beyond a reasonable doubt, both nonattendance and the absence of equivalent instruction at home. Affirming the convictions, the Iowa Supreme Court rejected the contention that the burden rested entirely on the state to prove a lack of equivalence. Instead, the court stated, "[t]he burden of going forward with the evidence [was] on the defendant to show that applicability of a defense" (*State v. Moorhead,* p. 63). Because the Moorheads failed to introduce any evidence that their home instruction program was equivalent to public school instruction, the court concluded it was irrelevant that the state had also failed to introduce any evidence to the contrary, and thus the state prevailed.

Similarly, where the court has placed the burden of proof on the state and the state failed to meet its burden, the parents have prevailed. For example, in *Sheppard v. State* (1957) an Oklahoma court held that where the burden was on the state to prove both nonattendance and a lack of equivalent instruction at home, the prosecution's failure to prove the latter element was fatal for the state's case.

The divided-burden approach is illustrated by the New Jersey Supreme Court's complex ruling in *State v. Vaughn* (1965). Remanding the case for a new trial, the court was Solomon-like in dividing the burden between the parent and the state. The court placed the initial burden upon the state to allege a violation of New Jersey's compulsory attendance law. Having done so, the burden was shifted rather dramatically onto the parents to introduce evidence that their child qualified under either of the statutory exemptions. As the court reasoned, it was peculiarly within the knowledge of the parents to describe their at-home instruction and, therefore, it was incumbent upon them to introduce evidence that their child was receiving equivalent instruction at home. The court did not thrust the burden onto the parents and leave it there, however. Once the parents introduced sufficient evidence to satisfy their burden of persuasion, the ultimate burden shifted back to the state.

The *Vaughn* rationale was also applied in *State v. Massa* (1967), another New Jersey home instruction case. Having determined the intent of the legislature required only academic equivalence, the *Massa* court concluded the only remaining question was whether the parents provided their daughter with an education equivalent to that available in the public schools. Having rejected social development as a criterion for evaluating equivalence, the court deemed the major portion of the state's evidence to be irrelevant. The court relied on the allocation of the burden of proof established in *Vaughn,* and found the state had not shown beyond a reasonable doubt that the parents failed to provide their daughter with an equivalent education.

In a more recent case, parents charged with violating the Alabama compulsory school attendance law argued that the law argued that the law was unconstitutional because it impermissibly shifted the burden of proof from the state to the parent defendants (*Hill v. State,* 1981). However, the court held that a statute that presumed a violation if certain elements were not met did not impermissibly shift the burden:

> It is now well established that a legislative body may provide by statute that certain facts may be prima facia or presumptive evidence of other facts ... such statutes are within the powers of the legislative body to enact, they are not considered an infringement upon the judiciary, and are not violative of any other constitutional provisions. (p. 433)

Category Three Cases: "Explicit" Statutes

The third kind of state statute explicitly provides for the home instruction alternative. As might be guessed, since this category permits home instruction, a far smaller number of cases have been decided in jurisdictions with Category Three statutes. The smaller numbers may also be attributed to the relative absence of ambiguity and adversity concerning the language of these statutes.

Four primary issues have been prevalent in Category Three cases. The most commonly raised issue, the burden of proof, was also notable in Category Two cases. Another recurring issue echoes an issue from Category One cases, namely whether home instruction constitutes a private school. A third issue, reminiscent of the Category Two question, "Who determines equivalence?," has developed where the parents have failed to fully comply with an express statutory requirement that home instruction be approved by state or local school authorities; the question here is whether the failure to strictly follow the technical requirements of the statute precludes as assessment on the merits of the home study program. Finally, a number of parents have challenged Category Three states's requirements concerning the qualifications of the home teacher.

In addition to these four common questions, constitutional issues have been raised in a few cases. The infrequency is not surprising; since home instruction is explicitly allowed, there is less pressure to seek constitutional recourse to open the door.

Constitutional challenges. In Category Three cases, constitutional challenges have been limited to First Amendment religious claims. In each case the court assessed the state's interest in compulsory education as being superior to the parents' religious interests.

In the first case, *Rice v. Commonwealth* (1948), the Virginia Supreme Court upheld the convictions of the defendants who claimed they were excused from complying with the compulsory education law based on their religious beliefs. The three defendants refused to send their children to public school because of their firm religious conviction that public school would expose the children to unwholesome influences and diseases, and prevent them, as parents, from teaching and training their children as the Bible commanded. Each of the defendants taught his children at home in a rigorous, religiously dominated atmosphere. Virginia's home instruction exemption was subject to the requirement that the instructor be approved by the local school superintendent according to qualifications established by the state board of education. While accepting the sincerity of the defendants' religious beliefs and their religious motives for instructing their children at home, the court refused to accept the argument that such religious interests excused them from complying with these statutory requirements. Readily distinguishing the *Meyer* and *Pierce* decisions, the court stated, "[t]he mere fact that such a claim of immunity is asserted because of religious convictions is not sufficient to establish its constitutional validity" (*Rice,* p. 347).

Whether *Rice* would have been decided differently in light of the Supreme Court's ruling in *Wisconsin v. Yoder* is doubtful, particularly in view of the West Virginia Supreme Court's 1981 decision in *State v. Riddle* was factually and legally similar to *Rice.* The sincerity of the Riddles' religious motives was not in question, and the quality of their home instruction was admittedly excellent. However, like the defendants in *Rice,* the Riddles had not complied with the statute that allowed home instruction conditioned upon approval by the county superintendent and county board of education. Relying on *Yoder,* the Riddles argued they were not required to comply with the statute because of their religious beliefs. The court, however, distinguished *Yoder* on two grounds: (a) the Amish were a self-contained community with long history, whose children were being equipped vocationally, socially, and spiritually to exist within that community and not the larger society; and (b) the Amish had sent their children to neighborhood schools for the first eight grades, which guaranteed the acquisition of sufficient basic skills to provide a foundation for adult life outside of the religious community. While not denying that the Riddles had presented a legitimate religious claim, the *Riddle* court found on balance that the interests of the state in preparing its citizens for a successful life (and conversely, so they would not become drains on the state), decidedly outweighed the parents' religious interest.

In the recent case of *State v. Buckner* (1985), parents challenged Florida's home schooling statute as unconstitutionally vague. The intermediate court of appeals held that the statute was not unconstitutionally vague, in that the "statute clearly prohibits an unqualified parent from teaching a child at home under the guise that a private school had been established" (p. 1230).

Private school. Whether home instruction constitutes a private school has been an issue in a significant number of Category Three cases. Like the argument surrounding the same issue in Category One cases, parents have tried to seek refuge in the generally less regulated option of private schools. Unlike Category One cases, the purpose of the argument has been to avoid statutory requirements (usually teacher certification) that in some states are placed on the home instruction exemption but not placed on private schools. For the most part, the authorities have successfully counterargued that the parents were conducting home instruction under the guise of a private school with the sole intent of evading the statutory requirements.

This issue was decisive in *T.A.F. v. Duval County* (1973). The appellate court affirmed the lower court's judgment that the two offsprings were truants and in need of supervision because they were not being educated as required by Florida law. Having the religious belief that race mixing was sinful, the parents withdrew their two children from school and instructed them at home in what they characterized as a church school. The court perfunctorily dismissed any claim of a bona fide religious interest.

In a subsequent Florida decision, the court reached a result identical with, but independent of, *Duval*. In *State v. M.M.* (1981) the appellate court reversed a lower court judgment that had found the appellee-children were not traunts. Concluding instruction at home by an uncertified teacher was not a private school, the appellate court noted home instruction and private schooling were interrelated, though distinct, statutory exemptions. While home instruction had some requirements, there was a virtual absence of any statutes or administrative rules regulating non-public schools. The court reasoned the legislature would not have established two such distinct exemptions, with separate requirements, unless it intended them to be mutually exclusive; to not read the exemptions as mutually exclusive would have undermined the legislative intent.

The validity of home study as a private school was also the central issue in an unreported 1981 Colorado decision. In *Gunnison Watershed School District v. Funk* (1981), the parents had removed their child from school and were instructing her at home because bus service had been discontinued to the child's remote, rural residence. The parents, neither of whom were state-certified teachers, purchased a correspondence course from the Christian Liberty Academy and applied for permission to teach their daughter at home pursuant to Colorado's two-pronged home instruction provision. For a number of reasons, none of which involved the lack of certification, the state board of education denied their request. Subsequently, the Funks declared they were operating a private satellite school under the name "Funk's Christian Liberty Academy." As observed by the court, there was only one child enrolled in the program, Naomi Funk, and instruction was given by her mother in one room of their house. Much like *M.M.*, the *Funk* court concluded that the legislature intended to create a distinction between home instruction and private school instruction, and this situation fell squarely into the category of home instruction. Most recently, the District Court of Appeals of Florida reiterated that a home school is not a private school (*State v. Buckner*, 1985).

As these cases indicate, the courts have rather consistently refused to blur the statutorily created distinctions between private schools and home instruction in Category Three states.

Burden of proof. The allocation of burden of proof has been decisive in a number of Category Three cases, all occurring in Missouri. The most recent case, *State v. Davis* (1981) followed the reasoning and holdings of the two earlier Missouri decisions (*State v. Pilkinton,* 1958; *State v. Cheney,* 1957). Charged with violating the state's compulsory school attendance law, the Davises were convicted solely on the basis of the state's evidence that their son was not regularly attending the local public school. The prosecution presented no evidence showing that the defendants had failed to provide the child with substantially equivalent instruction at home, and the defendants had not presented evidence showing their son was receiving substantially equivalent instruction at home. The defendants claimed that the burden of proof was on the state, not them. Agreeing with the defendants, the court reversed their convictions. Other courts have placed the burden on the parents; however, in none of these cases was the burden of proof the decisive issue.

Technical compliance. A number of cases in Category Three jurisdictions have been decided on the basis of a failure on the part of parents to comply with a specific requirement for home instruction such as approval of their program by state or local school authorities. Typically, the parents have argued that, although they were not in technical compliance with the statute, their home instruction program was equivalent to public school instruction and, thus, not in violation of the compulsory education law.

Courts have uniformly rejected this argument, strictly adhering to the statutory requirements. For instance, in *Akron v. Lane* (1979), the appellate court refused to consider evidence of adequacy where the defendant-parent had not received approval for his home instruction program from the authorized school official. The defendant in *Lane* had removed his hearing-impaired daughter from the public school because he was dissatisfied with her progress in special education classes and because the school district refused to place her in regular classes with the aid of an interpreter. Subsequently, the defendant provided his daughter with instruction at home from a private tutor, allegedly a certified teacher of the deaf. However, the defendant had not obtained the approval of the school superintendent as required by Ohio's compulsory education law. Consequently, he was charged and convicted for violating this statute. On appeal, the defendant contended that he was providing his daughter with equivalent education at home and, therefore, was not violating the law. The court summarily dismissed this argument and framed the issue as one of compliance with the specific requirements of Ohio's statute. Affirming his conviction, the court reasoned:

Mere equivalency between home instruction and public education is not an exception listed in the statute. The allowance of a home instruction exception is discretionary with the district superintendent of schools, subject to state direction and subject to appeal to the Juvenile Court . . . Whether defendant's home instruction program is equivalent to the education provided by the Akron Board of Education was, therefore, immaaterial to the instant prosecution. (*Lane*, p. 644)

Similarly, in *Gunnison Watershed School District v. Cox* (1981), the defendants argued that, regardless of Colorado's statutory requirements, their home instruction program was adequate and that, therefore, they were in compliance with the law. In an unreported decision, the court, using reasoning similar to *Lane,* declined to consider the adequacy of the respondents' home instruction program because they had failed to comply with the statutory requirements of either state board approval or instruction on a regular basis by a certified teacher.

In three other cases, a failure to comply with a specific statutory requirement has played a secondary role. Constitutional issues have played the primary role in these cases; however, once the courts resolved the constitutional questions (in each instance rejecting the defendants' arguments) the issue of noncompliance has then become crucial. For example, the Virginia Supreme Court, in *Rice v. Commonwealth* (1948), ruled " the religious beliefs of the defendants [did] not exempt them from complying with the reasonable requirements of Virginia [compulsory education] laws" (p. 347). The court went on to state:

Since the defendants made no effort whatever to have their qualifications [as instructors] approved as required by the statute, they are in no position to interpose their instructional efforts as a defense to their clear and admitted violation of the statutory requirements. (p. 349)

As recently as 1982, Virginia still required that home schooling only be provided by an "approved tutor" (*Grigg,* 1982). More recently the Virginia legislature passed a new law that eliminated that state's prior restrictions concerning home instruction.

The *Rice* pattern has been repeated in the two other decisions (*State v. Riddle,* 1981; *T.A.F.,* 1973). In both instances the courts first rejected constitutional claims and then refused to consider the adequacy of the home instruction programs due to the failure to comply with the statutory requirements. Thus, the courts in Category Three cases, like those in Category Two cases, have unequivocally refused to consider the adequacy of home instruction where statutory requirements were not satisfied.

SUMMARY AND CONCLUSIONS

Home instruction statutes fall into three general categories. One category consists of states that do not allow an exception for home instruction beyond the possibility of qualifying as a private school. Another category provides an implicit allowance for home instruction with statutory language like "equivalent education elsewhere." A final category consists of states with statutes specifically providing for home instruction. Within these latter two statutory classifications, the substantive criteria for home instruction programs and the procedures for obtaining approval for such programs vary significantly from state to state.

Each statutory category has given rise to a corresponding set of court decisions which cluster around certain identifiable issues. For instance, in Category One, a major issue has been whether home instruction qualifies as a private school. In response to this question, the cases have split almost down the middle.

Category Two, with its inherently ambiguous language, has spawned the greatest amount of litigation, as well as the largest number of distinct issues, including: (a) Does equivalent education elsewhere include home instruction given its lack of social contact?; and (b) Do parents have to prove equivalence or does the state have to prove the absence thereof? In response to the first question, the modern view is to disregard socialization and allow home instruction provided it is academically equivalent. No clear pattern has emerged in relation to the second question.

Cases within Category Three have involved a blend of issues from the two other categories. For example, the Category One question of whether home instruction constitutes a private school is a question that reappears, but for a very different reason. In addition, a defense has been proposed by parents that mere technical statutory noncompliance does not preclude adequate home instruction. In response to both issues, courts have vigorously enforced the statutory requirements. Where the statute has an explicit exception and specific requirements for home study, courts have adamantly rejected the arguments of parents that home study qualifies as a private school. Similarly, courts have insisted upon compliance with the procedural prerequisites specified in the statute.

Overriding and interrelating these statutory and case divisions are the constitutional parameters of home instruction. The two principal constitutional arguments are based on First Amendment free exercise of religion and the Fourteenth Amendment substantive due process. In response to First Amendment arguments, the vast majority of courts has rejected the religious claims of parents, leaving the Supreme Court's decision in *Yoder* as a narrow and largely unreachable springboard. Similarly, most courts have rejected the substantive due process arguments of parents, interpreting the Supreme Court's decision in *Pierce* as offering little support for home instruction. Parents relying on these and other substantive constitutional arguments have been successful in only a few cases. They have had more success with the void-for-vagueness doctrine, but the result, where they have succeeded, is typically more specific and sometimes more liberal legislation or regulations.

In gathering together a comprehensive survey and sustematic analysis of the statutes and cases on home instruction, this chapter delineates the contours of a patchwork and increasingly political legal solution beyond the rather consistent constitutional foundation. This variety is appropriate to the large extent that education is primarily a state function, with legislatures providing a framework for locally delegated implementation.

With the benefit of this comprehensive view of the statutory and judicial experience to date, states should consider providing a limited statutory exception for home instruction and attendant procedural due process protections. Such procedures should include notice, an opportunity for a hearing, and a clear set of standards. Statutory and case law experience suggests such standards include teacher competence, curriculum coverage, time requirements, and periodic progress reports (including but not limited to standardized test data). Socialization would not appear to be an appropriate standard for home instruction; to include it would seem to deny that opportunities for socialization vary within and beyond school settings. Applying these standards in an ad hoc, multifactor approach allows an accommodation for local conditions and differing combinations.

Finally, the New Jersey approach of burden shifting seems sensible and proper. Placing the initial, albeit nominal, burden of production on the state to show nonattendance, and once this is established, putting the burden of production on the parents to show compliance, accurately reflects the reality of each side's direct knowledge. Keeping the ultimate burden on the state to prove the child is educationally deprived is appropriate, when enforcement is criminal or quasi criminal in nature. Requiring reasonable cooperation of both sides is also an equitable approach. The balanced approach takes into account both the state's interest in education and the parents' freedom to choose. In addition, and perhaps most importantly, it permits a greater focus on the best interests of the individual child.

REFERENCES

Akron v. Lane, 416 N.E.2d 642 (1979).

Bangor Baptist Church v. Maine, 549 F.Supp. 1208 (D.Me. 1982).

Blackwelder v. Safnauer, 689 F.Supp. 106 (N.D.N.Y. 1988), *aff'd,*866 F.2d 548 (2d Cir. 1989).

Blount v. Dept. of Educational & Cultural Services, 551 A.2d 1377 (Me. 1988).

Burrow v. State, 669 S.W.2d 441 (Ark. 1984).

Commonwealth v. Kollock, 27 Pa. D.& C. 81 (C.P. 1936).

Commonwealth v. Renfrew, 126 N.E.2d 109 (Mass. 1955).

Commonwealth v. Roberts, 34 N.E. 402 (Mass. 1893).

Delconte v. State, 329 S.E.2d 636 (N.C. 1985).

Duro v. District Attorney, 712 F.2d 96 (4th Cir. 1983).

Ellis v. O'Hara, 612 F.Supp. 379 (E.D. Mo. 1985).

Farrington v. Tokushige, 273 U.S. 284 (1927).

Fellowship Baptist Chruch v. Benton, 815 F.2d 485 (8th Cir. 1987).

Grigg v. Commonwealth, 297 S.E.2d 799 (Va. 1982).

Gunnison Watershed School Dist. v. Cox, No. 81-JV-2 (Colo. Dist. Ct. Apr. 17, 1981).

Gunnison Watershed School Dist. v. Funk, No. 81-JV-3 (Colo. Dist. Ct., Dec. 30, 1981).

Hanson v. Cushman, 490 F. Supp. 109 (W.D. Mich. 1980).

Hill v. State, 410 So.2d 431 (Ala. 1981).

Howell v. State, 723 S.W.2d 755 (Tex. App. 1986).

In Interest of C.S., 382 N.W.2d 381 (N.D. 1986).

In re Andrew "TT", 504 N.Y.S.2d 326 (App. Div. 1986).

In re Adam D., 505 N.Y.S.2d 809 (Fam. Ct. 1986).

In re C.S., 382 N.W.2d 381 (N.D. 1986).

In re Charles, 504 N.E.2d 592 (Mass. 1987).

In re Falk, 441 N.Y.S.2d 785 (Fam. Ct. 1981).

In re Foster, 330 N,Y,S,2d 8 (Fam. Ct. 1972).

In re Franz, 390 N.Y.S.2d 940 (App. Div. 1977).

In re Lash, 401 N.Y.S.2d 124 (Fam. Ct. 1977).

In re Meyers, 119 N.Y.S.2d 98 (Fam. Ct. 1953).

In re Shinn, 16 Cal. Rptr. 165 (Ct. App. 1961).

In re Thomas H., 357 N.Y.S.2d 384 (Fam. Ct. 1974).

Jeffrey v. O'Donnell, 702 F. Supp. 513 (M.D.Pa. 1988).

Jernigan v. State, 412 So.2d 1242 (Ala. Crim. App. 1982).

Klicka. (1988). *Home schooling in the United States: An analysis.* Arlington, VA: Home School Legal Defense Association.

Knox v. O'Brien, 72 A.2d 389 (N.J. Super., 1950).

Leeper v. Arlington Indep. School Dist., No.17-88761-85 (Tex. Jud. Ct., Apr. 13, 1987.

Matter of Chapman, 490 N.Y.S.2d 432 (Fam. Ct. 1985).

Matter of Christa H., 513 N.Y.S.2d 65 (App. Div. 1987).

Matter of Kilroy, 121 Misc.2d 98 (N.Y. Fam. Ct. 1983).

Mazanec v. North Judson-San Pierre School Corp., 798 F.2d 230 (7th Cir. 1986).

McDonough v. Ney, 599 F.Supp. 679 (1984).

Meyer v. Nebraska, 262 U.S. 390 (1923).

Murphy v. State, 852 F.2d 1039 (8th Cir. 1988).

Nebraska v. Faith Baptist Church, 301 N.W.2d 571 (Neb. 1981).

Parr v. State, 157 N.E. 555 (Ohio 1927).

People in Interest of D.B., No. 87- CA- 1360 (Colo. App. Dec. 1, 1988).

People v. Levisen, 90 N.E.2d 213 (Ill. 1950).

People v. Turner, 263 P.2d 685 (Cal. 1953), *app. dismissed*, 347 U.S. 972 (1954).

People v. Turner, 98 N.Y.S.2d 886 (App. Div. 1950).

Perchemlides v. Frizzle, No.16641 (Mass. Super Ct., Nov. 13, 1978).

Pierce v. Society of Sisters, 268 U.S. 510 (1925).

Rice v. Commonwealth, 49 S.E.2d 342 (Va. 1948).

Scoma v. Chicago Board of Education, 391 F. Supp. 452 (N.D. Ill. 1974).

Sheppard v. State, 306 P.2d 346 (Okla. Crim. App. 1957).

Sheridan Road Baptist Church v. Dept. of Ed., 396 N.W.2d 373, 382 (Mich. 1986), *cert. denied*, 481 U.S. 1050 (1987).

State ex. rel Nagle v. Olin, 415 N.E.2d 279 (Ohio 1980).

State v. Anderson, 427 N.W.2d 316 (N.D. 1988).

State v. Buckner, 472 So.2d 1228 (Fla. App. 1985).

State v. Cheney, 305 S.W.2d 892 (Mo. App. 1957).

State v. Counort, 124 P. 910 (Wash. 1912).

State v. Davis, 598 S.W.2d 189 (Mo. App. 1981).

State v. Edgington, 663 P.2d 374 (N.M. App. 1983).

State v. Hoyt, 146 A. 170 (N.H. 1929).

State v. LaBarge, 357 A.2d 121 (Vt. 1976).

State v. Lowry, 383 P.2d 962 (Kan. 1963).

State v. M.M., 407 So.2d 987 (Fla. App. 1981).

State v. Massa, 231 A.2d 252 (N.J. Super. 1967).

State v. McDonough, 468 A.2d 977 (Me. 1983).

State v. Melin, 428 N.W.2d 227 (N.D. 1988).

State v. Moorhead, 308 N.W.2d 60 (Iowa 1981).

State v. Newstrom, 371 N.W.2d 525 (Minn. 1985).

State v. Nobel, Nos. 5791-0114-A (Mich. Dist. Ct., Jan. 9, 1980).

State v. Patzer, 382 N.W.2d 631 (N.D. 1986), *cert. denied*, 107 U.S. 99 (1986).

State v. Peterman, 70 N.E. 550 (Ind. App. 1904).

State v. Pilkinton, 310 S.W.2d 304 (Mo. App. 1958).

State v. Riddle, 285 S.E.2d 359 (W.Va. 1981).

State v. Rivinius, 328 N.W.2d 220, (N.D.1982), *cert. denied*, 460 U.S. 1070 (1983).

State v. Schmidt, 505 N.E.2d 627 (Ohio 1987).

State v. Shaver, 294 N.W.2d 883 (N.D. 1980).

State v. Toman, 436 N.W.2d 10 (N.D. 1989).

State v. Trucke, 410 N.W.2d 242 (Iowa 1987).

State v. Vaughn, 207 A.2d 537 (N.J. 1965).

State v. Whisner, 351 N.E.2d 750 (Ohio 1976).

Stephens v. Bongart, 189 A.131 (N.J. Super. 1937).

Svoboda v. Andrisek, 514 N.E.2d 1140 (Ohio App. 1986).

T.A.F. v. Duval County, 273 So.2d 15 (Fla. App. 1973).

Trower v. Maple, 774 F.2d 673 (5th Cir. 1985).

Trucke v. Erlemeier, 657 F.Supp. 1382 (N.D. Iowa 1987).

Waddell v. State, 347 N.W.2d 13 (Mich. 1987), *app. dismissed,* 483 U.S. 1002 (1987).

Wisconsin v. Yoder, 406 U.S. 205 (1972).

Wright v. State, 209 P. 179 (Okla. Crim. App. 1922).

Appendix: Home Schooling Requirements in the United States*

	Statutory language describing non-school options	Statutory requirements for the home teacher	Does statute require LEA Approval of program?	Does statute require pupil testing?	Home school (or Compulsory Education) Citations
Alabama	1) Instruction by tutor, or 2) qualify as church school	certification of tutor under option 1	yes, under option 1 only	no	Alabama Code 16-28-3
Alaska	1) tutored by certified teacher 2) enrolled in full-time approved correspondence course 3) educational experience approved by LEA, or 4) meet requirements for private or religious schools (current SEA policy)	teacher certificate under option 1	no, except under option 3	yes, for option 2 and 4 only	Alaska Statutes 14-30.010
American Samoa	no statutory provision				(American Samoa Code secs. 16.0302 through 16.0308)
Arizona	home instruction by parent or other tutor	teacher must score 80% on math, reading and grammer tests	no	yes	Ariz. Rev. Stat. 15-310 through 805
Arkansas			SEA approval	yes	Ark. Stat. Ann. 6-18-201
California	home school 1) Instruction by tutor 2) independent study arranged through school (current SEA policy)	tutor's certificate under option 1	no	no	Calif. Educ. Code s. 48222 & 48224

State				
Colorado	3) submit documents as a private school. 1) Instructed by certified teacher or 2) parent (or adult relative) must notify LEA regarding specified details on programs	teacher certificate under option 1	no	no under option 1; yes under option 2, at grades 3, 5, 7, 9 and 11.	Col. Rev. Stat. 22-33-184
Connecticut	"equivalent" instruction "elsewhere"	none	not by stat. but board regs require it	not by statue but LEA may do so	Conn. Gen. Stat. Ann. 10-184
Delaware	"regular and thorough" instruction elsewhere	none	yes	no	Delaware Code 14-2702
District of Columbia	"equivalent" instruction	none	yes	no	D.C. Code 31-401 through 31-413
Florida	"sequentially progressive instruction . . . by . . . parent"	none	no	yes	Fla. Stat. Ann. 232.01
Georgia	home study	parent must have h.s. degree or GED; other teacher must have college degree	no	yes	Official Code of Georgia Ann. 20-2-690
Guam	home instruction by parent or tutor	none	no, but Guam board rules require approval	no, but Guam board regulations require monitoring	Guam Code Ann. Tit. 17, secs. 6101 through 6109
Hawaii	"appropriate alternate educational program"	SEA regs. require tutor or parent to have B.A. degree	no	no	Hawaii Rev. Stat. 298-9

(Continued)

	Statutory language describing non-school options	Statutory requirements for the home teacher	Does statute require LEA Approval of program	Does statute require pupil testing?	Home school (or Compulsory Education) Citations
Idaho	"comparable" instruction	none	yes	no	Idaho Code 33-202
Illinois	School attendance only, but home can be a school People v. Levison 90 N.E. 2d 213 (1950)	none	no	no	ILL. Rev. Stat. Ch. 122, par. 26-1
Indiana	"equivalent" instruction	none	no	no	Ind. Stat. Ann 20-8. 1-3-17 & 20-8; 1-3-34
Iowa	"equivalent instruction by a certified teacher"	teacher certificate, but in 1988, the legislature imposed a moratorium on prosecution until July, 1989, if parents report on program	not by stat. but SEA regs required it prior to new law	no	Iowa Code Ann. 299.1
Kansas	School attendance only, but AG office informally advises home can be a school	none	no	no	(Kan. Stat. Ann 72-1111 through 72-1113
Kentucky	School attendance only, but state board regs. allow home to be a school	none	no	yes	(Ky. Rev. Stat. 159-010 through 159.990)
Louisiana	"home study"	none	no	no	LA. Rev. Stat 17:221(A)
Maine	"equivalent instruction . . . in any . . . manner arranged for by school committee and . . . approved by the commission"	none	SEA approval	not by statute but SEA regs. require it	Me. Rev. Stat. Ann 20A-5001A, 3A

State	Definition	Requirements	Approval	Testing	Citation
Maryland	"otherwise receiving regular, thorough instruction"	none	no	no (voluntary testing at local public schools)	Ann. Code of Md. 7-301(a)
Massachusetts	"otherwise instructed in a manner approved in advance by the superintendent or school committee"	none	yes	not by statute but LEA may do so	Mass. Gen. Laws 76-1
Michigan	school attendance only, but AG op. holds home can be a school. (A.G.Op. 5579 9/27/79)	yes (Private school teachers must be certified.)	no	no	(Mich. Comp. Laws 380.1561 through 380.1599)
Minnesota	home instruction	1) teacher certificate or 2) college degree or 3) use of accredited program approved by board or 4) child is tested annually at or above 30th centile	no	no, except under option 4	Minn. Stat. Ann. 120.10
Mississippi	home instruction	none	no	no	Miss. Code Ann. 37-13-91
Missouri	"home school"	none	no	no	Ann. Mo. Stat 167-031 through 167.042
Montana	"home school"	none	no	no	Mont. Code Ann. 20-5-109
Nebraska	School attendance only, but SEA allows home to qualify as 1) an "approved" private school; or 2) "exempt" private school where parents have sincere religious objection	1) teacher certificate or 2) meet board standards for exempt private school	no, but SEA approval required for option 1	statute gives board discretion to require tests	(Neb. Rev. Stat. 79-201, 79-1701, 85-607)

(Continued)

	Statutory language describing non-school options	Statutory requirements for the home teacher	Does statute require LEA Approval of program	Does statute require pupil testing?	Home school (or Compulsory Education) Citations
Nevada	"equivalent instruction"	1) teacher certificate, or 2) parent must consult with certified teacher, or 3) use approved correspondence program or 4) board waiver	yes	not by statute, but SEA requires it	Nev. Rev. Stat. 392.070
New Hampshire	School attendance only, but state board regs. allow home study in public school	none, but SEA require parents to be "qualified"	yes (by SEA rules)	no (but testing is recommended)	(N.H. Rev. Stat. Ann. 193:1 through 193.7)
New Jersey	"equivalent instruction elsewhere"	none	yes, but limited to review of subject matter coverage	no	N.J. Stat. Ann. 18A:38-25
New Mexico	"a home study program which provides a basic education program" operated by parent	none	no	yes	N.M. Stat. Ann. 22-1-2
New York	attendance "elsewhere" and instruction that is "substantially equivalent" by "competent" teacher	none	LEA has authority to determine equivalancy	no	N.Y. Educ. Law 3204, 3210, 3212
North Carolina	School attendance only, but home can be a school Delconte v. N.C., 329 S.E.2d 636 (1985)	none	no	yes	(N.C. Gen. Stat. 115C-358 through 115C-378)

State		teacher certificate	county and state both approve it		
North Dakota	school attendance only, but Dept. of Public Instr. Regs. allow home to be a school			no	(N.D. Cent. Code 15-34.1-01 through 15-34.1-05)
Ohio	"instructed at home by a person qualified to teach the branches on which instruction is required . . ."	no specific requirements	yes	no	Ohio Rev. Code 3321.04
Oklahoma	"other means of education . . . for the full term the schools of the district are in session"	none	no	no	Okla. Stat. Ann., Title 70, 10-105(A)
Oregon	instruction by a parent or other qualified person	none	no	yes	Oregon Rev. Stat 339.030
Pennsylvania	"regular daily instruction by a properly qualified private tutor" & satisfactory to district superintendent	none	yes	no	Pa. Stat Ann., Title 24, 1327
Puerto Rico	no statutory provision				P.R. laws Ann. tit. 18, secs. 71-81)
Rhode Island	"at home instruction approved by the school committee . . ."	none	yes	no	R.I. Gen. Laws 16-19-1
South Carolina	"instruction at a place other than a school" & approved by State Board as "substantially equivalent"	college degree or pass basic skills test, effective fall, 1989	yes	yes	S.C. 59-65-40
South Dakota	"Competent alternative instruction for an equivalent period of time . . . in the basic skills"	none	yes	yes	S.D. Comp. Law 13-27-1

(Continued)

Appendix: Continued

	Statutory language describing non-school options	Statutory requirements for the home teacher	Does statute require LEA Approval of program	Does statute require pupil testing?	Home school (or Compulsory Education) Citations
Tennessee	1) "home school" "conducted by parents . . . for their own children . . ." or 2) affiliated with and supervised by church school	H.S. degree or GED req'd to reach grades K-8, & college degree for grades 7-12 under option 1; no requirement for option 2	no	yes	Tenn. Code Ann. 49-6-3050
Texas	School attendance only, but home can be a school, Leeper v. Arlington Ind. School Dist., no. 17-88761-85, D. Tex., Apr. 13, 1987	none	no	no	(Tex. Educ. Code 4.25, 21.032-21.040)
Utah	"taught at home in the branches prescribed by law . . ."	none	yes	no	Utah Code Ann. 53A-11-102
Vermont	1) a "home study program" or 2) a "reporting private school" (state board allows home schools to follow rules for private schools)	none	SEA approval under option 1; none under option 2	no	Vt. Stat. Ann. Title 16, 11(21)
Virginia	Home instruction by parents if: 1) parent holds college degree. 2) parent qualifies as teacher,	yes, under options 1 or 2	yes, under option 4	yes	Va. Code 22.1-254.1

State					Citation
	3) child enrolled in approved correspondence course, 4) program approved by division superintendent				
Virgin Islands	home instruction by parent	none	V.I. govt. must approve program	no, but Dept. of Ed. meets with parents and children quarterly	V.I. Code Ann. tit. 17, secs. 81 through 97
Washington	"home-based" instruction with "planned and supervised activities" and which covers basic skills	1) parent has 45 college credits or takes course on home instruction at at postsecondary institution or 2) parent teaches under supervision of state certified teacher	no	yes	Wash. Rev. Code 28A.27.010
West Virginia	1) "instruction . . . in the home" or place approved by LEA and by a "qualified" person, or 2) file report on home school program	under option 1, home teacher must be qualified as public school teacher. Under option 2, teacher must have a H.S. degree and: a) 4 years formal education above pupil's or b) achieve acceptable score on NTE	yes, under option 1; no, under option 2	no, under option 1; yes, under option 2	W. Va. 18-18-1

(Continued)

	Statutory language describing non-school options	Statutory requirements for the home teacher	Does statute require LEA Approval of program	Does statute require pupil testing?	Home school (or Compulsory Education) Citations
Wisconsin	"home based educational program provided . . . by the child's parents . . . or by a person designated by the parent . . ."	none	no	no	Wis. Stat. Ann. 118.165, 118.15
Wyoming	"basic academic education program at home, & approved by LEA"	none	yes	no	Wyo. Stat. 21-4-101

*This table was prepared by the U.S. Department of Education, office of Educational Research and Improvement, office of Research, July 1988, and is based upon an examination of statutes, and verified by state departments of education. Approximately 80 percent of state departments responded to requests for modifications and suggestions.

For the sake of brevity, not all details of a state statute are included. Age of compulsory education, status of guardian as parent, durational requirements for the school day and school year, for example, are excluded. Likewise, exact wording of a statute is not always followed in order to allow brevity and comparability among states. For example, we consistently used the phrase "home can be a school" as shorthand to mean that a home can attempt to qualify as a private school under the requirements for private schools in the pertinent state. We also used terms, "SEA" to include either the state board or the state school chief; and the term "LEA" to describe local education agencies.

Note also that the table does not attempt to resolve legal ambiguities. Where a state or local education agency adopts rules that are not specifically authorized by the statute, there is always a question of the extent to which the rules are authorized. The table does attempt to indicate the situation where the agency is the source of a policy, if only to note the possibility of a legal challenge. Of course, a board with express authority to approve a home program will be in a better position to defend its more stringent requirements.

A similar legal ambiguity occurs where a statute authorized home schooling, and officials have (sometimes reluctantly) allowed homes to qualify as private schools as an option to meeting statutory requirements for home schooling. The widely prevailing view is that a home school may qualify as a private school, where a state law specifies only school attendance as a means of meeting compulsory requirements. However, in cases of conflict between two statutory provisions, courts will follow the more detailed provision. This would suggest that the home school provisions must be followed, and the option of qualifying as a private school is not available.

The U.S. Department of Education would appreciate receiving corrections and notice of changes in laws affecting this table. Mail to Patricia Lines, Office of Research, 555 New Jersey Avenue, Washington D.C. 2020-5646.

Author Index

A

Alford, R.E., 102, *118*
Apple, M., 75, *76*
Aries, P., 141, *156*

B

Bennett, W.J., 138, *156*
Benson, P.L., *39*
Berger, B., 137, 138, 148, *156*
Berger, P., 137, 138, 148, *156*
Bloom, A., 44, *60*
Blumenfeld, S., 70, *76*
Bowles, S., 75, *76*
Boyd, W.L., *118*
Bray, J., *39*
Burnap, G.W., 144, *156*

C

Campbell, D.T., 52, *60*
Carin, A.A., 53, *60*
Church, R.L., 138, 141, 147, 150, 151, 152, 153, *157*
Cohen, E., 75, *76*
Collins, R., 75, *76*
Cooke, B., 77, *97*
Coughlin, E.K., 20, *39*
Cremin, L., 154, *157*
Culver, R.B., 144, *157*
Cumbey, C., 70, *76*

D

Degler, C.N., 141, 142, 146, *157*
Delahooke, M.M., 47, 54, 55, *60*
Denzin, N.K., 30, *39*
Dewey, J., 121, *135*, 152, *157*
Dobbert, M.L., 77, 82, 84, *97*
Dorothy, L.W., *39*
Duffy, J.J., *157*

E

Eisikovits, R.A., 77, 82, 84, *97*
Ellson, E., 20, *40*

F

Falle, B., 51, *60*
Feinberg, W., 122, *135*
Findlay, J., 143, *157*
Frost, E.A., *40*

G

Gintis, H., 75, *76*
Gladin, W.E., 12, 14, 16, 17, 18, 22, 34, *40*
Glaser, B.G., 66, *76*
Gordon, E.E., 20, *40*
Gustafson, S.K., 13, 15, 17, 22, *40*, 56, 58, *60*

H

Haertel, E.H., 106, *118*
Hall, C., 140, *157*
Handy, R.T., 143, *157*
Hansot, E., 63, *76*
Hatch, N., 143, *157, 158*
Herzog, J.D., 77, *97*
Hirsch, E.D., 44, *60*, 138, *157*
Holt, J., 20, 28, *40*, 56, 59, *60*, 122–133, *135*, 154, 155, *157*
Hughes, M., 53, *62*

I

Illich, I., 126, *135*
Inhelder, B., 48, *60*

J

Jackson, S.L., *157*
James, H.T., 106, *118*
Jennings, M.K., 102, *119*

K

Kaestle, C.F., 145, 148, 150, *157*
Katz, M.B., 149, *157*
Kehoe, E., 102, *119*
Kellner, H., 137, 148, *156*
Kimball, S., 77, *97*
Kirschner, J., 143, 154, *157*
Kirst, M.W., 102, *119*
Klicka, C.J., 104, *119*, 159, 172, 173, *199*
Knight, E., 140, *157*
Knowles, J.G., *40*

L

Lancaster, J.B., 77, *97*
Landis, D., 44, *62*
Lasch, C., 134, *135*
Levin, H., 106, *118*
Linden, N.J.F., 47, *61*
Lindstrom, P., 70, *76*
Lines, P.M., 29, *39, 40*, 122, *135*
Lowi, T., 102, *119*

M

Madden, M.M., 50, *61*
Marek, E.A., *40*, 48, 57, *61*

M

Marin, P., 155, *157*
Marsden, G.M., 143, *158*
Marty, M., 143, *157*
Mattingly, P.H., 141 *157*
Mayberry, M., 13, 15, 16, 31, *40*
McGraw, O., 70, *76*
Mitchell, B., 44, *62*
Montgomery, L., 55, *61*
Moore, R., 10, 20, 33, *40*
Moggan, K., *135*
Morris, B., 70, *76*
Morris, R.C., *40*
Muller, H.N., *157*

N

Naisbitt, J., 20, 33, *40*
Noll, M., 143, *158*

O

Oakes, J., 75, *76*

P

Packard, F.A., 149, *158*
Peak, G.W., 102, *119*
Peterson, P.E., 102, 110, *119*
Piaget, J., 48, *60*
Pinnell, G.S., 44, *62*
Pitman, M.A., 57, *61*, 77, 82, 84, *97*
Pride, M., 26, *40*

Q

Quine, D.N., 20, *40*, 48, 57, *61*

R

Rakestraw, J.F., 46, 55, 59, *61*
Ray, B.D., *40*, 58, 59, *61*
Reed, F., 145, *158*
Reisman, J., 102, *119*
Reynolds, P.L., 56, *61*
Rosenblum, K.E., 27, *40*

S

Schemmer, B.A.S., 48, 56, *61*
Schlafy, P., 70, *76*

Scogin, L.A., 13, 15, 27, *41*, 47, 58, *61*
Sedlak, M.W., 138, 141, 147, 150, 151, 152, 153, *157*
Shepherd, M.S., *41*
Shulman, L.S., 43, 52, 57, 60, *61*
Smith, M.L., 57, *61*
Stanley, J.C., 52, *60*
Stevens, E.W., 141, *157*
Strauss, A.L., 66, *76*
Sund, R.B., 53, *60*

T

Taylor, J.W.V., 53, *62*
Tizard, B., 53, *62*
Travers, R.M.W., 53, *62*
Tuveson, E.L., 138, *158*
Tyack, D.B., 59, *62*, 63, *76*, 147, 149, 150, *158*

V

Van Galen, J., 18, *41*, 138, *158*

W

Ware, H., 144, *158*
Wartes, J., 13, 14, 16, 17, 20, *41*, 44, 45, 48, 54, 55, 59, *62*
Wayson, W.W., 44, *62*
Weaver, R., 20, *41*
Weiss, L., 75, *76*
Willis, P., 75, *76*
Wirt, F.M., 102, *119*
Worden, H., 142, *158*
Wright, C., 38, *41*

Z

Ziegler, L.H., 102, *119*

Subject Index

A

Academic achievement, 2, 19–20, 44–52, 58, 59
  contact with certified teacher, 46
  parent education level, 45, 47
  relation to parent's education, 20
  teacher certification status of parent, 47
  years student home educated, 46, 48, 51
Achievement, see Academic achievement
Affective development, 52–59
Alaska Centralized Correspondence Study, 12, 19, 28
Alternative schools, 138, 155, see also Free schools, and Fundamental schools
Anthropologists, educational, 77
Anti-Catholicism, 144
Authoritarian schools, 132

B

Bible, 142, 146

C

Calvert School, 19, 28
Childhood, 141, 155

Children's activities, 91–93
Children's rights movement, 126
Christian Liberty Academy, 19, 66
Civic religion, 143
Cognitive development, 48, 49
Common Christianity, 144
Common schools, see Public schools
Community network, 78–79
Compulsory attendance laws, history of, 160–164
Compulsory education laws, 22, Appendix, see also Legal status
Constitutional challenges, nonreligious claims, 167–172
  religious claims, 164–167, 192–193
Constitutional issues, 4
Critique of traditional schooling, see Traditional schooling
Cultural acquisition, 3
Culture acquisition, 78
Curricula, 18–19, 23–25
  correspondence schools, 23–25
  parents designing own curricula, 27
Curriculum agendas, 43, 44, 59, 60

D

Data management, 83–85
Demographic characteristics, 13–16
  education, 13–14
  income, 14–15

number of children in family, 15–16
race, 13–14
religion, 14, 15
Dewey, John, 121, 122, 134
Disabled, *see* Learning disabled children

E

Education, parents', 79
Emotional adjustment, *see* Affective development
Evangelical Christianity, 143
Methodism and schools, 143, 144

F

Family, 140, 141, 145, 151–152
Family business, 79–80
Farrington v. Tukushige, 162
Free schools, 127, 138, 154–155
Fundamentalist schools, 138

H

History, 9–10
Holt, John, 11, 20, 28, 122–134, 155
competition, 125
compulsory schooling, 127
disillusionment, 126
early work in educational reform, 123–125
Escape From Childhood, 126, 128, 130
Freedom & Beyond, 126
home of, 128
How Children Fail, 124
How Children Learn, 124
Instead of Education, 126, 133
Laissez faire individualism, 123, 125, 127
moral elite, 129
morally least fit, 127, 128, 132
nondirective pedagogy, 124
silent majority, 125
teachers, 126
What do I do Monday, 124
Home schooling, 137, 138, 139, 146, 147, 155–156
definition of, 10
reasons for, *see* Reasons for home schooling

Home schooling families,
demographics, 2
motivation for, 16–17
public schools, conflicts with, 67, 70–72
roles of mothers, 5, 65
social class, 5, 65
Home schooling laws, 104–155
Iowa, 110
Missouri, 109
Nebraska, 110
policy settlement, 111–116
regulatory tactics, 109
state regulatory tradition, 108–109, 114–115
Home schooling movement, 106–117
factions, 112
libertarian claims, 106
Michigan, 114
organizational skills, 111–113
political mobilization, 108–110
private schools and, 107–109
size, 107
Washington and, 112
Home schooling opponents, 113–115
Michigan, 114–115
NEA, 113
Wisconsin, 113–114
Home schooling parents, 130, 131, 134
educational levels, 65, 71
beliefs about learning, 73
religious beliefs, 67, 68–71, 75

I

Ideologues, 2, 66–71, 75
Illich, Ivan, 126
Individualism, 3
Informant interviews, 81

L

Lasch, Christopher, 134
Learning, 77–78, 81–82
Learning disabled children, 19
Learning incident, 82
Legal status, 11, *see also* Compulsory education laws
Library, 80, 89
Literacy education, 142, 146
Litigation, 4

M

Meger v. Nebraska, 161
Modernism, 140, 145, 148, 150, 151
   alienating aspects, 153
Moore, Raymond, 10, 20
Moral education, 146
Morgan, Kathryn, 124
Mother as educator, 142

N

Naisbitt, John, 10, 20
Northwest ordinance, 141

O

Opposition to home education, 75
   reactions of home schooling parents,
      ideologues, 69–71
      pedagogues, 73–74

P

Parent education level, *see* Academic
   achievement
Parent's activities, 89–90
Parent-school conflict, 147
Participation observation, 81
Pedagogues, 3, 71–74, 75
Pierce v. Society of Sisters, 160, 161
Pluralism, 2, 75
Politics of education, 102–116
   civil rights movement, 104
   consumer interests, 102, 104, 106,
     115
   ideological bargaining, 110
   interest groups, 102
   pluralism, 102, 110, 116
   professional interests, 102
Population, 20–35
   cautions on use of estimate, 35
   census, 20–21
   Florida, 34–35
   geographic variation, 31–33
   methodology for estimating, 22–30
   population trends, 10, 20
   surveys, 21
   verification of estimate, 30–35

   Washington, 34
   Wisconsin, 34
Primates, 77, 90
Private schools,
   and legal definitions of home schools,
     174–177, 193–194
Progressive education, 151–154
Protestantism, 142, 145, 147
   Unitarianism and schools, 143–144
Psychomotor development, 57
Public schools, 137, 138, 139, 141, 143,
     148, 153, 154, *see also* Home
     schooling families and public
     schools,
   age-graded, 148
   attendance, 141, 142, 149
   bureaucratizing tendencies, 148
     efficiency, 149, 151
   common faith,
     doubts, 150
   common schools, 137, 139, 143, 144,
     147, 150
     Whig Party, 147
   critics, 153–154
   disillusionment, 153–154
   enrollment, *see* Attendance
   mission, 150
   one-room school, 149
   as panaceas, 153
   parent control, 140
   professional control, 147
   proponents, 133
   public good, and, 3–4, 74–75
   reform, 115–116, 151–152
   religious faith, 138
   societal discontent with, 1–2, 3, 75
   state regulation, 148
   teacher, 155
   textbooks, 149–150

R

Reading, 80
Reasons for home schooling,
   ideologues, 66–67, 68–69, 70–71
   pedagogues, 71–73
Reform of public schools, *see* Public
   schools
Religious affiliation of home schoolers,
   15

Research design suggestions for future research, 20, 35–39
Research limitations, 45, 58, 59

S

School attendance, 64–65
Scriptural literacy, *see* Bible
Social development, 2
  and state statutes, 181–183, 198
Socialization, *see* Affective development
Standardized testing,
  state requirements, 173
State regulation of home education, 3, 4, 75
  home schooling, parents' reactions to, 71
State statutes, 172–198, *see also* Teacher qualifications
  compulsory attendance, 4
Support networks, 18
Systematic observation, 81–83

T

Teacher certification of parent, *see* Academic achievement
Teacher qualifications,
  state statutes and, 183, *see also* State statutes
Teachers in home schools, 17, *see also* Home schooling
Teaching methods, 73
Teaching styles, 18
Traditional schooling, 59

V

Values, 95–96

W

Wisconsin v. Yoder, 162–163
Women's role, burden, 146

LC 40 .H66 1991

Home schooling

DATE DUE			
OCT 07 '96	MAY 1 4 2008		
NOV 18 '96			
DEC 09 '96			
APR 2 1 1997			
OCT 1 3 199			
AUG 0 9 200			
MAY 0 1 2001			
DEC 0 6 2001			
DEC 0 1			
NOV 23			

sunday 12/1